ECONOMICS FOR A CIVILIZED SOCIETY

Also by Paul Davidson

AGGREGATE SUPPLY AND DEMAND ANALYSIS
(*with E. Smolensky*)
CAN THE FREE MARKET PICK WINNERS? (*editor*)
CONTROVERSIES IN POST-KEYNESIAN ECONOMICS
ECONOMIC PROBLEMS OF THE 1990s: Less Developed
Countries, Europe and the United States (*co-editor with
J. A. Kregel*)
EMPLOYMENT, GROWTH AND FINANCE: Economic Reality
and Economic Growth (*co-editor with J. A. Kregel*)
INFLATION, OPEN ECONOMIES AND RESOURCES: The
Collected Writings of Paul Davidson (*edited by Louise Davidson*)
INTERNATIONAL MONEY AND THE REAL WORLD
MACROECONOMIC PROBLEMS AND POLICIES OF INCOME
DISTRIBUTION: Functional, Personal, International (*co-editor
with J. A. Kregel*)
MILTON FRIEDMAN'S MONETARY THEORY: A Debate with his
Critics (*with M. Friedman, J Tobin, D. Patinkin, K. Brunner,
A. Meltzer*)
MONEY AND EMPLOYMENT: The Collected Writings of Paul
Davidson (*edited by Louise Davidson*)
MONEY AND THE REAL WORLD
POST-KEYNESIAN MACROECONOMIC THEORY: A Foundation
for Successful Economic Policy in the Twenty-First Century
THE DEMAND AND SUPPLY OF OUTDOOR RECREATION
(*with C. J. Cicchetti and J. J. Seneca*)
THEORIES OF AGGREGATE INCOME DISTRIBUTION
THE STRUGGLE OVER THE KEYNESIAN HERITAGE

Economics for a Civilized Society

Revised Edition

Greg Davidson
Assistant Director, Mission Operations and Data Systems Directorate
Goddard Space Flight Centre, National Aeronautics and Space Administration

and

Paul Davidson
Chair of Excellence in Political Economy
University of Tennessee

M.E. Sharpe
Armonk, New York

Library of Congress Cataloging-in-Publication Data

Davidson, Greg.
Economics for a civilized society / Greg Davidson and
Paul Davidson. — (rev.) ed.
p.   cm.
Includes bibliographical references and index.
ISBN 1–56324–893–X (hardcover : alk. paper).
ISBN 1–56324–894–8 (pbk. : alk. paper)
1. Economics.   2. Neoclassical school of economics.
I. Davidson, Paul.   II. Title.
HB171.D28   1996
330—dc20   96–10884
CIP

(c)   10   9   8   7   6   5   4   3   2   1
(p)   10   9   8   7   6   5   4   3   2   1

Printed in Great Britain

To Louise and Tamah, and of course
Arik, Gavi, and Zakkai

Contents

Preface to the First Edition

How did we come to write *Economics for a Civilized Society*? In many ways we have been working on this book for years, in our learning, teaching and writings. In our careers as a Professor at Pennsylvania, Rutgers and Tennessee, and as a student at Swarthmore and Harvard, we have frequently seen the intellectual history of economic thought fall to waste as it is distorted to fit within the current conventional wisdom known as 'neoclassical economics'.

At one extreme of neoclassical economics is the intellectual despotism of a discipline which is more ideological than empirical. More commonly we have found intelligent and well-intentioned economists whose work is needlessly constrained and ruined by the weakness of these neoclassical conceptual foundations upon which they have built their analysis. Ours is not the cynical message that economists do not know anything – the problems we see come more from the things that economists 'know' that just are not so.

Our goal is to provide a civilized approach to the important economic policy issues that face modern societies. Unfortunately, conventional neoclassical economic thought cannot penetrate the operations of an enlightened society. Yet Western societies have invested a great deal of intellectual effort in developing the database and analytical tools of this conventional analytical analysis. Hence we have tried to salvage what can be used, if properly modified for a civilized setting, of the conventional wisdom.

We therefore provide a civilized analytical structure which can support work already done in neoclassical economics, when the latter is modified to integrate valid critiques of the conventional wisdom. In so doing we hope not only to improve our understanding of the orthodox approach, but also to probe the crucial interactions between the self-interest basis of neoclassical economics and the civic values to which the orthodox approach is blind.

An understanding of the boundaries of conventional analysis and how one can go beyond this restrictive barbaric approach is not merely of academic importance. Whether we like it or not, current economic theory has become the bedrock of our public policy decision-making process as well as the basis for our philosophy of society and its laws. Economic theory not only affects our bank accounts, but it also, in large part, determines how our society is fed and housed, and even how much we think our society can afford to defend ourselves against epidemics or enemies threatening the very viability of our population. Conventional economic theory does influence our views of right and wrong, and can thereby change the context of our lives. Our hope is to provide guidance towards a more civilized approach to all these issues.

We would like to thank the following people for their comments on aspects of this manuscript: John Kenneth Galbraith, Robert Reich, Martin Kessler, Fred Zimmerman, Stephen Benko, William Kushner, Alan Plumley, Ellen Freeberg, John Powell, and Ellie Prockop. Others who have helped us with their comments on earlier aspects of what became the basis of this book include Amitai Etzioni, James Verdier, George Brockway, Dotty Robyn, Marty Linsky, John Dunlop, Malcolm Salter, Steve Kelman, Richard Zeckhauser, David Ellwood, Harvey Liebenstein, Shah Ashiqazziman, Peter Swiderski, Ken Sharpe, and Charles Gilbert. Not everyone mentioned above will agree with all of our findings but we appreciate the insights that their comments provided.

We would also like to express our appreciation to the late Sidney Weintraub who taught us, in separate economics courses almost thirty years apart, the importance of the statement of William Stanley Jevons that 'In matters of philosophy and science authority has been the great opponent of truth. A despotic calm is usually the triumph of error. In the republic of the sciences sedition and even anarchy are beneficial in the long run to the greatest happiness of the greatest number.' From Sidney Weintraub we learned much – but especially we learned that, although it is more pleasant and easy to agree than disagree, it is necessary to speak out against the fallacies which find their way into the conventional wisdom.

Finally, we wish to thank Louise and Tamah, whose contributions (editorial and other) would have earned them mention above, except that they also deserve special recognition for tolerating us as we frequently woke up at three in the morning to write down 'just one more idea'.

Washington, DC   GREG DAVIDSON
Knoxville, Tennessee   PAUL DAVIDSON

Preface to the Second Edition

We have completely revised our book *Economics for a Civilized Society*. It has been eight years since we wrote the original version, and in that time we have seen a continuation of the erosion of civilized institutions of the Western World. In the interim more facts that support our earlier analysis have emerged and are incorporated in our discussion.

Politician of both major parties in the United States and in the United Kingdom argue that they want to provide a legislative economic pro-gramme to promote a 'civil society' that emphasizes the importance of values of the family and the community. Unfortunately, today political decision makers are trapped by the rhetoric of conservative economics that focuses so strongly on market values that it derogates family and com-munity values. In *Economics for a Civilized Society*, we explore how we arrived at such a sorry state and by studying history we learn how we can again develop a prosperous and civilized global economy by developing civil principles that coordinate market values and civil values.

These past eight years have also seen many nations of the world throw off the authoritarian rule of communism and begin to experiment with free markets and democracy. The post-Cold War era has nations of the former East and West coming from opposite directions towards the same ques-tions regarding the fundamental nature of their society. The internal debate over the proper role for government and for free markets is a crucial one, and it raises questions that can not be adequately addressed using conven-tional approaches to economics.

We believe that *Economics for a Civilized Society* can provide the foun-dation principles that will permit all nations to develop a role for their government that provides their citizens with a prosperous civil society operating within a global civilized community of nations.

Knoxville   GREG DAVIDSON
Tennessee   PAUL DAVIDSON

1 In Pursuit of Civilization

A conservative philosophy of economics has dominated the political agenda of the 1980s and 1990s. This philosophy can be epitomized in the following question: What's the difference between love and prostitution? If we asked this question of those whose economic philosophy shaped American politics in the 1980s and 1990s, the answer is that prostitution is a valuable service that some people are willing to pay for, while love is not for sale and therefore is worthless. This philosophy of market valuations provides the basis for all values in conservative economics.

Conservative economics focuses exclusively on one of the two major types of human motivation: self-interest. Unfortunately the other source of human inspiration – what we refer to as civic values – is locked out of the conservative economic framework. Consequently, when debating national policy we can compare the costs and benefits of prostitution, but are blind to the importance of love.

Nations are built on the motivating forces of both self-interest and civic values. When self-interest and civic values are combined, they reinforce each other so that a nation can enjoy both prosperity and justice. Difficulties arise when society is governed by only one of these two forces because you can't buy justice in the marketplace, and similarly, you can't build prosperity on civic pride alone. A prosperous civil society combines self-interest and civic values so that the citizens may reap the benefits of each.

Unfortunately, in the last twenty-five years, we have come to view the nation's future in terms of choices between these competing parts of our heritage; self-interest *or* civic values. Liberals and Conservatives have each adopted a fragment of the national heritage as the centrepiece for their economic policies; social values for liberals and 'the bottom line' of self-interest for conservatives. As the political pendulum has swung, the policy choices that the nation has offered have, at best, provided improvements in one sphere at dreadful costs in the other. The liberalism of the Great Society programmes of the 1960s sapped the incentives behind the profit motive, just as the politics of self-interest in the 1980s and 1990s eroded and degraded civic values.

Unemployment and inflation are both evils. To deny jobs and income to those who want to work, that is, to *promote* unemployment in order to combat inflation, violates basic civilized values. To permit inflation, on the other hand, undermines the wealth earned by individuals acting in

1

accordance with their own self-interest. Liberals see the civic need for a fully employed society, even if this causes inflation and thus devalues the accumulated assets held by the wealthy. Conservatives, on the other hand, demand that inflation be stopped, even if this means that some people lose jobs and businesses lose profits as a result.

For more than two decades, the tragedy of economic policy has been the conventional wisdom that it is necessary to create sufficient unemployment to constrain inflation. The power of the anti-inflation (or pro-unemployment) philosophy was demonstrated as recently as early 1994. Policy makers at the Federal Reserve decided that inflation was a major threat since unemployment declined to 8.5 million workers (or 6.5 per cent of the labour force) in February 1994 from 9.4 million workers (or 7.4 per cent of the labour force) in 1992. These Federal Reserve policy makers (including two Clinton appointees) believed that it was more important to depress the growing economic prosperity to fight inflation than it was to continue growth in profits and jobs. The Federal Reserve raised interest rates to slow growth and reduce economic opportunities for the unemployed *who earnestly wanted to work*. This conservative approach is based on a false premise – namely that it is impossible to maintain a prosperous full employment society that is also protected from inflation.

A NATURAL RATE OF UNEMPLOYMENT?

The view that a free market society requires a significant portion of its population who want to work to remain unemployed has its origin in the Marxian notion of the need for an 'industrial reserve army of the unemployed' to keep workers in their place. In its recent conservative manifestation this industrial army of the unemployed has been resurrected by conservative economists under the less-emotive appellation of the 'natural rate of unemployment'.[1]

The concept of a natural rate of unemployment provides justification for Federal Reserve Policies that raise interest rates and encourages our government to move towards a balanced budget before full employment is achieved. Those who champion this natural rate concept are essentially claiming that it is bad for our society if businessmen hire more unemployed workers when market conditions provide profit opportunities for producing more output. This natural unemployment rate argument states that, by reducing the ranks of the remaining unemployed in response to possible profit opportunities, these self-interested businessmen will cause the economy to 'overheat'.

The 'natural rate' advocates argue that the Federal Reserve must destroy potential profit opportunities by raising interest rates whenever entrepreneurs hire a sufficient numbers of workers to reduce unemployment below its natural rate. It is better to keep more than 6 per cent of American workers unemployed than to hire them and in so doing make them productive, income-earning, tax-paying members of society. (The worldly wisdom of the policy makers at the Bank of Canada is that it requires 9.5 per cent of the employable labour force in Canada to be unemployed to contain inflation. Double-digit unemployment rates are also the prevailing wisdom of the natural unemployment rate of policy makers in most of the nations that make up the European Community as well.)

If some proportion of workers who want to work to earn income are required to be perpetually unemployed, then they must either starve to death or live as 'parasites' off government entitlements and/or private charity. The social welfare net of entitlements has permitted many governments to maintain the mask of civility while consigning a significant proportion of the working population to a standard of living below what a fully employed economy could afford.

If we eliminate welfare as we know it in order to help balance the budget and to force the unemployed to look for jobs that do not exist because of policies specifically designed to maintain a natural unemployment rate, and if private charities do not replace these entitlement payments, dollar for dollar, then only three alternative scenarios are possible.

First, unable to obtain any form of income maintenance, the unemployed will slowly starve to death. As they die, the rate of unemployment among the surviving members of society will fall below the critical unemployment rate value. To prevent inflationary overheating, the Federal Reserve will then be forced to destroy additional profit opportunities so that businessmen, facing slack markets, will discharge enough previously employed workers to refill the unemployment ranks to the amount necessary to maintain a natural rate. Under this scenario of 'starving the unemployed', additional employed survivors must be continually sacrificed to maintain unemployment.

Second, the unemployed can attempt to compete with the employed by lowering their wage requirements and/or improving their skills. If, however, the system always requires a significant portion of the population to be unemployed to prevent overheating, the newly employed will gain their jobs at the expense of the previously employed. Job search will merely be a game of musical chairs where the Federal Reserve undertakes to assure there are always fewer chairs than players.

Third, those who are cast upon the trash-heap of the unemployed without entitlements, may decide that it is in their self-interest to create an illegal entitlements system, i.e., to steal from the employed, rather than quietly starve to death. If, as the crime rate increases, society's response is to incarcerate these criminals, then the result will be more spending on entitlements for food, clothing, and shelter via prisons and orphanages. If, instead, society decides to expand the death penalty rather than locking up such criminals, and if we are successful in catching them, then the result will be to reduce the rankings of these unemployed more rapidly than under the first 'starving the unemployed' scenario. This will force the Federal Reserve to raise interest rates all the more rapidly to replenish the unemployment rate.

There are other possible policies that do not require a permanent army of unemployed and starving paupers to achieve a prosperous inflation-free economy. These alternatives hold greater promise for a civilized society. Our argument is not that the current safety net system to keep these paupers alive is desirable. Rather it is that a civil society can, and must, develop policies to assure employment for all and thereby deplete the army of paupers. Only if we accept a barbaric system that requires that we deliberately keep more than 6 per cent of the labour force unemployed, then, for both ethical and practical reasons, society must take care of the unemployed. It is cruel to develop welfare policies that punish the unemployed under the guise of motivating them to work, if, simultaneously, policy makers operate under the presumption that we must keep more than 8 million Americans unemployed. The best welfare system is to end the problem of unemployment and assure that everyone who wants to work for a living has an opportunity to do so. The best way to end welfare as we know it is to create the opportunity for every unemployed person to work their way out of poverty to the dignity of being a productive member of a civil society.

CIVILIZING CONSERVATISM

A few economists have advocated civil policies that do not require a permanent army of unemployed to achieve a prosperous, inflation-free society. To develop the discussion of these policies we must first understand the economic principles of a civilized society. Considerable progress in reducing the twin evils of unemployment and inflation can be achieved if we are willing to go beyond the choices posed by liberal or conservative economics alone. To fight unemployment *and* inflation we must make use of both self-interest and civic values in our economic governance. Until we adopt economic principles based on both self-interest and civic values, we will be doomed to political trade cycles of economic decline and social injustice interspersed with periods of relative prosperity. The transitory economic triumphs, if any, of any one Presidency or Congress will merely inflame the problems of the next. Since World War II, fleeting victories convinced first Liberals and then Conservatives that their hour of triumph paved the way towards a brighter future. The only constant has been the slow erosion of the resources and the economic greatness of America and the free world to deliver a growing prosperity to all members of our global civil society.

As a result of inconsistent and increasingly conservative governmental policies, we have witnessed a decline in our civilization, both as individuals and as a nation. The right to vote, which is surely one of the most basic foundations of our democracy, was exercised in the 1994 US elections by less than 40 per cent of registered voters.

The duty to pay taxes has eroded to the point where a third of the US population avoids paying their full share. In April 1995 (on the hundredth day of the Conservative Congress lead by Speaker Gingrich) the media implied that tax avoidance was socially acceptable (if not quite desirable) when it noted that about two dozen American billionaires would rather give up their American citizenship than pay an estimated $1.4 billion in taxes to the nation that gave them the opportunity to earn their billions. In order to replace the taxes that rich expatriates and others who do not completely comply with the tax law, the tax burden on honest taxpayers is more than eight per cent higher.

As a nation, we have lost the ability to cope with inflation without resorting to barbaric policies that work only if a significant portion of our population remains unemployed. We have accepted the notion that the working poor and the unemployed not only deserve their fate, but that they are to be blamed for it (as if only a character flaw could keep a person out of work and in poverty). We have watched the breakdown of one of the best accomplishments of American civilization, the post-World War II international economic order, without even a lingering memory of why we helped create it.

As our civic institutions erode, we lose our defences against the dangers that the passage of time may bring. History is filled with the wreckage of nations that did not realize the importance of maintaining their civilization until it was too late. The greatest danger facing any civilization is when its people forget the value of their own culture and institutions. When the Roman Empire fell to Attila in AD 453 the Huns were better educated and possessed the more civilized government; and the core of Roman society had already collapsed. Most great nations in history have eventually lost the spark that made their civilization great, and there is no reason to believe that America or any other democracy in our global economy can avoid this fate – but the more we understand the importance of civic values in our own lives, the more likely we are to maintain them.

Where does this hope come from? In the twenty-five years after World War II the United States *did* experience unprecedented economic prosperity in concert with a vibrant and progressive civic society. The benefits of economic competition were achieved in harmony with the benefits of civic and social values, and that prosperity helped propel most nations of the world along the same path of economic growth.

Today, the conservative philosophy has captured a position of media prominence, but civilized government still continues to be practiced in many places. For example, Thomas Peters and Robert Waterman's *In Search of Excellence* identifies a number of corporations which have successfully mixed organizational values with the pursuit of profit. In some of our political institutions there still remains a spark of civic spirit enlightening government combined with market incentives. For example, Title 4 of the 1990 Clean Air Act permits electric utilities that undertake to reduce significantly their sulphur dioxide emissions to reduce acid rain in the Northeast to earn marketable pollution rights that they can sell to other utilities who can not or do not undertake similar sulphur dioxide reductions. The effect is an overall reduction in regional acid rain, where the civic-minded utility receives some extra income as well.

A civilized society shows compassion and caring for all members of the community. It nurtures sensitivity to the needs of others and the desire to deal honestly and openly with all. A civilized society provides the opportunity for all to earn a livelihood, while it encourages excellence in all endeavours that people undertake independent of the monetary rewards for such activities.

A society which requires some members of the system be denied the sharing of economic gains and community participation in order for the economy to function is uncivilized. Economic policies that require certain groups in society be denied employment and a livelihood in order to discipline an inflationary economy are uncivilized. To base social prosperity on the hardship of others is a barbaric philosophy of government.

If a nation can thrive only on the hardships of some groups, it can not be called civilized – especially when the society is wealthy and has the capacity to produce far more goods and services than it currently does. Yet, some very influential bankers, financial writers, economists, and politicians have declared that unemployment is 'the price you have to pay for bringing down inflation', while others suggest that unemployment is 'part of the cure, not the problem'.

We often think of either self-interest *or* civic values as the important determinant of human behaviour, but too little attention has been focused on what happens when dollars and duty interact. To discuss the design of civilized public policies, we must first examine the analytical and philosophical views of those who advocate a system based solely on self-interest as well as the views of those who attempt to enlist civic values to help achieve specific policy objectives.

We recognize that our book is not the first to call attention to the limitations of self-interest as a governing mechanism for society. For example, under the communitarian banner, sociologist-economist Amitai Etzioni has organized a group to publicize the flaws of the paradigm of self-interest. Our argument, as developed in Chapter 3, does not focus merely on the limitations of the conservative argument. Rather it is based on a fundamental analytical distinction between the external incentives which motivate self-interest behaviour, and the internal incentives which motivate more complex social behaviour, such as loyalty, responsibility, the pursuit of excellence, love, and compassion. This concept of internal incentives permits us to investigate in some depth the nature of civic values and how these, when combined with self-interest, can provide civilized principles for improving our economic environment.

Chapter 4 provides a perspective on why conservative economists, whose analysis rests on self-interest as the sole motivating force, tend to provide advice which rarely works and is almost always uncivilized. Chapter 5 discusses the advantages and disadvantages of both a pure laissez-faire market system and a centrally planned system that is only oriented on civic values.

The remaining chapters will then develop a civilized approach to some specific major economic problems facing our nation as we approach the twenty-first century.

As may have become clear already, we are consciously making a distinction between liberalism and conservatism with which some conservatives (as well as some liberals) may not be comfortable. Some conservatives, such as the economist Milton Friedman, trace their philosophy back to that which went by the name of Liberalism in the eighteenth- and nineteenth-centuries. They see themselves as the 'true' liberals, in contrast to those who have stolen the title to serve quite antithetical ends. Friedman writes that 'the intellectual movement that went under the name of Liberalism emphasized freedom as the ultimate goal and the individual as the ultimate entity in society'. Other conservatives, however, for example, columnist

George Will, have accepted the conservative designation while condemning a solitary focus on free markets and self-interest. Instead conservatives such as George Will have also concerned themselves with the civic virtue of the citizenry – a topic which we identify with a Liberal approach.

Nevertheless, there are good grounds for making a useful distinction between an economic philosophy based solely on self-interest (which we label conservative) and one based only on civic values (which we call liberal). Those who believe in self-interested individuals operating in a free market as the primary form of social organization have far more frequently considered themselves conservatives than liberals – despite the semantic games some play. It is clear that if a politician advocates laissez-faire economic policies more strongly than his opponent, we would not think of calling this politician's economic policies 'liberal'.

Given this distinction between conservatives and liberals based on their reliance on either self-interest or civic values, we can unambiguously trace the linkage between conservative economics and the rise of conservative governments in recent years. In so doing we will be focusing on several basic questions:

(1) *Why economics?* Why is this framework of economics suited to undertake a study of the rules for operating a civilized society?

(2) What is so bad about relying on self-interest to provide civilized policies? What are the strengths and weaknesses of this form of motivation?

(3) Why do conservatives despise and fear government intervention? Why is the conservative view of the undesirability of government interference with individual behaviour a distorted view of the role of government in a civilized society?

(4) What are the dangers posed by organizing government around conservative ideas? How does a singular focus on self-interest obscure important changes that have occurred in our nation and our economy? What are the dangers to which a government based on conservative principles is vulnerable? What are the attributes of a civilized society that a conservative government does not sustain?

Our discussion must take place in a political context. The United States has been dominated by conservative economic policies in the 1980s and 1990s and by an overemphasis on our business culture. Our options for tomorrow are rooted in the trends of today. How did we get here, and what must we regain in order to strike a more even balance between self-interest and civic values? Why haven't we heard much from liberal economists during the Reagan, Bush, or Clinton years?

We start our discussion at the beginnings of American civilization.

ECONOMICS AND AMERICAN GOVERNMENT

WE THE PEOPLE of the United States, in order to form a more perfect Union, establish justice, insure domestic tranquility, provide for the common defense, promote the general welfare, and secure the blessings of liberty to ourselves and our posterity, do ordain and establish this Constitution of the United States of America.

The Preamble to the Constitution identifies the important parties in a discussion of American government – We the People. The Preamble provides guidance as to the meaning and purpose of our government. While the words may be broad enough to encompass several interpretations, they establish basic standards during all phases of the political cycle. The aspirations of our heritage are outlined: justice, domestic harmony, defence, prosperity, and liberty. Our public debate is ultimately oriented around these goals.

We approach the major issues of public policy differently today than in the age of the founding fathers, but we face many of the same concerns. A key difference is that today we speak of national policy issues in terms of economics rather than philosophy, using economic language to illuminate the problems that we face. Because of its logical structure and emphasis, conservative economics can only address issues of self-interest. Economics can be a useful guide to wise government, but it must be an economics that goes beyond the limited scope of conventional conservative economic theory. The language of national policy must be able to support the discussion of additional resources which become available only when there is a societal emphasis on both civic values – as expressed in the spirit of the US Constitution – and self-interest.

Why can't we keep economics separate from ideas of liberty and justice? There are studies of philosophy and law that have been devoted to these areas of liberty and justice for centuries. There are at least two reasons to expand economics into these areas. First, since Thomas Hobbes wrote *Leviathan* in the 1600s, the ideology underlying conservative economics has been applied to political philosophy. In recent years, a group of legal scholars have begun to implement an application of the textbook concepts of conservative economics in determining the nature of justice.

Bringing civic values into economic principles merely balances the export of the philosophy of self-interest from economics. But more importantly, government is coming more and more to depend on economics. By building on the strengths of the economics of self-interest we hope to civilize it so that the valuations behind our public debate will also reflect the values of civil society. Actually, the origins of economics have a wider social scope than most economists realize. The term 'economics' comes to us from Aristotle, who in his *Oeconomicos* discussed the political and social order of the basic economic unit of his time, the household estate. To Aristotle, economics was not only a matter of dollars and cents (or drachmas and obols), but also the foundation of a civilized society.

The conservative economics that has been used in our national political debate is too limited in scope to be a sole guide to public policy. Of all the areas of creative human intellectual activity, only economics still clings to its nineteenth-century foundations. Great advances have been made in mathematics, the arts, and the physical and medical sciences, as these studies have continuously re-examined their foundations. As a result of this re-examination, the metaphor of the universe as a precise, clock-like machine which was common to eighteenth- and nineteenth-century intellectual endeavours has been discarded. The conservative view of economics, however, is still too often guided and rationalized by an uncivilized, mechanical nineteenth-century economic analysis that advocates Social Darwinism and the law of the jungle as guiding economic principles.

The conservative focus solely on self-interest is destructive because the civic values that conservative economics ignores are very sensitive to public attitudes. If professors make the argument that public service, patriotism, or social justice are meaningless – and this message is echoed by business and community leaders – then the importance of civic values in motivating behaviour will be weakened. This is precisely the situation we face, and it arises from the incomplete picture of the world created by conservative economics. Our conservative government has not only overlooked the erosion of civic values, it has actually contributed to that erosion. The economic policy of planned recession and a natural rate of unemployment as practised by Presidents Ford, Carter, Reagan and Bush in the United States, and Prime Ministers Thatcher and Major in the United Kingdom to fight inflation are clear examples of the barbaric policies that have been inflicted on society. During the Clinton Administration, the attempt to use unemployment to contain inflationary pressures involved planning for a slow (less than full employment) growth path, euphemistically called a 'soft landing' by the talking heads in the political media.

By suggesting that an inevitable cost of a noninflationary economy is committing a significant portion of those in our society who want to work to persistent unemployment, conservative economics provides a philosophy that encourages the hemorrhaging of our civic values. The result is that, in the richest country in the world, society accepts the homeless, the poor, and the unemployed as a normal and necessary – even desirable – attribute of economic life. For a truly civil society, however, it is reprehensible for policy makers to required that some citizens be unemployed, and pushed into poverty as a normal and inevitable aspect of a healthy and vibrant economy.

No academic discipline shapes our modern world more than economics, and yet none has weaker foundations. Conservative economics is buttressed by hundreds of years of intensive study, and yet some of the basic principles and concepts have never been demonstrated. Conservative economics examines in very rich detail a world where self-interest is the only motivation – where no one will die for their loved ones, but where everyone has his price. Duty, loyalty and love exist in name only in conservative economics, but these values motivate only in proportion to the pleasure they yield and the market price they bring. This characterization of civic values, however, cannot explain the extraordinary behaviour we witness either during wartime, or when natural disaster strikes or even when 100 million citizens voluntarily pay their taxes despite odds which favour cheating.

Conservative economics distorts our view of the world, by focusing solely on self-interest. Self-interest can, *under certain circumstances*, inspire efforts to improve one's wealth while providing benefits to society; but our appreciation of self-interest must always be tempered with the explicit recognition that it must be constrained by civic values. Without these constraints, self-interest poses real dangers to any civilized community. Self-interest cannot inspire voluntary compliance with the law, and thus a society organized on the basis of self-interest alone leads inevitably to an intrusive and barbaric concept of government. This, in turn, incites the conservative plea to 'Get government off our backs!'

How did we get so far from 'We the People'? By investigating the conservative faith in self-interest and the conservative aversion to government, we can see how the attitudes behind the conservative plea have grown to undermine traditional civic values.

THE IMPORTANCE OF SELF-INTEREST

The pursuit of self-interest is at the heart of the conservative philosophy of economics. Adam Smith, one of the forefathers of conservative economics, wrote in *The Wealth of Nations*:

It is not from the benevolence of the butcher, the brewer, or the baker, that we expect our dinner, but from regard to their own self-interest. We address ourselves, not to their humanity but to their self-love, and never talk to them of our necessities, but of their advantage.

In this passage, Smith who is also the author of *The Theory of Moral Sentiments*, boils down human interaction to an exchange of wants: 'Give me that which I want, and you shall have this you want.' This view of motivation as being based on exchange was later expanded to include transactions which were made informally (or even unconsciously) but the basic premise remains: behaviour is shaped by the individual's calculations of the self-interest costs and benefits of undertaking any activity.

Even though the conservative philosophy focuses on individual self-interest, conservatives believe that the community can be served by individual wants. In this famous passage, Smith explains how the combination of wants could interact in beneficial ways:

Every individual is continually exerting himself to find out the most advantageous employment for whatever capital he can command. It is his own advantage, indeed, and not that of society which he has in view. . . . He intends only his own gain, and he is in this, as in many other cases, led by an invisible hand to promote an end which was no part of his intention. By pursuing his own interest he frequently promotes that of the society more effectually than when he really intends to promote it.

Smith's 'invisible hand' is a marketplace which effectively communicates individual wants and links them with those most able to satisfy them. Each individual is motivated to enter his most productive occupation in order to conduct more and larger transactions within the marketplace to satisfy more and more of his appetites. Thus, Smith argues, people pursuing their self-interest will strive also to be valuable to the community, leading to ever greater prosperity.

Even liberals, such as the economist John Maynard Keynes, have noted the advantages in encouraging the play of self-interest and providing for the free expression of private initiatives.

[Self-interest] is the best safeguard of personal liberty in the sense that, compared with any other system it greatly widens the field of personal choice. . . . It is also the best safeguard to the variety of life, which emerges precisely from this extended field of personal choice, and the loss of which is the greatest of all the losses of the homogeneous or totalitarian state. For this variety preserves the traditions which embody the most secure and successful choices of former generations; it colours the present with the diversification of its fancy; and, being the handmaid of experience as well as of tradition and of fancy, it is the most powerful instrument to better the future.

The conservative economic view of self-interest, however, remains fixed solely on the rosy side of self-interested behaviour. In describing behaviour in the economy, conservatives typically ignore the potential for deception and the use of brute strength to gain one's ends. In the marketplace of conservative economic theory it is assumed that businesses cannot wield any power over their competitors or customers. Individuals and businesses considering violence or deception will, according to conservative economics, calculate costs and benefits and conclude that it will not be profitable in the long run. Citizens will, it is claimed, protect themselves by ultimately withholding purchases from those who have cheated, deceived, or intimidated them.

Those who believe that cheating or deception cannot play an important role in the marketplace can not understand why, for example, the real world needs either a Food and Drug Administration or activists such as Ralph Nader. Conservatives assert that firms surely realize that dangerous products are unprofitable in the long run, and thus they would never put their name behind a product that threatens the public. Unfortunately, there are numerous cases where dangerous products have been marketed: Johns Manville and asbestos, GM's 'unsafe at any speed' Corvair, Ford's Pinto, and even fast food hamburger patties infested with the deadly e-coli bacteria.

Most reasonable people would agree that laws requiring manufacturers to recall sold products that are dangerous have made products safer today than they were when we relied solely on market forces to punish manufacturers of dangerous products. Once these unsafe products have been marketed, in the absence of recall legislation, it is in the self-interest of the business firm and its managers to deceive the public as to the inherent dangers of the product. The admission of fault even if it is due to human error (rather than deceit) threatens to inflict massive costs on the producer in the form of lost reputation and legal liabilities for damages. In his book, *Lawsuit*, famed lawyer Stuart Speiser provides a catalogue of historical cases of such denials by manufacturers.

In our society we have a number of methods of moderating business self-interest. Members of the US nuclear industry have acknowledged that the public pressure by environmental groups made American reactors safer from accidents such as the one that occurred in Chernobyl. In the former Soviet Union, without the prodding of environmental activists, the nuclear industry pursued its immediate self-interests in limiting short-run costs and in so doing ultimately exposed Soviet citizens – and other Eastern Europeans – to fatal health hazards. Although a conservative might argue that the Soviets had merely miscalculated the true risks and benefits of their industrial strategy, the safety measures which the American nuclear industry employs were chosen primarily because of public activism by concerned citizens rather than as a result of the calculations of industry managers.

In the aftermath of Chernobyl, the Soviet nuclear industry (and the Soviet system) did suffer the 'long-run loss of reputation' which conservatives count on to regulate business. It is unclear, however, whether this lesson will alter significantly the behaviour of the nations that followed the breakup of the Soviet Union. Certainly this after-the-fact loss of reputation will provide little solace to the victims of Chernobyl.

CONSERVATIVE GOVERNMENT

The political ramifications of conservative philosophy as expressed by its intellectual father, Thomas Hobbes, reveal the inevitable barbarism of conservative premises. Hobbes believed that only a dictator, a Leviathan, could stand up to the competing appetites of the people and enforce order and stability (if not justice). Since Hobbes believed that self-centred appetite was the only motivating force underlying human behaviour, and that this always resulted in a conflict of interests among individuals, it follows that the only viable social organization was one where a dictator places constraints upon the people. In the absence of a Leviathan, the perpetual conflict of self-interested individuals attempting to better themselves at the expense of their neighbours in Hobbes's barbaric 'state of nature' would make everyone worse off.

Conservatives have accepted Hobbes's stress on the need to impose order upon the appetites of the people, while abhorring his solution of a dictator. The conservative dilemma therefore is how to preserve the individual liberty of people who may themselves be trying to repress the liberty of others. Conservatives see the fundamental goal of society as restraining factions and individuals so that they are unable to violate the freedoms of others. From this has developed a concept of negative liberty – the idea that liberty does not mean active participation in civic life, but rather the absence of repression. Thus, the decline in voter participation is generally taken by conservatives to indicate voter satisfaction, since they are not voting *against* the status quo. From a civic perspective, however, the decline in voter turnout is a symptom of the decay in our civic values.

The free market is a very appealing concept to conservatives, because they believe that the free market can replace the Leviathan and impose order on the destructive cacophony of appetites in the economy. The freedom of the marketplace is supposed to be a freedom from oppression. However, as we shall see later, the free market *cannot* create order out of chaos. Something must restrain the self-interest of individuals or we will have Hobbes's war of all against all.

Proponents of conservative economics such as Milton Friedman, Ayn Rand, or Alan Greenspan see our society as facing only two choices for social organization: capitalist freedom or an authoritarian servitude. The capitalist society, based on the self-interested pursuit of individual appetites and achievement in accordance with the rules of the economic marketplace, is said to govern people only by their wants and their capabilities. The authoritarian society governs by decree from above, compelling obedience by the threat of overt force.

Looking at these two choices, conservatives assume that the benefits of liberty in a free society are only possible where there is first capitalism. We suggest that the conservative ordering is a reversal of the facts. Historically, when relatively open markets have developed, there were civilizing social and political institutions already in existence which have made this possible. Italy in the early Renaissance, and England and American in their industrial revolutions each had a very special heritage of civilized institutions which enabled them to maintain liberty, prosperity and justice in their societies for many generations.

The capitalism of conservative economics – without the moderating influence of a supportive civilized culture – is perilously unstable. If we respect people only for their capacity to produce and if we interact with others only to the degree that we can get something from them, then the existing civilized influences in our society will begin to erode. This inspires crime, violence and political revolution by those who cannot profit from existing market situations.

Karl Marx's focus on capitalist theory – as opposed to the more moderate reality of capitalism in existing societies – led him to conclude that capitalism will tend to sow the seeds of its own destruction. Marx has been proven wrong because society in its civilized practices has over time adopted policies which have moderated some of the worst shortcomings of a pure capitalist system.

Civilized government, however, comes not solely from enforcing sanctions against those who violate rules, but by the government of the people working with the people to encourage voluntary compliance with standards of conduct. Civilized incentives are crucial to establishing institutions that provide the levels of coordination and participation necessary to run our complex modern economy efficiently.

Without civic values, we are doomed to live either in an anarchic state of nature where only the powerful thrive, or under the barbaric domination of a government that manipulates its subjects like animals. As the nineteenth-century philosopher Jeremy Bentham put it:

Mankind is governed by pain and pleasure. Pleasures and pains, then, are the instruments with which the legislator has to work.

The barbaric spirit of Hobbes and Bentham lives on. After discussing the effects of the budget deficit on congressional spending in the *Washington Post*, George Will concluded with a modern 'axiom of conservative realism: in a democracy fear does the work of reason'. Like Hobbes, Will cannot envision human conduct which is not ultimately driven by barbaric stimuli. On the other hand we argue that individuals and (self-)interest groups can learn to control their appetites in pursuit of some common civic values.

The public policies that emerge from the conservative mindset are not necessarily cruel, but they are barbaric. Policies which offer both a carrot and a stick as incentives to self-interested individuals are seen as even-handed by conservatives. Primitive appeals to appetite and fear can not establish justice or assure domestic tranquility.

Soldiers willingly risk their lives in order to defend their families and their nation, not because they are being paid and/or threatened. Government based solely on policies of carrots and sticks to motivate their citizens can only lead to a domestic war of neighbour against neighbour, not the domestic tranquility to which the Constitution aspires.

Without enlisting civic virtues, we will never be able to secure the blessings of liberty and domestic tranquillity. Carrot and stick policies are more appropriate to spur animals into action than to enlist members of a civil society towards a common goal. Without enlisting civic values, the civilized promises of the United States Constitution cannot be met.

Conservatives policies run into unnecessary difficulties because of their inability to enlist the support of more civilized incentives than those of self-interest alone. Public policies using 'carrots' often result in a flawed result known as goal displacement. For example, a city decides to rid itself

of rattlesnakes in accordance with the precepts of conservative economics
– a bounty is offered for every dead snake brought to city hall. Soon the
poorest citizens, motivated by the bounty fee, start raising rattlesnakes!

Establishing understanding of (and compliance with) the intent of rules
requires common understandings. Indeed, one of the central attributes of
a civilized society is the ability to communicate by the use of a shared
dialect – a common language of actions and terms. Without the bonds of
culture and experience inherent in a shared dialect it becomes increasingly
difficult to conduct business or to regulate it. Accordingly, when different
cultures, possessing different standards of what is acceptable behaviour
coexist in the same society, this multiculturalism can impede the development of a coherent standard of civilized conduct. This does not mean that
the dominant culture must destroy the others. Rather what is required is a
social agreement on civic values that promotes tolerance and channels
conflict in ways that do not destroy core values. Since the civic values that
motivate each group come from its own particular culture, governing in a
multicultural civic society is a particularly challenging enterprise. While
we will touch upon the issue of combining civic values from different
cultures, the main theme of this book is the interaction of self-interest with
civic values.

We must emphasize that the bonds of civic heritage in a democratic
society are not shackles forced upon the people by governing power. Indeed,
a good example of a common industrial culture is that of the Japanese,
which shapes the conduct of business by maintaining a set of virtues that
businessmen willingly aspire to attain. The cure for goal displacement is
a society with sufficient coherence to place the self-interested incentive
force of carrots into the appropriate civilized context.

From the conservative position that society should be based only on the
self-interest of appetite and fear, it follows that any sort of welfare programme must be harmful. In this view, the more painful it is to be poor,
the more people will struggle to avoid poverty. The appetite for wealth
and the fear of poverty are the only fuel for the engines that drive the
conservative economy. In this hypothetical world, an independent work
ethic cannot exist. Since it is assumed that job opportunities are available
for all, any unemployment must be the fault of the unemployed. This is the
habitat of the so called 'welfare queens' and the rest of the menagerie of
cheats and wastrels. The conservative economic world is filled with malingerers, and the appropriate policy is to whip them into submission.

In the real world, where both hardworking and lazy people face poverty,
conservative solutions inflict pain on them all. Furthermore, the game is
rigged as long as we believe that there must always be 6 per cent of the

working population who do not have a job. Indeed, in an economy whose lacklustre rate of growth performance is not sufficient to lift the standard of living of all inhabitants year after year (as has been the case in the United States since the early 1970s), principles of self-interest encourage domestic crime, violence, and deceit of others as a quick solution to the economic problems of the poor. The barrier preventing a complete breakdown of civil behaviour is that many people still believe in the civic values that promote a civilized society.

When the economic system perpetuates poverty and unemployment among large segments of the population without hope of near term improvement, the democratic way of life is increasingly threatened. As economist John Cornwall notes, subjecting significant portions of the population to persistent bouts of unemployment erodes the work ethic. If this policy pursuit of a natural rate of unemployment is accompanied by removal of a social safety net justified on the argument this is necessary to cure 'welfare dependency' and end the molly coddling of welfare malingerers then, as Cornwall writes, the unemployed 'will learn to supplement their income by joining underground and underworld economies'.

The conservative assumptions of human behaviour motivated solely by self-interest shapes a political sphere in which government can act only through appeals either to a 'greed is good' notion or through ubiquitous enforcement which increases the risks and penalties of violating the law. Conservative economists do not concern themselves with the development, evolution, and strengthening of civilizing institutions which support voluntary rule-abiding behaviour. The only way the conservatives can maintain public order is through the use of carrots and sticks – the 'giveaways' and the 'government interference' that they themselves deplore.

DECLINE OF INSTITUTIONS

How can we put so much faith in the potential of the people to conduct their lives in a civilized fashion? We have already made mention of the decline in the norms which support our voluntary system of taxation, the willingness to resort to barbaric unemployment policies, and the breakdown of the post-war international monetary system. Furthermore, we believe that these areas of decline are linked not only with each other, but with a larger erosion of civic norms within our society.

Evidence of this erosion is being seen everywhere in our economic institutions. For example, adversarial litigation has come to replace more civilized forms of dispute resolution on crucial public questions such as financing of education, abortion, and environmental protection. The explosion of formal litigation in resolving our public debates not only indicates that many of our old institutions no longer function properly, but it also raises concerns that our legal institutions will not be able to handle this overload for much longer. Robert Reich writes of this threat in *The Next American Frontier*:

> There is a danger that the law itself will lose its legitimacy in the process. Legal judgments cannot create social consensus. Quite the reverse: law can resolve conflicts only through reference to shared principles.

As law loses its legitimacy, that is, as the civic core of society erodes, we are left with fewer civic resources, but the same divisive issues.

Other important institutions have also been mentioned as exhibiting signs of erosion. The loyalty to one's workplace that was once common in America has been weakened by the ephemeral corporate world where both workers and executives constantly move from job to job, or even worse, the productive labour force is continually 'downsized'. Managers of multinational firms encourage local communities to compete on the magnitude of local tax abatements for siting a plant in the community and thereby obtaining local community services without having the civic responsibility for paying for them.

The early post-World War II idea of a corporate IBM providing lifetime employment opportunities for those who work hard for the enterprise seems as distant to modern-day corporations in America as the War of Independence. Even in Corporate Japan where the idea of corporate responsibility to workers to guarantee lifetime employment still exists, there is evidence that this civilized business system is being gradually eroded.

For individuals, the opportunity to provide high level political service to the community has frequently become little more than a ticket to punch on the way to Wall Street and Corporate America boardrooms where the norms of fair trading have, since the 1970s, fallen suspect. Columnist William Safire noted several of these trends in the *New York Times* and concluded simply:

> We have two jobs; to make our institutions more worthy of respect; and then to respect them.

Our civilization may not yet be on the brink of collapse, but some of our institutions are. These institutions are not isolated from society at large

– losing a battle for Wall Street civic norms in an isolated case reduces the credibility of all Wall Street traders. The corruption spills over to other areas of business, polluting the existing social norms and thus weakening them. The cynicism that evolves from such episodes saps our civic values and propels us further down the road to barbarism.

So where do we get hope for civilization as we approach the twenty-first century? If there is hope for a civilized society, it must lie somewhere beyond the self-interest of conservative economics. The authors of *Habits of the Heart*, a sociological inquiry into the American character, trace the roots of the American spirit of civic values back to the founding fathers:

'Is there no virtue among us?' asked Madison. 'If there be not, no form of government can render us secure. To suppose that any form of government will secure liberty or happiness without any virtue in the people is a chimerical idea.'

If civic values do contribute to the health of our economic and social institutions, then we are left with the surprising conclusion that the hard-headed and pragmatic approach to solving the problems of government must involve pursuit of this civic virtue among ourselves. And by civic virtue we mean nothing more ethereal than excellence in the pursuit of civic values. Even conservative columnist George Will agrees on a definition of civic virtue as 'Good citizenship, whose principal components are moderation, social sympathy, and willingness to sacrifice private desires for public ends'. Those conservatives who talk of a return to the basic values of family and community must understand that these civic virtues must be nurtured and cultivated. They can not grow in a desert devoted to unregulated self-interest.

CIVILIZED GOVERNMENT AND CIVIC VIRTUE

Civilized society requires public cooperation by appealing to national ideals of fairness and justice in the pursuit of self-interest and efficiency. During the first oil shock in the fall and winter of 1973–4, for example, long lines developed at gas stations, creating frustration and wasting scarce gasoline. Contingent rationing plans were established, nationwide speed limits set, Sunday gasoline sales were banned, and President Nixon even ordered non-essential outdoor lighting – such as Christmas trees – to be turned off. At the same time, Nixon's conservative Council of Economic Advisors unanimously advocated resolving the problem by allowing the pump price of gas to rise. Gas lines would disappear as the poor and the those with less 'urgent' needs for gas were forced to conserve by the price increase. Those who could afford it would then have easy access to the available gasoline. The energy problem was thus not attributed to an external cartel operating in its own self-interest – but rather to the remaining price controls which hampered the free market.

The problem with this conservative approach of relying solely on higher pump prices to eliminate the shortage of such a basic commodity as gasoline was that it alone would not calm the panic atmosphere that beset the nation. Pricing gasoline out of some people's reach would merely have set the have-nots against the haves. It would divide the nation at a time when the economic threat was external to the community.

Suddenly, however, an innovative solution that did not require a price increase emerged from Oregon and within a few weeks spread nationwide. The civilized system that was adopted was that cars with licence plates ending in even numbers could fill up on even days and those with odd numbers on odd days. Almost overnight the lines and much of the frustration disappeared. The erosion of the public spirit was halted. People complied with this simple odd-even rule, not because they were forced to by their pocketbooks but because it was a fair and just solution. The capacity to take action as a community to resolve a common problem not only provided for a more just solution, but for a policy which was better able to enlist the voluntary compliance needed to implement a successful policy.

If we are to harness our capacity to create just economic solutions to our public policy problems we must do so from a philosophical perspective which – unlike conservative economics – recognizes the worth of civic values as well as self-interest, and uses both as forces to motivate behaviour to achieve a civilized economic society.

THE CIVIC TRADITION OF EXCELLENCE AND LIBERTY

Before Hobbes, there existed an intellectual tradition which acknowledged the need to blend civilized aspects of human nature with self-interest in successful ventures. Its advocate, the reader might be surprised to learn was Niccolo Machiavelli – who was well aware of some of the advantages created by the pursuit of self-interest. It was Machiavelli who first made the point (later echoed by Adam Smith) that competition and even conflict have beneficial applications:

Wealth derived from agriculture as well as from trade increases more rapidly in a free country, for all men gladly increase those things and seek to acquire those goods which they believe they can enjoy once they have acquired them. Thus it comes about that men in competition with each other think about both private and public benefits, and both one and the other continue to grow miraculously.

Machiavelli's view of human nature, however, was not limited to the inevitable conflicts of appetite. He made distinctions between the motivations of self-interest and civic values – distinctions that are entirely absent from the writings of Hobbes and modern conservatives. For example, Machiavelli noted:

Friendships that are acquired by a price and not by virtue are purchased but not owned, and at the proper moment they cannot be spent.

Aristotle, Machiavelli, Madison, and others in the civic tradition clearly distinguished the difference between goods which can be purchased for money, and goods which can only be obtained through other means such as virtue. (We will discuss these two sorts of goods in much greater depth in Chapter 3.) The civic tradition provides us with a conception of government which is different from the negative liberty of conservatism.

What are the attributes of a good society in this civic tradition? A civilized society will work to facilitate the development of excellence in *all* of its members. This means that our society should maintain the personal liberty of the people *and* encourage their full employment. One of the most important goals of a democratic civilized society is to provide the opportunity for employment for all who are willing and able to work. The central principle of civilized economics must be to promote an environment in which the benefits of market competition can be achieved in tandem with the benefits of civilization.

A civilized society recognizes virtue – that is, the pursuit of excellence for its own sake – as a fundamental motivation upon which civilization is built. 'If a thing is worth doing, it is worth doing well!' In contrast, a society where skills and characteristics are valued *only* by what can be received in exchange for them in a market will lack the civic spirit which makes organizations function effectively. It is not a surprise, therefore, to see that economists who advocate a policy goal of planned unemployment also conceive of workers who are shirkers and have to be motivated to provide an honest day's work by constant surveillance and the fear of joining the large army of the unemployed.

A civilized society, on the other hand, will encourage the establishment of excellence in the workplace by encouraging skills which are measured not only for their market value, but also for the level of human capacity which they demonstrate. Included among these excellences are not only technical and artistic skills, but traits such as loyalty, bravery, honesty, and compassion. The mottos of a civilized workforce are 'An Honest Day's Work for an Honest Day's Pay' and 'We Are Here to Provide the Customer with the Best Product and Service Humanly Possible'.

The ideals of excellence exist only *within* a community. Whether the excellence is that of being a good secretary, a good welder, a good Christian, or a good long-distance runner, the ideal of excellence is formed among the community of practitioners. Thomas Peters and Robert Waterman write in *In Search of Excellence* how the most successful firms depend on more than the simple financial incentives of self-interest economics in motivating their people:

> The top performers create a broad, uplifting, shared culture, a coherent framework within which charged-up people search for appropriate adaptations. Their ability to extract extraordinary contributions from very large numbers of people turns on the ability to create a sense of highly valued purpose.

Some proponents of conservative economics may recognize the value of inspiration, but they believe that spirit can be purchased in exchange for money or goods in the marketplace. Money is a very flexible medium, but the only loyalty it can enlist is the servitude which the conservatives abhor. A man working only because he is given something in exchange for his labour will shirk or cut corners whenever he thinks he is not being watched. Once it is recognized that civic values can also motivate workers, then it becomes apparent that a person working at their craft, or sphere of excellence, will provide additional advantages unforeseen by conservatives. A true craftsman works both for his employer and for himself.

A civilized society must promote *both* personal liberties and the full employment of resources. Without personal liberty, people are prevented from participating in the civic and social community in which civilized values are developed. If society excludes certain individuals or groups from participating in the public arena by either political discrimination or planned unemployment, then the evolving societal values will reflect this exclusion, fracturing society and raising the risks of violent protest, oppression, and other aspects of barbarism. A fractured society lacks the social coherence necessary to conduct its affairs without the intermediation of extensive and cumbersome mechanisms to force coordination, as Reich noted in regard to our overloaded legal system.

But personal liberty without the full employment of all of our national resources is still uncivilized. During the Eisenhower Administration, the Secretary of the Treasury declared that 'one of the Rights of a Free Society is the Right to Starve'. In a civilized economy no one who is willing to work for a living should be permitted to starve merely for lack of a job. Less-than-full employment of resources is not only wasteful, but it also strikes at the heart of community values and the spirit of excellence. Jobs provide people with dignity. Jobs also provide the basis for the practice of excellence in a very important sphere of the individual's life.

If a society is organized so that it routinely violates personal liberties or it deliberately operates at less than full employment, at least some of its citizenry will be at the mercy of barbaric forces. For it is barbaric to require that certain people in society be denied employment or personal liberty for the society to survive. A nation which thrives on the hardships of its members cannot be called civilized.

Note

1. A more technical specification of this same basic concept that directly links a specific unemployment rate with the containment of inflation is the Non-Accelerating Inflation Rate of Unemployment, or NAIRU.

2 The Demise of Liberal Economics and the Emergence of Conservativism

The demise of liberal public policy discussions in recent years can be traced to the abandonment of the spirit of civilization by many economists and politicians who previously labelled themselves as liberal. The 1960s culminated in a 'liberal' Administration that was simultaneously promoting the 'Great Society' of social welfare programmes and the Vietnam War. The unpopularity of this uncivilized war eroded the credibility of those who espoused the importance of civic values and led to the election of Richard Nixon who held particularly strong conservative views. At the same time, the promise of liberal economic analysis was betrayed in academic and intellectual circles by the erosion and near collapse of the core ideas that supported it.

Liberals lost faith in the power of civic values, and without civic values, the only resource left with which to shape a vision of the future was self-interest. By the 1980s, the L-word became a symbol of shame and ridicule. One example of this attempt to avoid the liberal appellation is the title of a 1987 book written by Princeton University professor Alan Blinder who was later appointed to the Federal Reserve by President Clinton. Blinder attempted to prove that liberals could be just as hard-headed about self-interest economic principles as conservatives. The title of Blinder's book was *Hard Heads, Soft Hearts: Tough Minded Economics for a Just Society.* (Blinder took it as axiom that it was a virtue for economists to have 'hard heads'.)

Starting in the 1960s, liberal economists attempted to rebuild their theoretical analysis on the assumption that people were motivated solely on the basis of self-interest. Liberals adopted the analytical and philosophical axioms of conservative economics – an intellectual and ethical framework based solely on the bottom line. Having adopted the conservative starting point, all that remained was to echo conservative conclusions.

The conflict between conservative logic and civilized ideals leads to a confused and bastardized version of liberal economics and liberal policy.

Since the 1960s economic analysis has adopted the conservative economic dogma that treats a nation as an aggregate of isolated self-interested individuals locked in perpetual struggle with each other. The monetary incentives that shape a portion of our behaviour have been taken to represent us in our entirety. Consequently, there can be no appeal to the public interest, to the spirit of 'We the People'. All that society can amount to is many separate individuals, each looking out for Number One. In the battle of ideas, those who maintained a liberal facade while accepting the conservative philosophy could provide only a weak imitation of conservative policies. 'Me too'-ism is never a successful political agenda or weapon to win the philosophical debate regarding public policy.

This erosion of civic virtue in liberalism can be seen in many areas. In 1961, excellence was the foundation of President Kennedy's charge to the National Aeronautics and Space Administration (NASA) to land a man on the moon and conquer the space frontier because it was there and not because it offered untold monetary rewards. Later NASA was faced with the erosion of the civic values which supported space exploration. The only argument remaining to promote the space programme was one based on self-interest. Thus NASA's supporters felt they had to argue that technological spin-offs from the space programme are so beneficial to the economy that they pay for the government's investment several times over.

But once a conservative economic position was adopted, it became difficult to argue for NASA funding as a means of pursuing economic self-interest (even if there is some evidence of the value of spin-offs and long-range technological investments). A former Office of Management and Budget Director, David Stockman, a self-proclaimed 'space buff', explained how the spin-off argument does not make sense from the conservative perspective:

> The way to improve medical telemetry or anything else was to reward private inventors, entrepreneurs, and investors with lower taxes. NASA was in effect claiming that the way to build a better mousetrap was to go to Jupiter.

If we lived in the world that conservatives imagine, Stockman would be right. But in our American civilization there are values beyond the self-interest of conservative economics. The true value of the space programme for Americans was best seen in the afternoon and evening of 28 January 1986, after the Shuttle Challenger had been lost with all of her crew. As the nation listened to the news, there was something more than lost profits on the bottom line that was being mourned.

The bottom-line vision of our economy has led liberals to a philosophical dead end. Once the premise was accepted that our resources would always be scarce and depletable, conflict over those limited resources was inevitable. Consequently, our society was destined to decay. Recognition of the potential abundance that a civilized society could promote was lost. A case in point is the 'limits to growth' doctrine that the Club of Rome promoted in the 1970s. Professor D. H. Meadows and his associates from the Massachusetts Institute of Technology predicted in their Project on the Predicament of Mankind that our natural resources would very shortly be depleted. Their vision was of 'a world where industrial production has sunk to zero. Where population has suffered a catastrophic decline. . . . Where civilization is a distant memory'. The 'liberal' Club of Rome suggested that programmes to accelerate economic growth should be abandoned since the inevitable depletion of our resources doomed any such programmes. What actually failed in the 1980s were the predictions of these liberals. Supplies of oil and precious metals flooded the market. Indeed, the failure of the liberal's predictions merely served to reinforce the conservative drift of liberal economics.

The loss of direction of liberal economics can be illustrated with MIT Professor Lester Thurow's book *The Zero-Sum Society*. Thurow used the example of a sporting event – where one team's gain must always be at the expense of another's loss – to demonstrate the zero-sum game concept analogy for society. The pluses for wins and minuses for losses always balance at zero. In effect, the teams are battling solely to win the game – the scoreboard is the bottom line. The moral is that just as in sports matches, there are winners and losers – some must lose so that others may gain.

Professor Thurow's zero-sum game concept does not recognize civic values as an important economic influence, and thus the analogy contains a fatal flaw; even sporting events are not necessarily zero-sum contests. The idea that 'It is not whether you win or lose, but how you play the game' is a civilized truth we tell our young. Often winning or losing is not as important as the particular excellence with which one plays the game. Kellen Winslow of the San Diego Chargers earned more respect by catching 13 passes and blocking a field goal to send a 1982 playoff game with the Miami Dolphins into overtime than many players have achieved by winning any game in their entire careers, even though his team did not even reach the Super Bowl. Winslow's excellence won him a victory that was not recorded on the scoreboard. Even his statistics for that day do not capture the entirety of his accomplishment. He simply achieved an excellence which cannot be appreciated in terms of the bottom line. In sports, and in our lives as individuals and citizens, our rewards come both from the payment we receive and from the excellences we achieve.

A zero-sum society implies that long-term prosperity for the United States depends on our capacity to endure considerable hardships for a significant period of time. This fits in with President Carter's 'crisis of confidence' address – the so-called malaise speech – but his zero-sum image failed to elicit any form of positive public response. This was not merely because President Carter offered a painful public policy while Ronald Reagan was offering a painless one, but also because recent liberal economic philosophy was shaped in the framework of conservative economics – of self-interest and not of civilization.

It is the absence of civic spirit that has turned liberal economics into a weak and strangely distorted shadow of conservative economics. Ironically, liberals like Thurow, who in earlier years recognized the inapplicability of conservative economic doctrine to resolving real world problems, began to base their arguments for social justice on people's self-interest – and not on civic concepts such as justice.

Without civic spirit, President Carter's final 'liberal' economic policy initiatives became merely a warm-up for Reaganomics.

THE PARADOX OF REAGANOMICS

In the 1970s, after the civilized core of liberal economics had been eroded, a modern version of the nineteenth-century conservative vision arrived on the national scene. The economics of the entrepreneur, shaped by writers like George Gilder and Jude Wanniski, and promoted by Ronald Reagan, swept the political agenda clean. The national heroes of the 1980s became the garage-workshop inventor, as typified by Steven Jobs of Apple Computer fame, Bill Gates of Microsoft and the corporate manager and deal-maker as personified by Chrysler's Lee Iacocca.

Civic virtues were presented as if they were attributes of self-interest. Gilder, in *Wealth and Poverty*, distinguishes the liberal economic doctrine of the 1970s (which he calls socialism) from his entrepreneurial creed as follows:

[Socialism] is based on empirically calculable human power; the other on optimism and faith. . . . When faith dies, so does enterprise. It is impossible to create a system of collective regulation and safety that does not finally deaden the moral sources of the willingness to face danger and fight, that does not dampen the spontaneous flow of gifts and experiments which extend the dimensions of the world and the circles of human sympathy.

This optimistic spirit, represented by candidate Reagan as a quality of entrepreneurs, struck a chord with the American public. At a time when President Carter was peddling malaise as a justification for ineffective government, this positive vision of the virtues of human aspiration was unbeatable.

The new entrepreneurial credo that 'incentives work' was adopted by the nation as a whole, with incentives being defined as being monetary (or what we define in Chapter 3 as external incentives). To create such incentives, tax rates were drastically lowered. The income tax rates of the wealthiest taxpayers plummeted from 70 per cent to 50 per cent in 1982 and declined again to 28 per cent in 1988 – a massive change in economic and social policy. The rationale for this massive tax reduction was that the entrepreneurial spirit was to be released from regulatory restraint and high marginal tax rates, so that the ingenuity of the human spirit could create new wealth. The faith of entrepreneurs in their creative handiwork and their ability to inspire their employees would guide Americans to an ever brighter and better future.

This gospel of opportunity was the single most important idea presented by the Great Communicator himself. President Reagan had initiated a cultural exchange (or revitalization) by rekindling a spirit of optimism and national self-confidence. The expression of national pride heard at such public events as the 1984 Summer Olympics and the Centennial of the Statue of Liberty would have seemed artificial and insincere in the 1970s.

One of the great paradoxes of the twentieth century is that Ronald Reagan campaigned for office on the issues that make the United States a civilized society – the importance of family and community values in guiding our behaviour – while his Administration promoted policies based solely on economic self-interest. The spirit underlying the Reagan vision was vastly different from the assumption of self-interest upon which conservative economics and Reagan's supply-side policy proposals was built. No wonder it was termed 'voodoo economics' by Candidate George Bush in the 1980 campaign. Reagan's vision and his economic platform were incompatible. No wonder that the tax cuts Reagan engineered in 1982 that were supposed to produce a balanced budget by 1985 fostered annual deficits in the hundreds of billions while creating economic prosperity and, until taxes were raised to reduce the deficit in the Bush Administration, a dramatic decline in unemployment.

Love of country and community, loyalty, and other civilized values were the dominant chords of Reagan's rhetoric but entirely absent from the conservative economics underlying his Administration's policies. The Reagan paradox might be traced to the pattern by which this White House was run – those responsible for presenting President Reagan to the public and those who made Reagan Administration policy were usually different people, and none were ever called upon to reconcile the two sets of messages that the Reagan Administration presented.

What President Reagan succeeded in doing was to integrate a message about the civilized virtues of human excellence with a conservative political agenda which, as it was enacted, would inevitably erode civic values. Consequently, while President Reagan's themes helped to revitalize the aspirations of the civilized American spirit, the conservative nature of his policies eroded the civic values which underlie his civilized promise.

This paradox explains the contrast between his vast personal popularity and the limited public support for his legislative programme and judicial appointments. The public responded to the President's civic message, but not to his Administration's policies which broke that civilized promise. Underneath the civilized human symbols were the same conservative economic focus on self-interest and the bottom-line. Reagan's policies were still based on the premise that people cannot be governed unless forced or bribed – that everyone on welfare is secretly laughing at the rest of us, that those drawing unemployment are merely lazy, and that the poor must face their poverty without relief.

George Bush was a colourless politician who discovered while running for President in 1988 that the only way he could erase a large shortfall in the opinion polls was to enlist the public's fear and hatred of a black convict, Willie Horton, who committed murder and rape while on furlough from a prison in the state where Bush's opponent was governor. This message of fear may have won the election, but it accelerated the polarization and fear that was breaking down America's civil society.

The effect of the misguided economic policies undertaken during the Bush Administration in 1990 (as we will discuss in later chapters) provided Bill Clinton with the opportunity to defeat Bush in the 1992 election. Clinton came from the conservative wing of the more liberal political party. Indeed, his campaign programme was entitled 'Putting People First'. The programme suggested that Clinton was not going to sacrifice those who wanted to work and play by the civil rules of society to the conservative fight against inflation. Unfortunately, when Clinton took office, no alternative to the conservative argument was made available to him by his aides.

DESPERATE CHOICES OF A BARBARIC WORLD

> That girls are raped, that two boys knife a third,
> Were axioms to him who'd never heard
> Of any world where promises were kept,
> Or one could weep, because another wept.
>
> W. H. Auden

History provides us with many examples of nations that have lost their civilization. As the result of our economic policies there are places in America where our people are ruled more by hunger and fear than the civic values of the Constitution. This grim reality not only shows how important it is to maintain the institutions that protect civilization, but also how conservative economics with its willingness to sacrifice human livelihoods to combat inflation makes us vulnerable to barbarism.

Machiavelli lived in a barbaric age, and his experience – suffering torture after his government was overthrown – made him examine the painful choices of a barbaric world. When a society's civilization has eroded, so that its institutions have lost their credibility – their virtue – then Machiavelli felt that there was no way for the people to pull themselves up by their bootstraps into a more civilized state.

> It is not enough to employ lawful means, for lawful methods are now useless; it is necessary to have recourse to extraordinary measures, such as violence or arms, and to become, before all else, prince of that city in order to be able to deal with it in one's own way.

At this desperate juncture when civilization has collapsed and barbarism rules, the only possible salvation Machiavelli sees is in one leader, in a Leviathan who can impose order in a barbaric world. This is the nature of the world described by both Hobbes and conservative economists. If all civilized incentives no longer exist, then in fact Hobbes's belief in the need for an absolute ruler *is* correct. Machiavelli's Leviathan would dominate the barbaric world and thereby have the power to re-establish civilized customs and laws. But conservatives do not envision any mechanism for re-establishing social order, because they do not recognize that society can collapse.

The implication for Machiavelli was very grim – once lost, civilization is not easily re-attained. In a world fallen into barbarism, the options are few and painful: remain in the rut of civil and social strife or risk the almost certain despotism of a tyrant.

'VALUE NEUTRAL' BARBARISM

Starting in the 1980s as the conservative rhetoric on the need for unemployment to fight inflation conquered America's public forums as completely 'as the Holy Inquisition conquered Spain' (to use one of Keynes's colourful phrases), the American government took steps towards eliminating job-training programmes in the inner cities. A natural rate of unemployment of 6 per cent nationally led to an unemployment rate of 18 per cent or more among the young minority males who live in the inner cities.

Conservative dialect indicated that government spending on job-training programmes was wasteful. Analysis based on self-interest concluded that businessmen in a free market can provide better job training for workers in the inner cities. The conservative 'supply-side' philosophy of the Reagan Administration saw that inner city unemployment problems were due to the lack of incentives for businessmen to create job training for disadvantaged people.

Fifteen years later, many former liberal commentators have joined conservatives in attributing the inner city problems of crime, poverty, and disease to the poor family environment created by absent inner city fathers. We agree that inner city values play a role in the current problems. No one is denying that a violent and brutal world has been created in our inner cities, but few question the role and influence that the conservative natural rate of unemployment policy has played in creating this situation.

In the 1990s, conservative economic policies again focus on self-interest and ignore civic values. Conservative rhetoric today suggests that the remaining welfare programmes that primarily benefit children of single mothers are the cause of the inner city problems. The conservative solution is to withdraw benefits to create incentives for mothers and children to get off welfare and into the job market. Yet the government is not willing to spend what would be necessary to stimulate the economy to create sufficient additional jobs to absorb those forced off welfare. Nor is the government willing to provide the resources necessary to provide these mothers with the job skills and child care needed while learning these skills.

If the 1990s welfare cuts are as counterproductive as the welfare reforms and reduction in job training programmes of the 1980s, then the prospect for increasing crime, poverty, and disease in our cities is frightening. And if that even more brutal and frightening world becomes real, then those who promote and enact conservative economic policy will once again deny intellectual responsibility for the damage they have done.

It is in regard to the fundamental questions of civilization and barbarism that conservative economics leaves us unprotected. Conservative economists believe that their analysis is on firm ground because of its 'value neutrality' (that is the assumption that all values are merely preferences, and consequently that economics is neutral in the choice between values). Conservative economists as people have values, but in their role as practitioners of economic theory, civilized values are absent. Two authors of a text on analytic methods, Harvard professors Edith Stokey and Richard Zeckhauser, provide a clear example of this value neutral perspective.

> Most of the materials in this book are equally applicable to a socialist, capitalist, or mixed-enterprise society, to a democracy or dictatorship, indeed wherever hard policy choices must be made. In deciding whether a vaccine should be used to halt the spread of a threatened epidemic we need not worry about the political or economic ideology of those inoculated. Nor will the optimal scheduling for refuse trucks depend on whether it is capitalist or socialist trash that is being collected.

There is a certain truth here. An analysis of the non-civic aspects of economic efficiency can be applicable to any society. The context of these bottom-line efficiencies, however, can be of great civic importance to us. The optimal scheduling of refuse trucks that applies to both capitalist and socialist trash can be equally useful in improving the effectiveness in transporting the victims to Auschwitz or the Soviet gulags. A conservative economist is limited to saying more is better – the value of additional efficiency cannot be qualified by its contents.

Conservative economics cannot come to grips with the idea that civilization can collapse even as standard economic indicators are rising, despite the vivid example of economic growth and barbarism provided by Nazi Germany. The problem is not with the morals of conservative economists but that their paradigm cannot handle questions of civilization. Consequently, such issues tend to be ignored. But if we are to make any use of economics in governing our nation, we cannot ignore the forces that maintain our civilization.

To abandon economics would be to waste a valuable tool; to practise economics in government without consideration for civic values would be to risk the degradation of our civilization. Only when we combine our understanding of civic values with the self-interest of conservative economics will we be able to reap the benefits of our entire national heritage.

NEW DIRECTIONS FOR THE TWENTY-FIRST CENTURY

The real choice between civilization and barbarism was posed first by Aristotle in examining the political economy of the polis – the civilized city states of ancient Greece:

> Any polis which is truly so called, and is not merely one in name, must devote itself to the end of encouraging excellence. Otherwise, a political association sinks into mere allegiance. . . . Otherwise, too, law becomes mere covenant – a guarantor of men's rights against each other – instead of being, as should be, a rule of life such as will·make the members of the polis good and just.

Even in Aristotle's time, there were some who aspired to remain true to the civic values of their nation and some who were content with a society based on self-interest and negative liberty – a society in which law is merely 'a guarantor of men's rights against each other'.

The philosophical issues confronting our founding fathers were not resolved forever with the writing of the Constitution. Every generation must reaffirm the meanings of 'We the People' and 'the blessings of liberty' or the civilized resources beneath the symbols will crumble. Our nation must pursue growth in maintaining our vitality, but we must also pursue something more. Peters and Waterman quote a leader in one of their 'excellent' companies:

> Profit is like health. You need it, and the more the better. But it's not why you exist.

Just as these authors found the pursuit of excellence as the keystone of business prosperity, so too we may find pursuit of the excellences of civilized economics at the heart of national prosperity. We believe it is time to stop the regression towards barbaric economics and barbaric economic government, and to return the public agenda towards a prosperous civilized economic system for the United States of America and the world.

3 The Political Economy of Civilization

> My bounty is as boundless as the sea,
> My love as deep;
> The more I give to thee the more I have
> For both are infinite.
> *Romeo and Juliet*, Act II, Scene ii

Newtonian physics postulates that every action has an equal and opposite reaction. Similarly, it is a conservative argument that every economic benefit must exact a cost somewhere else. Conservatives view everything in the world as a trade-off, or as the current slang goes: TANSTAAFL ('there ain't no such thing as a free lunch').

The love that Shakespeare's Juliet expresses defies the economic principle behind the no free lunch philosophy. The idea that there can be rewards from social interaction that benefit all is nowhere to be found in conservative economics.

For conservative economists, motivation is explained solely by a literally insatiable appetite to consume or acquire regardless of the costs imposed on others. People are said to have appetites – 'preferences' – that conservatives associate with all human values. Loyalty or love are merely appetites that may be compared and freely traded in exchange for other consumption goods.

Economists are not the only ones who follow this conservative philosophy – some psychologists also focus on self-interest, attributing all motivation to mere appetite. Christopher Lasch noted in *The Culture of Narcissism* that 'when therapists speak of the need for "meaning" and "love", they define "love" and "meaning" simply as the fulfillment of the patient's emotional requirements'. What could such psychologists have to say to Juliet?

If this self-interested appetite were really the only motivation for human behaviour, then Juliet's words would have no meaning for us. Juliet's feelings, however, are neither fictional, strange, nor unique. Love is just one of many motivations that are fundamentally different from the TANSTAAFL transactions of conservative economics. Juliet's love for Romeo improved the well-being of both (despite the fact that circumstances conspired to end their romance in tragedy). Similarly, the civic values which hold our nation together can potentially inspire behaviour that yields a positive sum for society.

PREFERENCES AND MOTIVATION

Why do some people prefer bacon to sausage with their eggs for breakfast, while others prefer only toast and coffee? Why do some parents participate in the local Parent-Teacher Association while others spend their evenings at the movies? Economists assume that each of us have our own individual set of innate and complete preferences, and that each of us can order our individual priorities in an unambiguous way among *all* conceivable alternatives. This ordering axiom is a fundamental tenet of conservative economics. It presumes that each individual's preferences are explicit and complete (that is, everyone knows everything that they want and how much they want it in all possible circumstances today and for every future day for the rest of their lives as well as for future generations of their progeny). Consequently, no one is ever faced with a choice where they are torn by indecision – Hamlet cannot really be puzzled by the choice: 'To be, or not to be?'

In conservative economics, nothing can be said about why preferences change. Economists do not investigate changes in preferences – this is said to be outside the realm of the 'hard science' of economics. Conservative economists leave preference formation and change to the weaker 'soft sciences' such as sociology and psychology. By developing a theory void of preference formation, conservative economists have allowed an inherent weakness in their explanation of human behaviour to bias their measurement of motivation.

Economists cannot measure preferences directly. Instead, it is asserted that people respond to incentives and reveal their preferences through their market actions. For example, the public can be said to 'prefer' chocolate ice-cream over medieval mandolin music because they spend a larger share of their income on it. Economists can even explain how preferences vary: if the price of chocolate ice-cream goes up, economists will predict how this changes the demand for the mandolin music and its price. Conservative economists assert that by tracking the movement of goods, the desires which make up motivation can be measured. These market measurements, however, introduce bias (in a statistical sense) into the determination of value by exaggerating the impact of those goods whose values are most easily measured, and thereby undervaluing other goods and services that are not normally traded in the marketplace despite their having significant civic value. Thus 'hard' economic data will be consistently wrong wherever civic values are important for motivating the actions of members of a community. This bias comes from the assumption that all preferences ultimately involve market transactions or exchanges, real or implicit, rather than recognizing that actions can be induced by both market and civic values.

Some goods and services derive their worth solely from social relations. These cannot be considered 'for sale' without losing their value. Imagine what would happen if a judge who was about to rule on a case attempted to auction off his decision. What legitimacy would remain to support the judge's verdict, even if neither litigant could meet his asking price, and thus no deal was consummated? Justice, the blessings of liberty, and other social goods are not easily detected by the market measurement tools of economists, and so they are systematically undervalued in conservative economic analysis. If people do not pay for something, then conservative economists must conclude that the good is worthless.

There are many things besides love and justice which cannot be valued in the marketplace without being debased; hence the conservative representation of motivation based solely on market price and preferences is incomplete. Indeed, policy shaped by conservative economics will be consistently biased in favour of motivating by self-interest. Therefore, the guidance of conservative economics is not able to lead us to the benefits of both self-interest and civic values.

INTERNAL AND EXTERNAL INCENTIVES

It is not sufficient merely to rail against the prevailing orthodoxy of a philosophy based on self-interest to establish the case for a more civilized approach to economics and public policy. Others before us have also noted the weakness of a conservative philosophy based on self-interest. What they have lacked, however, is an analytical foundation upon which to base their alternative approach. The following analysis is intended to provide the structure necessary to encapsulate previous critiques (as well as our own) in a form which can challenge the conservative approach on their own conceptual turf.

In everyday human behaviour we recognize that people are motivated by many different incentives reflecting self-interest and/or civic values. When the incentive for an action comes solely from a source external to the performance of that action, as might be the case with a wage payment to perform an unpleasant job, the payment is an external incentive. Only self-interest is reflected in the transactions involving external incentives.

When an incentive comes solely from the performance of an action *per se* (and not in exchange for something else), as with craftsmanship for its own sake, then the reward is internalized within the craftsman, and is thus defined as an internal incentive. The internal incentive of civic values comes from performing an action, not in exchange for something else.

When we speak of internal incentives we are *not* referring to social pressure in the form of the threat: 'Do this or the community will shun you!' (Nor do internal incentives motivate an action in exchange for a future reward or reprieve.) The plea 'Do this and I will love you' is an external incentive. Not only will social and emotional threats fail to enlist internal incentives, but the very process of treating civic values as external incentives will degrade and corrupt the existing internal values. Instead, internal incentives work by communicating pre-existing rules of behaviour so that self-interest is not called into play.

Traditionally, conservative economists, in an effort to appear as 'hard-headed' scientists devoid of any value judgments in their professional work,[1] treat all incentives as if they were external. If all incentives are external, then conservative economists believe that they can semantically transform these incentives into observable 'objective' facts. These external incentives are easy to measure, since they are based on transactions which are often documented in the form of contracts or market prices. Accordingly, these measurable external incentives are the basis for conservatives explaining the revealed preferences of members of the society. People's motivations are reduced to being based on an actual or implicit calculation of costs and benefits from the viewpoint of self-interest.

Internal incentives are something quite different. Internal incentives that shape our lives with an influence which is more than simple appetite include love, duty, honour, responsibility and the striving for excellence in all endeavours. Internal incentives are harder to measure, since they depend more on social context. The desire to work harder at one's craft to achieve the recognition of one's peers will not, in any way, demean the accomplishments of other artisans working in the same area. The result, however, will be an industry known worldwide for its achievements of excellence.

Internal incentives have some special advantages that external incentives lack. Civic values do not necessarily wear out with use, and they can prove mutually reinforcing ('The more I give to thee the more I have,' proclaims Juliet). The honour and esteem a community of peers awards for professional excellence does not exact a cost somewhere else – often, this

respect will ennoble both those who are honoured as well as those extending the honour. In contrast, when all incentives are treated as if they are
external, internal incentives tend to be undervalued or ignored.

Self-interest alone can never explain many human choices. What possible market price could make a rational economic man decide to die for
his country? Conservative economic theory implies that external incentives – market prices – are not only a feasible method of enlisting soldiers,
but in fact the best way to maintain an army. This view provided the basis
for Professor Milton Friedman's argument that we should enlist as soldiers
only those who choose to work in the army for the prevailing wage. In
wartime, however, a system built on self-interest cannot maintain civic
spirit. During the Civil War, for example, citizens in the North who were
drafted for military service could hire someone to serve in the army for
them. This policy of allowing wealthy citizens to discharge civic duties
through the payment of external incentives did not work – resulting in draft
riots in the streets of New York, and a degrading of patriotic motivation.

The conservative view that a mercenary army is always best is in stark
contrast to Machiavelli's strong concern that a free and civilized people
take military duties on themselves, a concern taken by the founding fathers
and put into the Constitutional right to bear arms. Machiavelli doubted the
viability of a society dependent on the hired poor to defend the posses-
sions of its wealthy members. Values beyond self-interest will be necessary to motivate an army which will bravely face death in defending the
nation.

Conservative economists may argue that we have misrepresented their
views, and that theirs is not merely a science of self-interest. They often
assert that love, loyalty, craftsmanship, and patriotism are integrated into
their analysis as individual *preferences*. What they means by these words,
however, is something entirely different from the reality of these values in
a civilized society. Take the value of loyalty, for example. For conservatives to say that one has a preference for loyalty means nothing more than
that one is loyal only in proportion to the pleasure it yields. In the conservative lexicon, loyalty at all costs is an oxymoron. Although conservative economists may claim that this surrogate sentiment accurately represents
the reality, we conclude that true virtues have characteristics which cannot
be purchased in the conservative free market. An analysis based solely on
external incentives inevitably boils down to the Hobbesian world of self-
interest.

The inability of conservative economics to account for behaviour based
on community and loved ones as motivating forces fundamentally distorts
its view of how society operates. A conservative approach obscures vital

issues of public policy because it discards the most crucial motivations: the incentives that can hold society together or tear it apart.

COMMUNITY

External goods, like all other instruments, have a necessary limit of size. Indeed, all things of [external] utility are of this character; and any excessive amount of such things must either cause its possessor some injury, or, at any rate, bring him no benefit. [It is the opposite with goods of the soul.] The greater the amount of each of the goods of the soul, the greater is its utility.

Aristotle, *Politics*

It was Aristotle who first recognized the distinction between internal and external incentives. His remarks in regard to external incentives are consistent with the position of conservative economics as to preferences and the law of diminishing returns.

But Aristotle also describes another form of motivation which exhibits different characteristics. Writing for the political leadership of his time, Aristotle was also attuned to the motivation of Juliet – 'The more I give to thee, the more I have'.

Aristotle uses the term 'the goods of the soul' to refer to internal incentives. He is not referring to the Christian 'soul' in this passage, but rather to the essence of man 'the political animal' (or literally, 'an animal intended to live in a polis'). Internal incentives are rooted in what has been called organizational culture, or more broadly, social norms. These norms are centred around a social hub, which may be a nation, a family, a profession, or an organization. Aristotle makes explicit the connection between internal incentives and civic values. The Greeks referred to the social hub as the *polis*, and they saw it as the heart of their civilization. Where such a community exists, shared values within an organizational or social tradition produce internal goods which the members of the polis enjoy. In our social and professional lives we participate in many communities.

This conception of community does not exist in conservative economics. It is also absent from public policy discussions based on the conservative economic paradigm. Economist Mancur Olson views a community as a collection of individuals constantly calculating the individual benefits of membership in the community, and comparing these with the benefits they would receive if they left the community. This representation of a community is misleading because it attempts to slice incentives that are entirely based on community into individual choices. Where there is a strong sense of community, abandonment is not even considered as an option – as those who have given their lives for their country have demonstrated.

While Professor Olson's view may provide an insight into the behaviour of political one-issue coalitions, it is the growth of such coalitions (often called special interest groups) in our political system that in recent years contributed to the erosion of our civilized community. We must be careful not to extend this concept of political coalitions to groups or organizations where civic values play a strong role. The power of a community, as with the Amish in Pennsylvania, or among members of the Civil Rights movement in the 1960s, is never achieved by many individuals separately weighing the benefits from membership. The legend of the rugged individual exists more in American mythology and Hollywood Westerns than in American history. The Constitution begins 'We the People' and not 'Each of Us'.

DIALECT

Dialect: the form or variety of a spoken language particular to a region, community, social group, occupational group, etc.
Webster's New World Dictionary

Every community has its particular dialect, that is, its own interpretation of words, phrases, and concepts. Dialects include everything from shop talk to in-jokes, from regional dialect to the language of meanings established by religious teachings. The particular dialect of a community can reveal much about its strengths, weaknesses, character, and membership. Just as language defines nationhood in the international realm, so does a shared dialect indicate the existence of a community among or within nations.

The dialect established by a community can reinforce values by providing guidance as to what is expected of its members. Even one word can provide the context that makes a community thrive. Peters and Waterman attribute the excellence of Bell Telephone to:

Theodore Vail's seventy-five year old insistence that the company was not a telephone company but a 'service' company.

A shared language reinforces the feeling of membership in a community and also provides signals as to what that membership means. Lee Iacocca writes:

It's important to talk to people in their own language. If you do it well, they'll say 'God, he said exactly what I was thinking.' And when they begin to respect you, they'll follow you to the death. The reason they're following you is not because you're providing some mysterious leadership. It's because you are following them.

Civic values are continually iterated and modified through the development of dialect which comes about as a result of social and personal interaction.

In an economy that works well, the dialect of one community will tie into the dialects of other groups so that all of the separate dialects form a compatible whole. Former Secretary of Labor John Dunlop wrote:

> Each of the actors in an industrial relations system – managerial hierarchy, worker hierarchy, and specialized public agencies – may be said to have its own ideology. An industrial relations system requires that these ideologies be sufficiently compatible and consistent so as to permit a common set of ideas which recognize an acceptable role for each actor.

The norms and expectations of those within an industry can be discovered in the meanings of the words with which the groups communicate.

Our standard industrial practices do not work unless all parties have a shared language of definitions and rules of the game. The self-interest of an employee or subcontractor is always in opposition to the interest of his employer, since the former wants to do the job with as little effort as possible and the employer wants the best job regardless of effort. Without common understanding, they will both expend a great deal of effort in arguing over every decision to be made in carrying out the project. Frequently, the development of a professional code of ethics and long-term personal relationships between parties is necessary for them to develop mutually and adopt a common language of meanings.

The development of a shared dialect is not limited to parties with similar or mutual interests. Even adversaries may develop understandings as to the meanings of the slightest nuance of each other's behaviour. Even in warfare, the common understandings of enemies still benefit each by establishing the parameters by which the conflict may be pursued. For example, innocent civilians and especially children are not to be made deliberate targets of destruction. Any level of trust between individuals or groups brings the risk of betrayal, but cooperation even among adversaries holds the potential for producing additional rewards for all. Even in a Darwinian environment it is often the cooperative species that prosper.

If dialect is essential to understanding, then the dialect adopted in discussing specific policy problems in this book and elsewhere will also be important. We must be aware of what our words really signify. Although our discussion must be abstract to be generally applicable, to be useful it must deal in particulars. It is important to keep this distinction in mind; no one ever dies for an 'internal incentive' *per se*. Where people give their life, it is for particular reasons intricately wound up in the interstices of their personal role in their own community or family.

We discussed in Chapter 1 the difficulties in pinning down the labels 'Liberal' and 'Conservative' in even a general sense. We have taken on an even greater challenge in referring to civilization and virtue. When we describe something as being civilized, we hope to be saying more than merely that we approve of it. When we use the adjective 'civilized', we are making reference to a harmonious combination of self-interest and civic values as established in the ideals and institutions of a society. When we write of virtue, we mean the pursuit of excellence (or internal incentives) in the context of previously established social roles and ideals.

Conservative economics is supported by its own dialect: 'the free market', 'laissez-faire', and 'the bottom line' in common usage, and concepts such as 'marginal cost' and 'optimal allocation' for economists. In order to challenge the paradigm of conservative economics it is necessary to establish a compatible vocabulary for those aspects of economic and social behaviour that conservative economics does not address. Thus we are attempting to create a dialect through the terms 'internal incentive', the 'community', and even 'dialect' itself. In this we are following Hobbes, who in the first 11 chapters of *Leviathan* expounded the basic premises of conservatism in the definition of a multitude of terms, from 'Good' ('the object of any man's appetite or desire'), to 'Reason' ('nothing but reckoning – that is, adding and subtracting'), to 'Compassion' (grief arising in an individual 'from the imagination that the like calamity may befall himself'). Our analytical dialect is much less comprehensive than that of Hobbes, but we believe that it provides the basic structure needed to construct an alternative analytical paradigm to that of Hobbes and the conservatives while maintaining a constructive dialogue with conservatives.

The crux of public issues is often revealed in the dialect of both sides. In *What Price Incentives?* Professor Steve Kelman of Harvard's Kennedy School of Government highlights how paradigmatic interpretations of the world leave economists and environmentalists 'talking beyond each other'. Environmentalists may oppose pollution taxes even if they acknowledge their economic efficiency and (external) incentive effect, because such taxes help to legitimize the role of polluters and their right to outbid others who wish to maintain a clean environment. Any step in the direction of pollution taxes contradicts the environmentalist vision of norms and roles, and thus weakens their community. Consequently, even if environmentalists completely understand the benefits of economic efficiency, they will still be motivated to reject pollution taxes and maintain faith with their community (and to continue to enjoy the internal incentives that their membership provides).

Dialect can also be the means through which a new community is created. Three million Israelis and millions of other Jews worldwide share the common bond of Hebrew – a language which existed only in the context of religious ceremony until Ben-Yehuda, a Lithuanian scholar, emigrated to Jerusalem in the late nineteenth-century and began single-handedly to revive Hebrew as a spoken language. Other societies are working to repeat Ben-Yehuda's success, with Gaelic in Ireland and with Catalan and Basque in Spain. From boot camp to college orientations, the introduction of a new dialect can be a powerful tool in establishing a new sense of community.

Finally, dialect can provide the means with which to combine several communities, and thus enlist a wide range of civic values in the service of a single ideal. The authors of *Habits of the Heart* rightly note the genius of Martin Luther King, Jr in shaping the community of the civil rights movement. King juxtaposed the poetry of the scriptural prophets with the lyrics of patriotic anthems:

> I have a dream that every valley shall be exalted, every hill and mountain shall be made low. ... This will be the day when all of God's children will be able to sing with new meaning, 'My country 'tis of thee, sweet land of liberty, of thee I sing.'

King's oration reappropriated that classic strand of the American tradition that understands the true meaning of freedom to lie in the affirmation of responsibility for uniting all of the diverse members of society into a just social order.

King's words remind us not merely of the power of civic values, but also the value of their content. For King, freedom was not the negative liberty of conservatives, but rather something which combined the values expounded in the scripture with the values of the American civic heritage. The essence of King's idea of civilization was a free community rich in the 'blessings of liberty':

> When we let freedom ring, when we let it ring from every village and hamlet, from every state and every city, we will be able to speed up the

day when all of God's children, black men and white men, Jews and Gentiles, Protestants and Catholics, will be able to join hands and sing the words of that old Negro spiritual. 'Free at last! Free at last! Thank God almighty, we are free at last!'

THE STRATEGIC IMPORTANCE OF DIALECT

Words can be strategic weapons in the conflict over public policy. The following quotation comes from a business publication, *Nation's Business*, rallying opposition against the establishment of the Occupational Safety and Health Act (OSHA). It demonstrates the strategic corruption of language in industrial relations:

Imagine yourself sitting in your office, a few months from today. A young man barges in. You recognize him as a man you once refused to hire. He had no education and no potential talent you could use. His main experience consisted of cashing welfare checks.

But he shows you he's now a representative of the federal government – an 'inspector' with the Department of Labor. And he threatens to have you fined $1000 a day if you don't do as he says.

The young man – who knows nothing about your business – then tramps through your plant, without a warrant, ordering you to take costly steps to improve 'safety and health.'

Such scenes could be duplicated throughout the country should a new proposal being deliberated on Capitol Hill be signed into law.

The hidden agenda of *Nation's Business* was to promote the idea that government will only hire incompetents, and that there couldn't possibly be anything wrong with the plants to be inspected. The meaning of 'inspector' and 'safety and health' (quotation marks in the original text) to *Nation's Business* and the constituency to which it was appealing is clearly different from that intended by those who established OSHA. *Nation's Business* was trying to establish a negative connotation for these terms in the minds of its constituents. There is one community for *Nation's Business* and its constituents and a different one for OSHA framers and their supporters. These separate communities do not form a compatible whole. Instead, they come into conflict in an environment of uncertainty and shifting rules, roles, and norms.

There is no clear boundary between a tactical corruption of dialect to pursue economic goals and the same techniques used to pursue political goals. The conservative anti-government rhetoric gained strength in the 1970s by combining economic and political purposes. In an article entitled 'Language Matters' Michael Pertschuk of the Advocacy Institute argued that many groups have 'adapted libertarian themes and language to cloak their political objectives'. Examples Pertschuk provides include:

> The National Rifle Association (freedom to defend one's family) and the tobacco industry (freedom of choice); the flourishing business lobby (freedom from oppressive legislation) and the medical right (freedom from socialized medicine); mining, timber and real estate interests (freedom from unjust 'takings') and opponents of civil rights laws (freedom from quotas). . . . Triumph of ideas? No: triumph of words.

Pertschuk notes that conservatives have developed language tactics that include (a) associating free markets with community values of family and freedom, (b) associating all government with bureaucracy, waste and corruption, and (c) shifting the meaning of certain words. For example, in the 1950s the term 'special interests' denoted business lobbies. Today the term is applied to civil rights groups, environmentalists, etc., rather than business which by omission is endowed with the public interest.

As the conservatives seized the dialect initiative, conservative rhetoric against government intervention has grown in strength and intensity. In pushing for the Contract with America in 1994, Representative Newt Gingrich sent a memo to Republicans with a section entitled: 'Language, A Key Mechanism of Control'. In this document, the current Speaker of the House of Representatives told his readers to characterize Republicans with words such as change, truth, moral, courage, family, peace, and duty, and Democrats with words such as sick, corrupt, decay, and traitors.

In 1995, President Clinton suggested that those who engineered the infamous bombing of the federal building in Oklahoma City could have been motivated, at least in part, by the vicious harangues of radio talk show hosts. Former President Bush sent a letter of resignation to the National Rifle Association (NRA) because he:

> was outraged when, even in the wake of the Oklahoma City tragedy, Mr Wayne LaPierre, executive vice president of NRA, defended his attack on federal agents as 'jack-booted thugs'. To attack Secret Service agents or ATF people or any government law enforcement people as 'wearing Nazi bucket helmets and black storm troopers uniforms' wanting to 'attack law abiding citizens' is a vicious slander of good people.

Despite the publicity given Bush's resignation, the NRA initially refused to retract this description of government law enforcement agents. Mr LaPierre of the NRA was quoted in the *New York Times* as responding: 'The American public needs to know the truth . . . I am confident that . . . our words and actions will be completely vindicated.'

When the NRA describes government law enforcement agents as 'thugs' or a talk-show host exhorts his audience to shoot for the head if a federal agent of the Bureau of Alcohol, Tobacco and Firearms enters their residence, as talk-show host G. Gordon Liddy did, the dialect being used clearly implies that government employees are subhuman bullies who deserve to die.

This manipulation of dialect is not a new phenomenon. Perhaps the most stark example in the past century involved the Nazi depiction of the Jews as vermin, subhuman pests who ought to be eradicated. Yet conventional economic books do not deal with these issues of converting dialect to one's own self-interest economic and political purposes. Conservative economics rules out the possibility of inflaming hatreds, of creating a war of us against them, because it assumes that no one can change the 'preferences' of self-interested individuals.

Nation's Business in its fight against OSHA and the NRA in its fight against gun control, are fighting a very real war of words. Unfortunately, one of the first casualties in such a conflict is the dialect of common understandings that might have helped both sides understand how government must pursue its necessary functions as a civilizing influence without threatening the liberties of the individuals it is sworn to protect. When dialect becomes divisive the resources dedicated to purely antagonistic conflict will have to be increased as a more uncertain environment necessitates greater efforts to protect against a larger number of potential threats.

Additional costs are imposed on both adversaries, and on society as a whole. Imagine a war where neither side knew the word for 'surrender' in the language of the other – the loser would not be able to capitulate, thus dragging the fight on at a cost to both until one side was annihilated rather than trying to reach a negotiated peace.

Dialect can be more important than 'pure economic facts'. Unions have sometimes rejected a wage offer if it is understood to be a concession, whereas the exact same wage offer may be approved if it is seen as a 'new package'. Of course, differences in self-interest among groups can not be paid merely in the coin of flowery rhetoric. Over time, experience will establish new meanings for the words of management and unions, and these meanings will shape the course of labour negotiations as much as will concerns of dollars and cents.

The presence of a shared dialect indicates the existence of an extended community and thus the existence of mutually generated internal goods that makes providing a helping hand to disadvantaged members of the community a civic value. The word 'entitlements', for example, originated in policy discussions to mean providing a *legal* right to a specified form of help to every individual of a specific section of the community that society has agreed is disadvantaged and deserving of help. Thus for example, retired persons over 65 years of age who paid taxes into the Social Security Fund for at least 40 quarter-years were legally entitled to old-age payments, while those over $70^{1}/_{2}$ years, whether retired or not, were legally entitled to receive such payments. Similar criteria were set up for the poor, those with disabilities – and other groups who, under specified conditions, were granted legal entitlement to special payments and other benefits from the civilized society at large.

Recently, however, conservatives have subtly altered the meaning of 'entitlements' in the public dialect to a word that splits the former civilized community. Rather than representing the liberal view of entitlements as a civil responsibility for providing a helping hand to those less fortunate, conservatives have convinced the citizens that other people's entitlements merely increase the income of the lazy and prodigal grasshopper parasites in the community at the expense of the hard-working, industrious ants. Others who receive entitlements are ripping-off the system. In an economy ruled only by self-interest motivations, however, one's *own* government 'entitlement', whether it be in the form of a government payment or special tax treatment, is seen as a reward for one's own hard work.

When one party unilaterally changes the meanings of previously shared terms such as entitlements, then that party betrays the mutual trust and weakens the shared dialect. Not only do all members of the community no longer share the meaning of the disputed term, but, in any further discussions, the meanings of every word of the betraying party and the betrayed are also cast into doubt.

The spread of the breakdown of the common civil dialect is facilitated when the economic system deliberately hobbles growth via policies that pursue a natural rate of unemployment. (Even the term 'natural rate' attempts to reassign responsibility from deliberate conservative policy to a natural outcome.) Since the 1970s as this natural rate philosophy took root and flourished, the evidence shows that middle-income and poor people have tended to become poorer as upper-income people became richer. In 1995, conservatives call this intentional slowing down of economic growth a 'soft landing'. (In the 1970s, the somewhat harsher term of a 'growth recession' was used.)

With the consequent sub-par performance of the economy compared to its full employment potential, workers, who are still employed and still playing by society's rules, find it difficult to provide a rising standard of living for their families. Often it requires two members of the household to work merely to keep up the standard that was obtainable with only one worker in the family in earlier years. For example, in early 1994, the *New York Times* asked a former sheetmetal worker, who had lost his high-skilled job during the 1991 recession, what he thought of the fact that in the first year of the Clinton Administration three million new jobs were created. The worker responded: 'Yeah, between my wife and myself we have four of them!' This worker was now employed as both a school bus driver and an attendant at McDonald's. His wife also worked for McDonald's and, in the evenings, stocked the shelves in a Toys 'R Us retail store. The four salaries combined were slightly less than what the worker had previously earned as a skilled sheetmetal worker. Yet the early years of the Clinton Administration were still an improvement over the four years of the Bush Administration during which less than two million new jobs were created.

In recent decades, the civic values of the working population have been eroded by the economic self-interest necessity of trying to provide for one's family in an economy where the opportunities to earn income are deliberately set at a level that all who want to work can not find gainful employment. The result is to create a dispirited electorate stripped of any feeling of belonging to a civil community and motivated solely by self-interest. This disheartened constituency struggling to balance family budgets can be readily convinced that 'entitlements' are nothing short of stealing from their pocket to keep the poor, aged, disabled, and unemployed scoundrels in the lap of a lazy and indulgent luxury. In these circumstances, the fact that 80 per cent of the people are in favour of the government balancing its budget is understandable, even though it would only make conditions harsher for all. In an uncivilized society, misery loves company.

Dialect is a very special human institution that exists wherever humans do. A shared language can be a valuable asset that benefits all parties by reducing transaction costs and by being part of the process of generating the internal goods that the community produces. One of the great strengths of any community is the acceptance of a shared language by all its members. As our civilized dialect has been manipulated for a particular conservative political agenda, the result has been poor economic performance and a disaster for basic civic values.

THE VOLATILE INTERACTION OF INTERNAL AND
EXTERNAL INCENTIVES

A successful civil society will reap the benefits of both self-interest and civic values. Both internal and external incentives must be enlisted, but the values of self-interest do not necessarily combine easily with the values of a civil community.

The introduction of external incentives can sometimes diminish the effectiveness of already existing internal incentives. Psychologist Barry Schwartz of Swathmore College provides the example of some elementary school students who were given tokens as a reward for reading books. Although the number of books read in school increased, the books they chose to read became shorter, the level of comprehension declined, and reading outside class decreased.

The market philosophy in which everyone has his price implies certain norms and roles that may infringe on a existing civil community. In certain instances, even the offer of a market transaction can contribute to the erosion of civic values. If Romeo had offered Juliet gold ducats to sleep with him, something of immense internal value would have been lost. The difference between love and prostitution is vast, but if we are to use the market measurement tools of conservative economics, then the difference that will be measured is that prostitution is valuable (people demonstrate a 'willingness-to-pay') and love is worthless.

When government policy is based only on self-interest, it can degrade the civic values of its citizens by treating their civic concerns as if they were solely financial. Professors Philip J. Borque and Robert Haney Scott of the University of Washington in Seattle suggested that there was a 'simple way' to resolve the controversial issue of nuclear waste disposal by allowing the free market process to work:

> Open, competitive bidding by states on government contracts [to store hazardous waste] would resemble a market process. Providers of the site would be compensated for their perceived social costs.

In other words, these economists advocate telling concerned citizens something like this:

> We recognize your concerns that nuclear waste disposal may increase the risk of cancer for you and your children. How much do we have to pay you to forget all that?

The answer for a civilized society is not in dollars. Even if citizens of a town made a deal for a million dollars each, what would happen as cancer cases began to develop? Even if the cancers are not related to the nuclear waste site, imagine the tensions between those struck with tragedy and those spared to enjoy their new wealth with impunity. How would parents feel, having accepted a million dollars, if their child was born with severe birth defects?

This conservative economic solution was actually proposed in a March 1987 Senate bill put forth by Bennett Johnston of Louisiana and James McClure of Idaho. One hundred million dollars was offered to any state or Indian tribe willing to accept a high-level nuclear waste dump. The offer was immediately denounced as a bribe, and Nevada Governor Richard Bryan went so far as to refer to it as 'nuclear blackmail'.

The most humane *and* efficient way to handle serious controversies is not to try to buy our way out, but to go through the messy and difficult political process, so that the relevant citizens themselves may participate in coming to a just solution. That eventual solution may involve payment to the community, but only as part of a process which enlists the civic resources of the community as well. The purpose would not be to reach a solution merely by adding up the individual preferences of the citizens, but rather to have them shape a solution as a community that has worked to obtain the best knowledge available to make a civilized decision. External and internal incentives must be combined with great care if we are not to waste either.

INSTITUTIONS

I am not an advocate for frequent changes in laws and constitutions, but laws and institutions must go hand in hand with the progress of the human mind. As that becomes more developed, more enlightened, as new discoveries are made, new truths discovered and manners and opinions change, with the change of circumstances, institutions must also advance to keep pace with the times. We might as well require a man to wear still the coat which fitted him when a boy as a civilized society to remain ever under the regimen of their barbaric ancestor.

The Jefferson Memorial, Washington, D.C.

We live in a world of change in which the external and internal incentives that motivate human behaviour are constantly evolving. The environment is continually reshaped by developing technology, the ebb and flow of natural resources, and evolution of civic values. Government is one process by which we manage our affairs during this social and economic evolution.

Societies sustain a productive harmony between internal and external incentives through the development of institutions – that is, pre-established laws, customs, practices, or formal mechanisms which simultaneously distribute internal incentives and protect the community from the erosion of values over time and from the corrupting influence of external incentives. For example, the institution of a dowry helped to provide an effective mechanism for capital formation and wealth distribution while protecting the social and emotional integrity of marriage from the potentially corrupting influence of external incentives. But the dowry also illustrates how an effective institution for one period in a society's evolution can become undesirable as the society's values and economic environment change.

One example of a public institution which has evolved to resolve an everyday problem is the regulation of driving. For millennia there was no need for rules to determine traffic lanes. But with the development of carriages, and later automobiles, the ensuing congestion made it inconvenient (and dangerous) to permit each individual to exercise his choice as to which side of the road to ride on, or which side to pass a slower traveller. And so gradually 'rules of the road' were developed which spelled out proper procedures for use of roads. Although these rules were simple, they eliminated some real problems and made transportation significantly more efficient.

As the economy developed, the needs of travellers evolved and were met by frequent elaborations and additions to the original rules of the road. In the 1920s an African-American inventor named Garrett A. Morgan developed and sold the idea for traffic lights to General Electric. Traffic lights effectively utilize internal and external incentives through the combination of a clear and fair determination of the right-of-way with the self-enforcement carried by the dangers of running a red light.

The introduction of traffic lights brought enormous efficiencies, but also led to further evolution of our driving institutions. In borderline cases, some people broke the new rules of the road, and thus it was necessary to change the role of police in our society (to the point where the main contact many people have with police is in regard to driving).

Other more complex concerns have also evolved as a result of the technological and civic changes in driving. Our driving institutions and technology have become so effective that hundreds of thousand of vehicles can be coordinated within a single city. This very efficiency increased the usefulness of cars until their number in certain cities has grown beyond the capacity that the existing institutions and infrastructure can handle. Other problems have emerged and been resolved – remember the gas lines during the Energy Crisis, and the adoption of the odd-even rationing scheme. The perpetual process of evolution, adaptation, and further evolution continues.

A well-developed institution will support the basic values of the community and enhance economic productivity. For example, a competition which recognizes excellence for its own sake is an institution which goes back at least as far as the first Olympiad in 776 BC. The shared pursuit of excellence strengthens the community. The shared experience can not only encourage a striving for excellence along traditional routes, but increase productivity by encouraging innovative ideas. The display of these innovative approaches leads to their transmission throughout society. Thus the enjoyment of the civic values of Olympic competition were successfully combined with the external incentives of enhanced productivity.

As with the evolution of species, however, there can be evolutionary dead ends for institutions as well as advances. For example, after the development of the 360 computer, IBM Chairman Thomas Watson, Sr asked vice-president Frank Cary to design a new research and development system to prevent a repeat of the chaos that occurred during the development of the 360 computer. Unfortunately, the institution Cary designed did more than eliminate chaos – it also stifled creativity. As Peters and Waterman recount:

> Cary did what he was told. Years later, when he became chairman himself, one of his first acts was to get rid of the laborious product development structure that he had created for Watson. 'Mr Watson was right,' he conceded. 'It [the product development structure] will prevent a repeat of the 360 development turmoil. Unfortunately, it will also ensure that we don't ever invent another product like the 360.'

Cary was fortunate in having the opportunity to correct his earlier error. Society will eventually abandon mistaken efforts to develop new institution – the challenge is to identify the institutions which are not working and repair them before they further erode.

The internal incentives of an institution can be a powerful force, but without effective guidance the values can evolve in unhealthy way. Sometimes a society will develop counterproductive values from which come internal incentives that promote neither external efficiency nor the vitality of the community:

Poorer performing companies often have strong cultures, too, but dysfunctional ones. They usually focus on internal politics rather than the customer, or they focus on 'the numbers' rather than on the product and the people who make and sell it.

The basic theme behind the 1990s idea of re-engineering the corporation is simply to force firms to scrutinize their own institutional habits and procedures in light of new information as to what is in the interests of their customers.

THE TIPPING MODEL OF EROSION

Professor Thomas Schelling of Harvard has developed a 'tipping model' which can be used to examine one way in which the erosion of norms can occur. Schelling's model describes how a small number of individuals possessing different preferences from the rest of the community can take a certain action, thereby changing the environment so that others in the group find it in their self-interest to take the same action, further changing the environment, until the entire group takes the action originally preferred by but a few.

An example is the game of poker, an institution which is often represented as a zero-sum game in economic terms (where the gains of the winners are exactly offset by the losses of the losers). But if this is a friendly game of poker among members of a strong social group, then at the end of the evening both winners and losers will have benefited from playing. It is only when a few of the players abandon the principles of the civil poker community and start to cheat that the environment turns sour and they are all left with a zero-sum competition. The cheaters, in effect, degrade the existing civic values and in so doing establish a new regime in which it is likely that more of the players will begin to cheat (since the incentive to win money becomes proportionately more important as the internal incentives from playing by the civil rules are diminished). The warning of the tipping model is that a small erosion may sometimes trigger an avalanche.

An important attribute of a civil community (and a measure of its long-run viability) is its ability to keep self-interest in check and maintain the discipline needed to prevent cheating. It is our experience that poker games are generally honest not because there exists adequate surveillance and credible sanctions, but because the norms of behaviour are that you simply do not cheat in a friendly game of poker. Similarly, the vitality of a civilization lies in its capacity to maintain the strength of its institutions so that self-interest cannot begin to tip the nation towards barbarism.

EROSION OF A NATIONAL CIVIL COMMUNITY

Civilization can be weakened when (1) internal incentives are eroded as individuals devote themselves to the sole pursuit of self-interest, or (2) the values of the group are corrupted, in that the rewards of the group can come only at the expense of others. In the latter case we can say that the community has developed uncivilized or corrupt values. Nevertheless, the internal incentives of such uncivilized communities can encourage behaviour to further its barbaric ends. In order to deflect attention from economic problems, Serbian leader Slobadan Milosevic appealed to the internal incentive of racial hatred and thereby started the brutal Serbian Wars against Croatia and Bosnia. Khomeini's Iran, Nazi Germany, and the Ku Klux Klan all drew upon internal incentives to motivate their followers towards acts of violence.

The internal incentives of such barbaric regimes do not reflect civilized virtue, as the rewards came only at the expense of others – in violation of our positive-sum premise for civilized societies. Just as all barbaric regimes require particular victims in order to justify the shortcomings of their social order, the conservative economic philosophy typically requires an underclass of lazy and undeserving to explain the existence of the persistent unemployed and the poor among us.

In this sense, therefore, if one can discern a set of values evolving around the ideology and dialect of conservative economics, its incentive scheme cannot be labelled virtuous or civil. Since conservatives conceive of systems of zero-sum games, any definition of excellence that they may develop implies that the winners have beaten 'the losers'. The ideal figure in the conservative cosmology is shrewd, hard-working and innovative, but he may also be amoral, manipulative, and deceitful when circumstances require it. In a civilized society, on the other hand, what is required is both shrewd, hard-working, innovative entrepreneurs and artisan workers who operate within and honour the civilized rules of the economic game.

Positive action must be taken to maintain and invigorate a civilized community – otherwise, there is a tendency either for it to erode or to become corrupt. Once this occurs, society finds it difficult to restore and revitalize its civilization. As Professor Benjamin Barber puts it:

Communities that do not grow and evolve become brittle and frail –
become something other than communities. To be genuinely free, a
community must be just; to be sustainable, justice must be embedded in
community.

Corrupt societies tend to sow the seeds of their own destruction, because
they silence the new ideas that might bring new life, and they set into
motion the desire for revenge which will motivate their victims. However,
this tendency may take years, or even generations to manifest, providing
very little consolation to those who live and die under the oppression of
a corrupt society.

During the early stages of erosion, it is still possible to attempt reforms
and revitalize civilized behaviour. It is, however, necessary to behave
within the existing set of norms. Appeals to ethical ideals cannot be used
as motivation to re-establish the very same values that have been lost in
the first place. For example, the advertising campaign for military recruit-
ment which was begun during the Carter Administration initially did not
try to appeal to American youth on the basis of patriotism, but rather in
terms of self-interest. 'Be all that you can be!' was the slogan as the
emphasis was on the career development advantages of military service
('It's a great place to start!'). As the counter-culture of the Vietnam era
faded and a new patriotism developed, the Armed Services have been able
to expand their advertising campaign to include appeals based more on
military virtues ('It's not just a job – it's an adventure!'). Over a period
of years – and in sync with changes in the national community – the
Armed Services succeeded in transforming the earlier message of career
advancement into one which could revitalize military virtues in our
society.

People in a society where the civic values have been eroded frequently
will not recognize any difference between the current norms and the original ones. Indeed, the greatest problem with the successful erosion of
civic values is that it is not readily seen by members of the community.
For example, our voting participation has declined, as the democratic process
has come to be regarded as either a battleground for special interests or a
horse-race between candidates ruled by their media consultants. As a people
we have allowed ourselves to accept the notion that our votes really don't
matter. At no point have we recognized that an important civic value was
being lost. While we recognize that voter participation is at the lowest
level in decades, we do not see this as an important change in the way we
govern ourselves. In other words, the institution has remained outwardly
the same, but the inner meanings have changed.

THE STRENGTH OF AMERICAN CIVILIZATION

We have been fortunate in our history that America has always had abundant civilized resources. The unique American experiment in civic democracy was made possible by the inherited norms and principles which allowed our founding fathers to collectively create a new nation. Professor Benjamin Barker of Princeton writes:

> Our greatest asset is our spirit: the spirit of political liberty and civic activism evident in the towns Tocqueville toured on his journey across America in the early 1830's; the spirit of adventure that once opened up the West; the spirit of giving by which Americans have always shown themselves prepared to help their neighbors and participate in voluntary associations without calculating the return on their altruism; the spirit of tolerance that permitted the victims of a hundred worldly persecutions to find sanctuary here, and that made America a nation that saw equality as a function of will rather than birth; the spirit of patriotism that inspired the young to serve their country without the promise of a free ticket to college; the spirit of democracy that made liberty not merely a private matter but a matter of respect for the dignity of others.

The civic heritage established by our Founding Fathers, and elaborated upon by the American people during the growth of our nation, have guided the development of the American civilized community.

Even when the harsh external incentive force of the Great Depression struck America, we did not turn to the fascist solutions of Germany, Italy, Japan and Spain. The members of the German and Italian ethnic communities in the United States saw themselves as American first. They were not moved by appeals from their European kinsmen. Even the Japanese Americans, interned in camps for much of the war, served with great distinction in the US Armed Forces. Our civilized resources were sufficient to pull us through without resorting to such drastic – and almost inevitably fatal – measures.

CIVIC VIRTUE

In a productive and civilized economy, every member of society plays a role in maintaining the viability of our institutions, even as we participate in their evolution. Machiavelli's term for pursuit of excellence in this civic role was *virtù* – or virtue. In economics for a civilized society, virtue is the practice of actions which generate and reproduce internal incentives, or more broadly, a virtue is an action that strengthens the civil community. An act of kindness that inspires others to achieve the same standard of conduct is an act of virtue. A healthy marriage conveys credibility to the conception of marriage in the community, thus reinforcing civic values.

A society that strives continuously for full employment enhances the value of belonging to the community, while a society that justifies unemployment and loss of income as the necessary and inevitable cost of a comfortable survival for the rest of the community erodes the very basis of its civilization.

Civic virtues require full participation of all members in the process by which social values change and evolve. These processes involve formal political mechanisms such as voting and jury duty, and economic activity such as workplace interaction, customer-business relations, and government institutions handling economic dislocations.

Civic virtue includes being a good team player – but this team role also includes the responsibilities to develop new ideas, to promote civilized behaviour, and to work against the erosion of existing civilized values. By practising one's excellence – in a profession, as a parent, or in athletic endeavors – a person may set an example that promotes the civilized values that he or she is pursuing.

There is also the form of leadership by which one establishes a new civil community from the start, thus creating a new set of guiding principles under which to organize a cooperative effort. The birth of a new community for a business or agency is a very special event, a combination of politics and poetry. In the realm of corporate kingdoms, inside our larger society-wide community, often it is an individual leader who creates the community virtues of his or her own organization, as described in *In Search of Excellence*:

All the companies we interviewed, from Boeing to McDonald's, were quite simply rich tapestries of anecdote, myth, and fairy tale. And we do mean fairy tale. The vast majority of people who tell stories today about T. J. Watson of IBM have never met the man or had direct experience of the more mundane reality. . . . These days, people like Watson and A. P. Giannini at Bank of America take on roles of mythic proportions that real persons would have been hard pressed to fill. Nevertheless, in an organizational sense, these stories, myths, and legends appear to be very important, because they convey the organization's shared values, or culture.

This individual leadership is entirely absent from conservative economics, even though this type of leadership is commonplace in the business world. In conservative economics a good manager merely chooses the optimal combination of available inputs to produce maximum profits. Civilized leadership, however, is composed of more than the computer-like choice of optimal combinations imagined in conservative economics.

Citizenship and leadership are both civilized virtues which we can practise in our families, our jobs, our neighbourhoods, and in our national governance. Through enlisting civic virtues our public policies can work more efficiently and can help to establish a more just society. The Preamble of the Constitution guides us towards the meaning of our government and our purpose as a people. Without civic values in economics – our chief tool of government – we will never be able to achieve justice, domestic tranquility, a secure national defence, prosperity, or the blessings of liberty.

Note

1. There is a difference between 'having' civic value judgments that shape our daily behaviour when dealing with others and incorporating these values into one's professional analysis of how people behave.

4 What's Wrong with Economists?

THE TUNNEL VISION APPROACH OF CONSERVATIVE ECONOMICS

Economists, like psychologists, believe that their .expertise lies in the understanding of human motivation. If we know what motivates people then we can use *incentives* to encourage people to behave in a socially desirable manner. Most economists analyze the world using a set of notions known as the classical model where economic problems are viewed strictly from the perspective of business and personal self-interest; civic values are ignored. Consequently traditional conservative economic policies have a major flaw; they often fail to provide civilized solutions to our pressing economic ills.

BUSINESS AND GOVERNMENT IN AMERICA: PARTNERS OR ADVERSARIES?

The belief that developed countries must choose between either an unfettered private enterprise system or a completely governmental regulated economy is false. As Harvard Professor and Secretary of Labor Robert Reich observed:

> Americans tend to divide the dimensions of our national life into two broad realms. . . . Our civic culture embodies a vision of community, premised upon citizenship. Its concern with democratic participation and the sharing of wealth stems from a conviction that such commitments enrich life and affirm the interdependency of individual lives. . . . The business culture embodies a moral vision of its own – one of individual responsibility and freedom. According to this vision, the market offers a superior organizing principle for society because it promotes the common good while preserving individual autonomy.

As we have argued, in a civilized real world, both civic and business attributes are integral parts of all our successful private and public institutions. As Peters and Waterman note in their book, *In Search of Excellence*, the most profitable companies are characterized by the possession of a particularly strong *esprit de corps*.

In recent years, the self-interest aspect of individuals and businesses has been overemphasized by politicians, civil servants, and financial media writers in public discourse regarding our pressing economic problems. This tropistic application of a severely limited view to resolving important problems of our society by people in high places in not new. Walter Bagehot, the pragmatic nineteenth-century editor of *The Economist*, complained that the policy makers of his day did not attempt to determine whether the theoretical principles underlying their decisions were appropriate for developing financial policies and practices. Bagehot wrote about these policy makers:

> They could not be expected themselves to discover such principles. The abstract thinking of the world is never to be expected from persons in high places; the administration of first-rate current transactions is a most engrossing business, and those charged with them are usually little inclined to think on points of theory, even when such thinking most nearly concerns those transactions.

Even today, those responsible for policy development rarely have either the time, or the inclination, to think seriously about points of abstract theory. It is not surprising, therefore, that their perspective has led to rationalizing policies that completely fail to meet their objectives. For example, the 1981 Reagan 'supply-side' tax cut proposal invoked the self-interest conservative economic theory to show that the annual federal government deficit would be completely eliminated by 1985. Instead the deficit increased to unprecedented levels.

Even when policies derived solely from self-interest economics do succeed in one area, they do so by invoking uncivilized solutions which create or exacerbate problems elsewhere in the system. For example, in 1986 inflation was a minuscule 1.1 per cent. In the following year inflation increased to 4.4 per cent. Inflation continued to rise so that by 1990, inflation was 6.1 per cent. To tame these inflationary tendencies the Federal Reserve periodically raised interest rates between 1987 and 1990. The result was ultimately an increase in unemployment, bankruptcies and the recession of 1991–2 that helped to elect President Clinton under a campaign promise to change the economic direction of the nation.

Policies founded solely on this conservative view of how the economy operates often not only distort the civic values which hold society together,

62   *Economics for a Civilized Society*

but produce results which are counterproductive to the economy. For example, the keystone to President Clinton's initial economic policies was the conservative notion that it is essential to reduce the annual government deficit and balance the federal budget in order to ward off future inflation. This encouraged demands for raising taxes and reducing government expenditures. Raising taxes to pay for ongoing projects creates slow growth and decreases employment opportunities, especially if the Federal Reserve raises interest rates, as it did in 1994, to create an unprofitable business climate.

Cutting government spending on ongoing programmes, on the other hand, not only causes additional unemployment but it can also be damaging to the future productive growth of the economy. For example, cutting back on government projects to improve mass transportation, highways, harbour, and airport facilities will increase delays, accidents, and raise the future cost of transporting goods to market, thereby requiring higher prices. Reductions in spending on environmental clean-up projects (for example, sewerage treatment facilities under the Clean Water Act) or reducing government spending on medical research and education increases exposure to future health hazards which eventually exact a cost in terms of lost work days, health care, and even lives. Attempts to balance the budget by reducing federal aid to education will make more difficult the accumulation of technological knowledge for our young people just as the world is becoming more dependent on technology for better goods, jobs, and prosperity.

In all these cases, the long-term results of a short-sighted conservative vision to reduce deficits will be to burden the economy with higher costs and more inflation in the future. It is not deficits *per se* that are an economic problem. Deficits may be needed to maintain a fully employed economy. We must make sure that the deficits are spent on things that enhance our productivity and living standards rather than being frittered away in personal income tax cuts as the Reagan supply-side deficits of the 1980s were.

Conservative dogma is deeply ingrained into the public perception of economic problems, despite the shallow logical foundations upon which conservative doctrines are based. Accordingly, in order to open public discussion of a civilized economic analysis, it is necessary to demonstrate the specific ways in which this predominant ideology impedes the way we examine the 'facts' in public forums.

WHO CARES IF ECONOMIC THEORY DOES NOT REFLECT THE REAL WORLD?

Institutions and the economic system

Humans have elevated themselves from the law of the jungle to a civilized state by designing institutions to provide innovative responses to unforeseeable changes in the economic environment. Even among humans, the spectrum of economic development from primitive tribes to complex, economic democracies is closely related to the degree that the various human communities have developed socio-economic institutions to interact with, adapt to, and even regulate, the economic environment to serve the needs of mankind.

This power to control the economic situation is a double-edged sword. Used well, as it was during the decades following World War II, it provided enormous increases in prosperity and in living standards around the globe (see the statistical analysis of Table 10.1 of Chapter 10, p. 180). Used poorly, as it has been since the early 1970s, it can result in a slow growing or stagnating economy where the current generation is unable to significantly surpass the average living standard of their parents. And if our civilizing institutions are continually abused there is the potential to create real economic misery and havoc (as in The Great Depression).

Thus, economic analysis of real world systems cannot ignore the institutional setting in which economic activity takes place. Yet practitioners of classical economics believe one of the primary virtues of their analytical system is that it is devoid of any institutional content and hence equally applicable to *all* the economic problems of *all* living creatures. Believing they are 'hard' scientists, classical economists have attempted to establish the existence of immutable economic 'laws' which all living creatures must obey, in the same way that the law of gravity must be obeyed not only by humans in developed economies, but by primitive tribes, all animal and plant life, and even inanimate objects. As Nobel Prize winning economist Robert Solow has stated:

[M]odern economics has an ambition and a style rather different from those I have been advocating. My impression is that the best and the brightest in the profession proceed as if economics is the physics of society. There is a single universally valid model of the world. It needs only to be applied. You can drop a modern economist from a time machine – [or] a helicopter . . . at any time, or any place, along with his or her personal computer; he or she could set up business without even bothering to ask what time and which place. .... We are socialized to believe there is one true model and that it can be discovered or imposed if only you make the proper assumptions and impute validity to econometric results that are transparently lacking in power.

In the world we inhabit, as Solow implies, there are no universal economic laws. Instead, economic behaviour can be altered by civilizing institutions, so that economic principles are neither timeless nor independent of the civic setting and the prevailing institutions. The conservative self-interest model cannot provide the universal solution for all our economic maladies, for all times, despite claims to the contrary by many economists.

Do the facts fit the theory?

When confronted with real world economic data, the explanations of the conservative model often clash with the facts. For example, conservative economists assert that the rate of inflation is directly related to the excessive rate of growth in the money supply. The facts, however, show that between 1977 and 1981 the money supply grew by approximately 32 per cent while the price level rose by 40 per cent. Between mid-1982 and mid-1986, on the other hand, the money supply rose by over 40 per cent, while the price level only increased 12 per cent.[1] Yet, this conspicuous failure of the conservative model to predict the decline in the rate of inflation between 1982 and 1986 despite the higher rate of growth of the money supply (and larger government deficits) has not undermined its powerful standing in the profession. Nor has it discouraged conservatives from insisting that the only way to fight inflation is to limit the money supply growth to 3 per cent a year and to eliminate the federal deficit.

Nor can it be claimed that the period from 1982 to 1986 is a statistically oddity. During the period 1987 to 1994, the money supply grew by 58.4 per cent while prices rose by 35.2 per cent, and the deficit expanded from $169.3 billion to $251.7 billion. Between 1990 and 1994, the money supply increased by 40.0 per cent; prices rose by 13.4 per cent and the government deficit declined from $278 billion to $251.8 billion. It should be apparent that the data do not support the classical notion that there is a strong and immutable relationship between increasing government deficits, increasing money supply growth and inflation. Despite the transparent lack of explanatory power (as Solow noted) the classical model is still held by people in high places to explain how the economy must operate to prevent inflation.

Contradictory facts and incorrect forecasts can be, and usually are, explained away by conservative economists with the claim that predicted consequences of their analysis will occur 'in the long run' with a 'long and variable' lag over time. Hence if events appear to be incompatible with the theory, it is simply because the full impact of any action has not yet occurred. In the long run, after a long (but unspecified) time lag for things to work their way out, it is claimed, the prediction will ultimately come true. Counterfactual empirical evidence can always be dismissed since we are not yet in the long run.

THE 'HARD SCIENCE' APPROACH TO ECONOMICS

Outcomes are inevitable

In 1968, MIT Professor and later Nobel Prize winner Paul Samuelson wrote that in their quest to provide a hard scientific basis for the economics discipline modern economists must believe in a 'unique long run equilibrium [i.e., an inevitable outcome for the economy] independent of the initial conditions'. Underlying this creed, is the presumption that the economic system operates under what Samuelson called 'the ergodic hypothesis'.

The word 'ergodic' does not often come up in ordinary discourse except among mathematicians and some physical scientists. Consequently the intelligent lay person may not comprehend the devastating tunnel vision that this ergodic hypothesis imposes on Samuelson's hard-science economist. In using this ergodic terminology, Samuelson is, as he readily admits, drawing an analogy with nineteenth-century statistical mechanics where the ultimate long run 'equilibrium' outcome of a system is independent of the initial conditions. For example, the ergodic presumption permits physicists to predict that an unhindered pendulum will always come to the same (long-run equilibrium) point of rest at the bottom of its path no matter where in the swing we start it off from. In economics, the 'ergodic' analogy of the swinging pendulum is that an unhindered economy will always come to the same long-run position of rest (at full employment), no matter where in the business cycle swing the system starts from.

It is this belief in an ergodic economics that permits conservative economists to postulate the existence of unique, inevitable outcomes and therefore makes economics a *hard* science – on a par with nineteenth-century physics. This seemingly innocuous presumption of the existence of unalterable long-run economic equilibrium outcomes implies that there are natural laws which govern the operation of the economic system propelling it towards a stable, desirable (often termed 'efficient') solution, just as the natural law of gravity propels a swinging pendulum towards the midpoint of its swinging arc. Consequently, if ergodicity is postulated for economics, then all the predictions of conservative economic theory can be expected to occur here on earth *in the long run* – if we only trust the invisible hand of natural laws to operate in the absence of government interference.

Keynes's reaction to the usefulness of such natural long-run equilibrium concepts as the basis of policy was clear:

But this long run is a misleading guide to current affairs. In the long run we are all dead. Economists set themselves too easy, too useless a task if in tempestuous seasons they can only tell us that when the storm is long past the ocean is flat again.

To believe in the natural inevitability of economic outcomes is to deny that humans can have control over their economic destiny. Accordingly, a considerable amount of mischief can be rationalized under the rubric that economics is an ergodic 'hard' science. If one accepts the view that the economic pendulum is always swinging towards a full employment prosperity or at least towards the natural rate of unemployment, then any attempt by the government to improve the current situation to create jobs for all who want to work will only hinder the long-run ability of the economy to right itself.

Samuelson provides an interesting example of how this presumption of a unique long-run equilibrium position can influence our view of the economic scene. Because of the ergodic hypothesis, 'hard-headed' scientific economists believe in a long-run market-determined distribution of income independent of the initial income distribution (just as the pendulum's equilibrium is always at the bottom of the swing independent of how far from this position we start the swing).

Suppose that this natural equilibrium distribution of income leads to the rich living in huge mansions while the poor sleep in the streets of the cities. A government (not under the influence of hard-headed economists) might try to redistribute income towards the poor so that they can at least obtain some shelter from the elements. In a long-run classical world of economic science, however, the unique equilibrium solution would prevail. As Samuelson puts it, 'if the state redivided income each morning, by night the rich would again be sleeping in their comfortable beds and the poor under the bridges'. Accordingly, the conservative 'hard science' view of economics justifies the existing income distribution – no matter how inequitable – as part of the normal working out of the natural laws of economics.

The dominance of this 'hard' science economics

The 'hard science' claim of conservative economics recommends itself to the self-interest ideology of the powerful, for it rationalizes the existing distribution of income, wealth, and power as the *natural* outcome of some immutable law of nature. This is no accident, for as Machiavelli wrote, money can not buy friendships but it can secure alliances. The financial requirements of higher education in recent decades have made the academic profession vulnerable to the temptations posed by grants, provided by the rich and powerful – including recent conservative governments – for economic research. To be a continuing recipients of such grants, one must be able to provide still another 'proof' of the desirability and inevitability of the laissez-faire market outcome.

In an earlier day, before research grants were an important financial consideration in university budgets, diverse academic views and discussions were tolerated and even encouraged on campus. Nowadays, as both private and public universities are run by administrators with an eye on the business culture focus on the bottom line, alternative lines of investigation which may enrich intellectual stimulation and development but which do not bring in significant outside research money tend not to be encouraged. Under such a system, conservative economic theory, with its implicit justification of the existing distribution of income and wealth, tends to dominate professional discussions as 'successful' economists follow the 'invisible hand'.

ECONOMIC OUTCOMES ARE NOT INEVITABLE

To repeat, ergodicity asserts that economics, like Newtonian mechanics, involves 'timeless' natural laws which control the behaviour of all subjects within the scientific discipline. Thus, just as Newtonian physicists believe that the dinosaurs, and all other living creatures past and present (and future), have always obeyed (and will obey) the law of gravity on the planet Earth, so do conservative economists assert that all past, present, and future living creatures obey the same 'timeless' laws of economics as they engage in the processes of production and trade. In this conservative view, governmental laws and rules that attempt to alter the long-run 'natural' outcome of ergodic economic processes are as useless as a government edict that would outlaw the law of gravity in order to make Earth the centre of the solar system.

Those who believe that economics is a hard science eschew any hard thinking about the vexatious problems we face. Nature, guided by immutable economic laws, will provide the inevitable outcome – without government's help.

The truth, however, is that unlike the world of the physical sciences where all living creatures obey unchanging natural laws (such as the law of gravity), there are no universal economic 'laws' that govern all animal behaviour in economic affairs, or even all human behaviour.[2] Thus economic principles are not ergodic even among species – much less over time within the human species. Since economics is a soft science, then what is essential is to think hard and long about the economic processes that are responsive to civilizing influences. Humans can work together to mold their economic destiny.

WHAT HAVE ECONOMISTS DONE FOR US LATELY?

Lincoln once said that God must have loved the poor, he made so many of them. To which, one might facetiously add, that conservative economists are only doing God's work by providing a rationalization for recent policies which have created more poor in our midst. Since about 1970, conservative economics has generated a rationalization for reversing a 35 year movement towards policies that promote full employment, a more equitable income distribution and a reduction in global poverty.

President Roosevelt's New Deal supplemented by Keynesian policies had in fact moved the world closer to a full employment environment and a much more equitable distribution of the nation's economic bounty. The statistics on unemployment and the distribution of income in the United States show that for more than a quarter of a century following the Great Depression progress was made towards eliminating unemployment as a major economic problem and simultaneously reducing the percentage of the poor in the US. Lower income households received a proportionately larger share of the growing economic pie. As President Kennedy noted: 'A rising tide lifts all boats'.

When by the late 1960s the problem of inflation became substantial, these objectives of full employment and a more equitable income distribution were jettisoned. Since then deliberate policy decisions have unleashed economic forces which reversed the progress that the United States made towards becoming a more civilized economy. Unemployment has again become a chronic problem, even in the prosperity swing of the business cycle.

At the same time, as Table 4.1 shows, the distribution of income has

Table 4.1   Per cent of personal income going to rich, middle class, and poor in the United States, and the unemployment rate, 1947–1993

	1947	1967	1986	1993
Rich	43.0	40.4	43.7	48.9
Middle class	52.0	54.0	51.6	47.5
Poor	5.0	5.6	4.6	3.6
Unemployment rate	3.9	3.8	7.0	6.8

become more unequal. Between 1947 and 1967 the poorest 20 per cent of the population of the United States saw their share of the total income of the economy increase from 5.0 to 5.6 per cent. Since then it has declined to less than 4.6 per cent in 1986 and to 3.6 per cent in 1993. The share of total income going to the middle class (middle 60 per cent) in America increased from 53 to 54 per cent between 1947 and 1967; it slipped back to 51.7 per cent in 1986 and fell to 47.5 per cent in 1993. The share of income going to the richest fifth of the American population, on the other hand, fell from 43 to 40.4 per cent between 1947 and 1967, but under recent policies it has climbed back to 43.7 per cent in 1986 and to 48.9 per cent in 1993.

In sum, for more than two decades after World War II government policies created a close to full employment economy and also produced a more equitable distribution of income. This trend has been more than reversed in the subsequent decades. Even during the period of prosperity under President Reagan the rising tide did not lift all boats. This growing inequality in income is not only economically unhealthy for an economy that depends on mass production and domestic mass consumption for its prosperity but it also contributes to the erosion of the civic values of the community. The creation of a large and growing class of losers juxtaposed against a small class of fabulously wealthy winners can only weaken the fabric that holds a civilized community together.

The generation of people entering the work place immediately after the Second World War were able to look forward to a higher standard of living than their parents – thanks in large measure to the civilizing New Deal and Keynesian policies designed to deal with the problems of that era. Since the end of the 1960s, the likelihood of earning a higher standard of living than one's parents has significantly diminished for many American families as barbaric natural rate policies rationalized by classical analysis were hammered out to deal with the new economic problems.

ORTHODOXY, CIVILIZED ECONOMICS, AND OUR MAJOR ECONOMIC PROBLEMS

The major problems in economics are divided into two categories: micro-economics and macroeconomics. *Microeconomics deals with the difficulties inherent in a single market* or small group of markets, for example, the market for chain saws, or petroleum products, etc. *Macroeconomics*, on the other hand, *deals with the difficulties inherent in the total national or global economy*; for example, with questions of inflation, employment, income distribution, etc. Although there is an obvious relationship be-tween a tree and a forest, nevertheless the microbiology of a tree is dif-ferent from the macrobiology of forests. Similarly, the microeconomics of individual markets is related to, but different from, the macroeconomics of the national economy or a global economy.

Ultimately, it is the macroeconomic problems which have an indelible impact on our lives as members of a civil society. Inflation or persistent unemployment among those willing to work tend to threaten the stability and the sense of community among members of a society. Traditional methods of coping with these problems often exacerbate one attempting to solve the other. In the resulting maelstrom, the benefits of living in a civilized society are often jeopardized. Accordingly, the rest of the chapters in this book will be spent discussing macroeconomic issues – and civilized solutions. For if we can get our macroeconomic house in order, we may find it easier to resolve our microeconomic problems.

Nevertheless we would be remiss if we did not at least suggest that even at the microeconomic level, a single-minded emphasis on the importance of self-interest in a free market environment may produce undesirable micro-solutions. When government does not look for civilized solutions to the fundamental microeconomic problems of our highly interdependent society, the results can be barbaric. As the following examples demon-strate, 'deregulation' which unleashes self-interest in a free market is not always a good thing.

IS DEREGULATION A UNIVERSAL MICRO-SOLUTION?

In recent years, there has been a movement towards 'deregulation' of all markets in the expectation that unregulated markets and a pricing system unconstrained by any government rules will provide better services for the public.

In a more academic tome than this one we might delve deeply into the fallacy of accepting a conservative microtheory which presumes that un-less proved otherwise, micro-markets perform efficiently in providing the greatest amount of benefits for the lowest costs. The discussion would show that failure of free micro-markets to perform 'efficiently' is an al-most ubiquitous phenomenon; and hence we can not simply rely on the invisible hand of free markets to achieve the efficient solution that econom-ists daydream about.

There are no simplistic and universal solutions to achieving good market performance. Each market must be studied on a case-by-case basis. Per-formance criteria that are acceptable in our society must explicitly be developed and checked for compatibility not only with business standards but with civic goals as well. Then clear rules and regulations can be developed which prescribe acceptable economic behaviour within a civil-ized system.

In the limited space remaining in this chapter, we will take three cases to illustrate why 'free markets' need not provide desirable results. These three illustrations are: networking, congestion, and the development of UHF television transmission facilities prior to the innovation of cable television.

NETWORKING

As a civilized society, what do we want from the transportation and com-munications networks that bind our geographically dispersed population together as a nation? The feeling of belonging to and participating in one's nation is maintained by the ability to move around and communicate easily with the other members of our national community. In an earlier era the explicit policy of public utility regulation of transportation and communica-tion enterprises was to require these firms to provide a universal service where all members of our civil society should have easy access to the networks of these common carriers. This simple principle of universal service permitted the United States to sustain our view of ourselves as 'One Nation, Indivisible'. Despite a widely scattered population coming from a multitude of ethnic backgrounds, we could communicate and travel easily in a gigantic 'from sea to shining sea' melting pot. The American civil community was strengthened by this provision of inexpensive access to a great transportation network of railroads (before World War II), or air transport (in the postwar period) and telephone and written communica-tions networks.

To make sure that all communities had a minimum level of access to these networks at roughly comparable prices, public policy encouraged cross-subsidization. People who lived in high density areas (where the per capita access costs per person was very low) paid more than the cost of providing their service in order to insure that other members of the community in far flung regions (where costs of extending the network was higher) could be linked-in at affordable prices. The result was a national network which strengthened the sense of community.

In the last two decades, however, a conservative movement for common carrier deregulation was initiated. It sets groups of citizens against each other by encouraging, under the mantle of economic efficiency, the dismantling of significant outlying portions of the service networks which had promoted the American community. Those persons in high density (i.e., urban) areas were told they were chumps for 'wastefully' cross-subsidizing the members in the hinterlands. If the citizens in the outlying areas could not, or would not, pay their higher costs for access to the network, then they should not be provided with such service. Making each person pay for the cost of providing services to his location, it was argued, would be efficient compared to a system of public utility regulation which promotes cross-subsidization in order to pay for as wide a network as possible to serve all the people. Never mind that the universal service principle helped generate a feeling of belonging to the American civil community and permitted access to poor and rich alike.

In a healthy civil community, individuals do not continually measure the benefits of exiting from the responsibility of paying to maintain a network that pays for universal access for every member of the community with the costs of remaining part of the group. Exiting merely to avoid the costs of maintaining the network was not considered socially acceptable – and hence the community retains its viability and strength.

The reader might recognize that a similar argument underlies the need for all members of the community to participate in the financing of public education even if a citizen does not have children in the public schools or a citizen desires to provide a private education for their offspring. Only if all the members of the civil community recognize that they can not opt out of paying for the public educational system, can a literate public be maintained and strengthened.

The conservative argument is that all regulation is bad and therefore deregulation is always desirable does not recognize (1) the effects of violating community values by denying adequate network service to all, while maintaining preferential access to service for the rich or for those located in high density or low cost areas, (2) the costs of the decline in regional economic vitality in the hinterlands due to the lack of network facilities, or (3) the cost of additional congestion due to the increase in traffic on the heavily used routes where costs are low as the network disintegrates. Indeed, unrestrained competition on the heavily used routes might so seriously weaken the 'common carriers' that firms which initially provided low cost operations (for example, Frontier Airlines, Peoples Express, SBS Skyline, etc.) would ultimately fail leaving the consumers' fate in the hands of a remaining cartel.

We have not yet experienced all the results of deregulation of our transportation and communication network, yet it should be clear that deregulation has not provided the utopia promised by its advocates in the 1970s. Deregulation may have gone too far and created problems that outweigh any cost-saving efficiencies (such as additional travel times through hub airports), increased use of less safe commuter planes, and even uneven geographical development (based on access to hub airports). Unfortunately, we cannot know whether the concern is justified for we have not developed benchmark criteria to compare what the society wants from these sectors to compare with actual performance or what the effects of alternative policies may be. At least in the days of public utilities regulation, society's goals of providing every area with access to networks was achieved. Today, in our era of deregulation, the only criteria is a metaphysical one, whatever the market does provide must be what the people want.

Accordingly, despite deregulation of the telephone industry, one can not logically demonstrate whether the consumers of telephone services are either better off than they were when long-distance telephone service was organized as a public utility. Some consumers of telephone services have improved their economic situation because of deregulation, while others have suffered a degradation in service and significant increases in the cost of maintaining telephone service in their homes. Telephone rate structures and possible discounts have become so complex that only the heavy users (typically business and wealthier individuals) have the resources to learn to play the system in their own self-interest. Average consumers find it difficult if not impossible to know if they are paying the lowest price available for the quality and quantity of service they are receiving.

It is not at all clear that deregulation of the telephone system has been a universal good – or that it is better for society than what could have been developed under a regulated system which encompassed both the business and civic values. We must, therefore, be able to discuss the issues of regulation in the realm of civic values – it is not enough to dismiss regulatory rules with the argument that the free market knows best.

The trend in the 1970s and 1980s away from regulation of specific industries in what is claimed to be in the public interest (for example, airlines, utilities, banks, etc.) was typically rationalized on the basis that deregulation *per se* would improve performance. There is no doubt that this deregulation movement altered the pre-existing market situation, creating winners as well as losers. There is no evidence indicating that the resulting market situation has improved the economic situation of all market participants compared to what could have been obtained under a civilized system that promoted universal service principles. Of course, the previous regulatory system was not perfect, nor did regulatory agencies always make decisions that were in the public interest. This is not to deny that foolish regulatory rules can be as bad as unthinking deregulation. But just as eternal vigilance is the price of liberty, so watchfulness is a necessary condition to make sure economic institutions continue to adapt to new environmental conditions in order to fulfil the public service roles that they were designed for. There is no substitute for hard thinking about hard problems in search of a civic solution.

CONGESTION

The overuse of public facilities can cause congestion and lead to traffic delays. Everyone who uses a bridge, public park, train, airline, internet connection, or any other shared facility may contribute to congestion and degradation in the quality of service during periods of peak use. Those who use the facilities thereby impose a burden on other users. The conservative solution for the congestion problem is for those who can pay the most for the use of the facilities to outbid the others for exclusive use of the facility during peak usage periods. Thus, for example, if more people wished to use a bridge than the bridge could hold, the priority in the sequence of crossing would go to those who were willing to pay the most for the use rather than wait. (As is most 'efficient' conservative solutions, the poor are most likely to be at the end of the line.) Under this market solution, for example, ambulances would not be able to obtain the traffic right of way to cross the bridge by using their siren; instead, the conservative economic solution would be for the ambulance driver to pay all road users a sum sufficient to bribe them to move out of the way. The civilized view, on the other hand, is that the victim in the ambulance must have priority in order to save precious seconds – regardless of whether the victim is rich enough to afford to bribe others to get out of the way. Most readers would think this solution is civilized and proper; but, conservative economic logic suggests that the 'siren solution' is inefficient and thus not beneficial. According to conservative philosophy, this should be an example where government interference (by enforcing the rule that emergency vehicles have the right of way) is deleterious. Here then is an obvious case where a society, because it wishes to be civilized, has ignored the conservative solution.

Conservatives may argue that the siren solution is a special case. This is fine by us; if conservatives are willing to admit the existence of 'special cases', we can then discuss how far these special cases extend. Our discussion of external vs. internal incentives attempts to identify what makes such special cases prevalent, and therefore how to derive general principles which identify 'special cases' in all modes of economic life.

Even in non-life-threatening situations, most civilized societies choose to resolve the congestion problem via the first-come-first-serve principle, rather than by the free market solution of going to the highest bidder. Most readers would want reservations honoured when they go to a hotel or restaurant even if there are more people wanting to use the facilities than can be accommodated. Bribing the head waiter or the reservation clerk to cut ahead of reservation holders may provide an economically efficient solution, but it is one which most of us would find to be uncivilized, unpleasant, and undesirable. Similarly, in inclement weather, the civilized solution to the congestion problem is to queue up in taxi stands, not to push people aside or outbid them for cab service. Ultimately it is this civilized behaviour that moderates our individual self-interest and allows businesses to survive and thrive in any highly evolved economy.

THE DEVELOPMENT OF UHF TRANSMISSION FACILITIES

By the 1960s, the VHF spectrum space for over the airwaves television transmission was completely filled, while UHF space was completely empty. The conservative solution to this congestion problem on VHF was to auction space to the highest bidders among television broadcasters. The reasoning was that when the price for VHF space was raised sufficiently, broadcasters would find the cheaper UHF space an excellent substitute for their transmissions. The only problem was that because no one was transmitting on UHF, television sets were not built to receive UHF signals. The consumer could, of course, pay extra to have a UHF receiver custom built into the TV – but since there were no programmes on that part of the spectrum, it was not in the buyer's self interest to do this. Since UHF transmission could not be received by TV in American homes, it was not in the self-interest of any broadcaster (or advertiser) to use that part of the spectrum. Here then we had a variant of the chicken-egg dilemma. If only UHF transmission was widely available, consumers would want TV's with UHF receivers, and if only consumers had such TV sets in their homes, broadcasters and advertisers would be willing to use this part of the spectrum. The free market could never resolve the dilemma.

The United States government, recognizing the desirability of expanding broadcasting transmission to all the nation, solved the problem simply mandating that all newly produced TVs had to contain UHF receivers. The mass production economies of providing UHF reception on every set, allowed UHF reception to be built in at a minimal increase in the purchase price of a TV. In a very short period of time, as householders bought second TVs for their homes, or replaced old ones, the entire nation was receptive to UHF broadcasting. It was now in the self-interest of entrepreneurs to use UHF channels if VHF ones were not available. The VHF congestion problem was resolved, simply and in a civilized manner.

A similar case can be made for the government regulation requiring the installation of dual air bags in all new cars as a safety rule for a civil society. If the installation of air bags was left to the market, then it would be an optional extra for a new car buyer. This fitting of cars upon order basis would substantially increase the cost of a car so equipped. Once the government mandated that all new cars produced after a certain date must have dual air bags, then the economies of mass production reduced the cost of cars with bags. As time goes on and new cars replace the older equipment, all members of the community will enjoy a greater level of safety at a minimum cost.

CONCLUSIONS

The real lesson to be derived from these microeconomic illustrations is that businesses are not compelled to compete in accordance with natural market laws beyond humans' capacity to alter. Every market must have some set of 'rules of the game'. In a civilized society, social institutions play an essential moderating role on the law-of-the-jungle behaviour in pursuit of external incentives.

Since the dawn of recorded history human progress has been associated with the development of community rules and institutions to resolve conflict without violence. The common understandings of the rules of the game – as specified in the interpretation of law and in the establishment of customs – plays a decisive role in constraining behaviour and helping to determine outcomes.

There is no monolithic government, just as there is no faceless abstract market. There are specific people who often recognize that they are interacting in the pursuit of their own self-interest. Often the same people play influential roles in both governmental agencies and private industries. The rules under which we operate the economic system are in a constant state of flux, and the economically powerful can often have a significant say in how things change. Assuming away the importance of the interaction between the laws of our society and the people who shape and mould our social as well as political mores and economic rules of behaviour, is to deny the human condition.

A civilized society itself, is a public good. Civilization would not have been purchased by individuals acting alone and calculating costs and benefits of their civilized actions. Unless a certain critical mass of a population simultaneously and collectively adopts civilized standards of behaviour, the full rewards of civilization can not be enjoyed by anyone. Once adopted they are enjoyed by all – even those who do not toil to create the civilizing environment.

Moreover, civilization is not something which can easily be purchased on a piecemeal or incremental basis. Consider the concept of justice for all – a keystone for any civilized society. If a society permits justice to be meted out solely as to whether the benefits of the decision outweigh the costs of this specific decision, then the integrity of the principle of justice to all will soon be eroded. In a civilized society, for example, the judicial system may have to provide a specific decision which in its own context is not popular because it does not provide specific benefits to the current population. Nevertheless this decision may be necessary in order to promulgate the principles of a civilized society.

The answer to the question of 'What's wrong with economists?' is that conventional economic theory is flawed by its omission of civic values. Conservative diagnoses of economic problems overlook critical interactions, and therefore the choices that conservative economists present to policy makers are sometimes false ones. As a consequence, conservative policies often do damage that conservative economists are not even equipped to recognize.

Notes

1. Between 1977 and 1981, the federal deficit increased from $45 billion to $58 billion (reaching 2 per cent of the GDP), while between 1982 and 1986 the deficit increased from $120 billion to $238 billion (or approximately 5 per cent of the GDP).

2. A major implication of the fact that we do not obey any immutable economic law in our economic behaviour is that the economic future, unlike the astronomical future, is uncertain. Hence economists cannot reliably forecast where the economy will be even a few weeks or months from now, or even the stock market's value tomorrow. (Instant riches awaits anyone who can forecast correctly even a few minutes ahead.) Astronomers, on the other hand, using the unchanging law of gravity and previous observations of the positions of the heavenly bodies can confidently predict the position of the planets days, weeks, years, and even centuries into the future.

    Because economics involves non-ergodic phenomenon, all economic prediction is an art form, not a science. Like any of the arts, some practitioners are much better at it than others. The use of expensive and impressive computer hardware and software in formulating economic predictions does not guarantee excellent forecasts any more than the use of the most expensive paints and canvas assure one will produce an art masterpiece.

5 The Entrepreneurial Market System vs. State Socialism

A pure market system operating solely on the principle of self-interest and a pure state planning system designed only to promote civic values possess significant faults as well as some advantages. Table 5.1 sums up these differences between the advantages and disadvantages of State Planning vs. a Market System.

The major faults of a laissez-faire market system are a tendency to experience significant and prolonged periods of unemployment, and/or inflation, and an arbitrary and inequitable distribution of income and wealth. On the other hand, the advantages of decentralized decision-making by self-interested entrepreneurs operating in a market system are the provision of incentives for improvement in product quality and product diversity. The market system can provide an environment where change and hard work can be encouraged through the use of market price incentives operating on individual's self-interest to encourage greater productive effort.

A centrally controlled state planning system, on the other hand, may be able to deal effectively with the problems of unemployment and a capricious income distribution that plagues laissez-faire market systems. Since state planning does not traditionally use market incentives to encourage efficient completion of tasks by management and workers, however, the major weaknesses of these centrally controlled economies can be inefficiencies (especially overstaffing), the absence of product diversity, and a potential lack of a spirit of innovation and the desire to work hard by individuals. If individuals are motivated primarily by self-interest, then centrally planned economies will not encourage efficiency and diversity, and especially the diversity that comes from technological innovation. In a society where all important decisions regarding incomes and prices are decided centrally, there is no appeal to the human motivation of economic self-interest to encourage hard work, quality of products, and the production of a wide variety of goods. Consequently, planned economies are often faced with the dilemma of a fully employed population who are earning income but are unable to buy the goods and services they desire. As Keynes noted, a system of State Socialism 'seems to solve the problem of unemployment at the expense of efficiency and freedom'.

In the eyes of its inhabitants, whenever the faults of either system loom

79

Table 5.1   Comparison of market and planned economies

Market oriented (capitalist) system	State planning system
Advantages	*Advantages*
1. Incentives for diversity, innovation, working hard	1. Full employment
2. Conservation of resources	2. Equitable distribution of income and wealth
Disadvantages	*Disadvantages*
1. Unemployment	1. Lack of diversity
2. Arbitrary and inequitable distribution of income and wealth	2. Wasteful production methods (overmanning) and shirking

large relative to its advantages, the public tends to call for reforms aimed at pursuing the benefits of the other system. Accordingly, the economic pendulum swings first one way and then the other over the decades, often with the gains from modifying the existing system offset by absorbing the disadvantages of the alternative system.

The interwar years in Great Britain and the Great Depression in the United States, for example, accentuated in the public mind what Keynes noted were the 'outstanding faults of the economic society in which we live . . . its failure to provide full employment and its arbitrary and inequitable distribution of income and wealth'. To correct these major flaws of a market system does not require a radical change in the system. What is needed, according to Keynes, is a modified system that is 'moderately conservative in its implications'. Although the correction involved an extension of the traditional functions of government where the State would 'exercise a guiding influence' on total spending in the community,

> this need not exclude all manner of compromises and devices by which public authority will cooperate with private initiative. But beyond this no obvious case is made out for a system of State Socialism which would embrace most of the economic life of the community. It is not the ownership of the instruments of production which it is important for the state to presume. If the State is able to determine the aggregate amount of resources devoted to augmenting the instruments and the basic reward to those who own them, it will have accomplished all that is necessary.

What is required is for the government to accept responsibility for assuring that total demand is sufficient to encourage private sector entrepreneurs to be willing to hire all who want to work. (As a corollary to this demand expansion responsibility, oversight regulation of domestic and international financial markets might be required to prevent speculative financial disruptions to total demand growth.)

With the virtual collapse of a mostly laissez-faire market system during the Great Depression in the United States (and most other capitalist countries), there was initially a popular movement towards a 'Keynesian' system of aggregate demand management that reached its pinnacle with the Kennedy–Johnson tax cut of the 1960s. Through the mid-1960s, this modified market entrepreneurial system, with some minor hesitation and backsliding, tended to achieve fuller employment and a less inequitable distribution of income.[1] While this mixed market system reduced the magnitude of the flaws of unemployment and unequal income distribution compared to the system of the 1930s, the problem of inflation and a slowing down of the rate of innovation became more apparent. It was at this time that communist leaders such as Khrushchev believed that the communist system could bury capitalism.

As the inflation of the postwar market system threatened to increase, the public yearned to return to an earlier capitalist era when inflation was neither as severe nor prolonged. In the late 1970s under President Carter (and Mrs Thatcher in the United Kingdom), and later under Presidents Reagan, Bush, and Clinton, the pendulum swung back to a more laissez-faire approach. Deregulation became the buzz-word of this more conservative conventional wisdom. Many of the regulations that had been earlier placed on the banking system and financial markets to prevent speculative excesses were removed. Typical 'Keynesian' demand management via fiscal policy was curtailed. Monetary management by the Central Bank became 'the only game in town' for affecting the macroeconomic problems of unemployment and inflation.

The result, over the last two decades, of financial deregulation and systematic reduction of the deliberate intervention of the elected federal government to promote expansion in total demand has been a tendency towards sustained levels of higher unemployment. At the same time there have been great strides in the introduction of innovations and a greater diversity of consumer goods. Unfortunately, there has also been a tendency towards a greater inequality of income both within Capitalist nations and across nations in the international Capitalistic parts of the world.

A different dilemma developed in the planned economies of Eastern Europe and China. By the late 1970s it was obvious that these planned economies suffered, as Keynes said they would, from tremendous inefficiencies in production and a lack of diversity and innovation. With the ability to watch television programmes emanating from market economies that showed the cornucopia of goods available in such systems, the residents of planned economies looked out enviously at the advantages of the market-oriented, entrepreneurial system. Rather than attempting a slow orderly transition that would maintain their civic values while incorporating the principles of self-interest, however, many in Eastern Europe thought it was desirable to impose what was called 'shock therapy'; that is to cut out any vestiges of civic values and to make an instant conversion to a self-interested market system. The hope was to obtain almost instantaneously the fruits of a market economy, while it was expected that the economic system would still provide full employment and an equitable income distribution.

The result was that the greater the shock treatment the more likely that the patient was put in jeopardy by creating a market system that combined the worst features of the market and planned economies combined. In general the more 'shocked' the economy, the greater the resulting unemployment and the more inequitable the resulting distribution of income so that fewer and fewer inhabitants were in a position to afford the innovations and diversity of goods that were achieved. Consequently, there has been a continued immiseration of large segments of the population supported by what remains of a tattered social safety net in these former planned economies.

The more successful entrepreneurial systems of Western Europe, North America and Japan had taken decades to develop a stable civil institutional framework for restraining market power within the framework of a domestic economy. These stabilizing institutions, while sharing some common features, differ significantly in their design among specific nations as they develop all sorts of civilized compromises between the civic values and private self-interest initiatives. To work effectively, these nation-specific institutional designs must be compatible with the cultural background and heritage of the populations concerned.[2]

As we approach the twenty-first century, the problem facing all modern nation economies is how to systematically modify and redesign their economic systems that have been backsliding for the past two decades. In the emerging global economy the challenge is to evolve a civilized market system to achieve a more fully employed economy, with stable prices, where the distribution of income within each country and among nations is not completely determined by the self-interest proclivities (what economists call 'rent seeking' tendencies) of individuals and groups that have amassed significant market power.

Achieving these objectives will require substantial modifications of the economic institutions that have developed in recent decades in the leading market-oriented nations. As the quarter century after World War II demonstrated, given the rules of the game for producing a civil progressive economy, entrepreneurial systems tend to be successful at delivering both the goods and the civilized environment because they are capable of innovation and adaptation to changing conditions. Because these civil economies are not centrally controlled, market systems can continuously evolve and re-invent themselves as long as the government restricts itself to a moderately conservative 'guiding influence' in achieving a civilized societal environment of full employment without inflation.

In the global economy of the twenty-first century, however, orderly adaptations will have to go beyond national institutions. It will also require the major trading nations to develop international institutions so that if any one market-oriented economy fails to achieve full employment without inflation, it can not pass its unemployment or inflation maladies on to other nations.[3] Nevertheless before international civilized economic institutions can be developed, each nation that expects to participate in a global market community must first get its domestic house in order. This book is dedicated to providing some guidelines for promoting government guidance of individual initiatives at both the national and international level.

Notes

1. With the success of these demand-augmenting policies, a movement favouring another type of government intervention began involving the regulation of individual product and labour markets to limit individual entrepreneurial decisions.
2. Even with the recent evolutionary reversal to a greater emphasis on self-interest that has occurred in market economies since the 1970s, the remnants of the civilizing institutions has so far buffered the economy from the worst barbaric effects of this backsliding towards a laissez-faire system.
3. See Chapter 10 *infra*.

6 Why Taxpayers Pay their Taxes

In 1974, armed with a graph drawn on a paper napkin, economist Arthur Laffer and White House Chief of Staff Richard Cheney initiated the re-shaping of American society. What sounds like the first line of the most implausible political thriller ever written is actually a factual (and frightening) demonstration of the overwhelming influence that economic ideas can have on our nation.

For conservatives, paying income taxes has an external disincentive effect on workers and businesses. Why work, conservatives ask, if the government takes so much of your income in taxes? Consequently, conservative solutions for getting people to work harder focuses on tax reform by cutting tax rates. Thus, under Ronald Reagan, cutting taxes became a 'supply-side' measure to increase people's willingness to supply greater productive effort to produce more goods and services. As John Kenneth Galbraith often characterized it, supply-siders believe that the rich do not earn enough after-tax income and therefore propose to cut their taxes to make them work harder and expand their businesses. The poor, on the other hand, are seen as having too much income, and hence we have to reduce their income and thereby create an incentive for the poor to get off their duff and search harder for a job and work harder when they get one. The few critics of this 'supply-side' policy called it 'trickle-down' economics.

By significantly reducing the taxes of the rich by more than cutting welfare to the poor and by increasing total government spending, the Reagan Administration stimulated total demand for the products of industry. The policy was successful in expanding production in American industries and, via imports, in production abroad. The world recovered from a great recession, but the distribution of income in the United States became significantly more unequal. As a result, despite an improving overall economy, many of the poor in the inner cities found their after-tax income lower than it was in the mid-1970s.

Conservative economists, worry about how taxes affect the behaviour of individuals motivated solely by self-interest. Conservatives are quick to explain how taxes 'distort' the free market outcome (a strategic use of pejorative dialect). From our perspective, an important issue involving any tax reform proposal is the need to support and strengthen the institutions that will maintain voluntary taxpaying in a civilized society. Our approach to tax reform is in the context of the civilized sphere where civic duties and self-interest cold-cash calculations interact. An oft forgotten aspect of the tax protests of the American Revolution was that they were not directed at taxes *per se*. The battle cry was 'No taxation without representation!' – that is, without civic justice. Civilized tax reform is organized around a coordinated application of external and internal incentives to earn credibility, change attitudes, and build institutions that maintain the norms that underlie this important duty of citizenship.

We first focus on the conservative argument that by reducing tax rates we create an incentive for people to work harder and longer so that government budgets can be balanced. This conclusion was tested in the 1980s and was proven false. Next, we will examine how conservative economists account for why people pay taxes and contrast that with an approach that combines self-interest with civic values to motivate people to voluntarily obey the tax laws of our country. Finally, we will outline a number of civilized policies that address the public policy concerns with taxes and taxpayers which we have identified.

Supply-side economics, which traces its lineage back to Arthur Laffer's cocktail napkin, came as a backlash against the excesses of the eroded liberalism of the 1970s. Supply-siders were a group of conservative economists who believed that prosperity resulted from the activity of daring entrepreneurs who (when unhindered by high taxes and government regulation) create a flood of new and productive businesses even in the absence of any change in the aggregate demand for goods and services. This virtuous creation of a new supply of goods was contrasted with the image of a ponderous 'liberal' bureaucracy managing the economy through demand-side interventions to increase total demand for the products of private enterprise. Six years after the Laffer–Cheney meeting, the ideas of Arthur Laffer were to guide the government of our nation in determining tax policy.

In the intervening years, the Laffer Curve was drawn on many other cocktail napkins to make the simple point that tax rates, especially on the wealthy, were too high. The explanation of the graph was that 'there are always two tax rates that yield the same revenues'. For example, if the income tax rate was zero per cent, no revenues will be raised. If the tax rate was 100 per cent, there would be no external incentive to work since no one would keep anything they earn. If no income is earned then revenues will be zero. At these extreme income tax rates, Laffer's logic is impeccable. Laffer, however, goes on to extrapolate tax revenues for all points between a zero per cent and a 100 per cent income tax rate. At some point between these two extremes, Laffer argued, tax revenues would be maximized. Laffer never said what the revenue maximizing rate was or how it could be determined. Nevertheless, Laffer was certain that by lowering tax rates from whatever level they are today, the nation would move in the right direction.

Other supply-side economists expanded Laffer's message by arguing that high tax rates encouraged cheating by making it profitable for taxpayers to underreport income and to engage in transactions which were not easily traceable by the Internal Revenue Service (IRS) tax collectors. As long as tax rates were 'high', supply-siders argued, the payoff for cheating or noncompliance in terms of unpaid taxes would exceed the costs of getting caught. If, however, tax rates were lowered, then the profit from cheating would be reduced, thereby encouraging more people to comply with the tax laws.

Finally, high tax rates encouraged people to invest in what were claimed to be 'unproductive' but legal tax shelters. Lower tax rates would make such sheltered investments relatively less profitable, encouraging investors to switch to other more productive – but taxable – investments. (Of course, if the tax shelters were truly non-productive, then they should have been removed from the tax laws entirely – but this latter point was not made by the supply-siders.)

In sum, given the 'high' tax rates existing in 1980, supply-side economists argued that any reduction in rates would raise tax revenues by increasing work effort, reducing noncompliance, and by moving investment from tax sheltered to taxable projects. In 1981, supply-siders predicted that a 25 per cent across-the-board reduction in tax rates would lead to a balanced budget by 1985.

Supply-side economics took the nation by storm. Supply-siders were seen as economic Santa Clauses giving every taxpayer a permanent Christmas present – lower taxes. As a predictive theory, however, supply-side economics was responsible for the largest economic miscalculation in history. Instead of the balanced budget confidently predicted to occur by 1985, the total national debt held by the public doubled from $700 billion in 1980 to $1.5 trillion in 1985 while the annual federal government deficit ballooned from $74 billion in the recession year of 1981 to $212 billion in 1985. Eight years later at the end of the Reagan Administration, the national debt exceeded $2 trillion dollars. By 1994, the national debt had grown to $3.5 trillion although the deficit had declined for the third year in a row to $203 billion.

The enormity of the forecasting error by supply-side economists has led some to believe that supply-side economics was merely a red-herring designed to detract attention from a hidden agenda; namely (1) to reverse the trend towards a more equitable distribution of income begun during President Roosevelt's New Deal; and (2) to run enormous deficits to precipitate a public outcry to reduce the size of big government. This hypothesis gains some support from David Stockman's confession in his autobiography, *The Triumph of Politics*. Two months before the 1980 election Stockman recognized that Reagan's proposed tax costs would not lead to a balanced budget. Instead, he expected deficits on the order of $100 billion by 1985 – a very optimistic estimate, as it turned out. Stockman perceived annual deficits of this magnitude 'more as an opportunity than as a roadblock' in an attempt to carry out the conservative agenda of reducing the size of government.

There is no doubt that this was achieved. The Reagan supply-side policy led to the belief that we as a nation could not maintain funding for many civilized programmes. By 1995, almost everyone in political office was spouting the conventional wisdom that for the sole purposed of balancing the budget sometime in the twenty-first century, it would be necessary to reduce the size of government.

Stockman's confession of this ulterior motive is a particularly damaging comment of the substance of supply-side ideology. Stockman was not only one of supply-sider Jude Wanniski's strongest converts, but he had provided 'incisive criticisms and cogent amendments' for the first edition of the supply-side treatise *Wealth and Poverty* (according to author George Gilder).

Economic ideas, whether for good or evil, shape our social as well as our economic lives. Even though the supply-side tax rate reduction proposals never met the budget balancing promises of its advocates, we continue to find our public policy directed at the goal of reducing tax rates. In 1987, the United States reduced income tax rates with the top rate falling from 50 per cent to 28 per cent under the guise of tax simplification.

An exception to this demand for a lower tax occurred in 1993, when President Clinton and a Democratic Congress increased the top tax rate to 39 per cent for those earning over $200,000 per year. Conservative supply-side predictions to the contrary, this tax increase (that conservatives call 'the largest in US tax history') produced 7.3 per cent growth over two years while continuing the trend towards lowering the deficits begun in 1992.

Since the Second World War there has never been even three consecutive years of deficit reduction prior to the years 1992 through 1995. Regardless, supply side economic pressures to reduce taxes as part of any deficit reduction scheme lives on in the 1995 Republican Congress. Representative Richard Armey has advocated a flat personal income tax on wages and salaries with no taxes on income received in the form of dividends, interest, profits, or capital gains. Armey justifies these lower taxes on primarily wealthy persons by indicating that the rich, whom he considers the 'engine of growth' will work harder and thereby promote better economic growth and reduced government deficits.

SUPPLY-SIDE ECONOMICS AND TAX COMPLIANCE

The Reagan Administration concentrated efforts on relieving the burden of taxpaying. Reagan's tax policy was promoted not only as a way of improving the economy, but also as a means of balancing the budget by eliminating 'unfair' (high) tax rates and thus improving tax compliance.

Conservative proponents of tax reform and simplification attributed the growth in noncompliance to the fact that in the 1970s inflation pushed most Americans into significantly higher tax brackets without any increase in real income. People found themselves earning more money but paying proportionately even more in taxes. Because of inflation people's after-tax income often bought less than they could afford in the 1960s. Tax compliance and hard work were being eroded by the progressive tax brackets inherited from the liberal legislation of the 1940s to the 1960s.

Supply-side economics argued that the lower (and less progressive) tax rates were not only a panacea for boosting economic growth, but would encourage tax compliance as well. The forces determining employment, inflation and economic progress will be dealt with later. In this chapter we will examine tax compliance and see how the supply-side solution misses the core of the tax noncompliance problem.

WHY TAXPAYERS PAY THEIR TAXES

What motivates some people to pay their taxes and others to cheat? In our view, civic values and not just calculations of after-tax income play a significant role in determining how hard people work and whether they willingly pay their taxes. In contrast, conservative philosophy asserts that efforts to earn income are necessarily unpleasant. People will therefore work less if they receive less after-tax pay; or they will cheat more if they face higher tax rates. Rational self-interested individuals, by definition, do not care about the civic values of tax compliance. Self-interested individuals will pay taxes only if motivated by the external incentives of low tax rates and strong enforcement with severe penalties. Conservatives cannot explain the 'non-rational' behaviour of people who see a civic duty in paying taxes.

This conservative proposition carries with it some perverse political ramifications. As *Forbes* magazine puts it, 'People pay taxes largely because they perceive revenue collectors as vicious ogres without souls'. *Forbes* goes on to state that any deviation from this barbaric role for tax collectors will only impede the functioning of the tax system. Internal Revenue agents are cast as enemies who harass citizens and pick their pockets.

In conservative doctrine each individual's decision to cheat on taxes has an insignificant effect on total government revenues and thus the services which that individual can expect to receive. If taxpaying is viewed as a collective purchase of government services, then the price each self-interested individual would be willing to pay, under their conservative philosophy, should be close to nothing, because each citizen receives virtually the same government services whether he or she pays taxes or not.

Conservatives also argue that the taxes paid and the effort of record-keeping paperwork associated with taxes creates a burden (or 'tax wedge'). According to supply-siders, the tax wedge forces transactions out of the record-keeping 'money' economy and into the 'private' underground economy (where the tax collector cannot see the transaction) as 'off-the-books' cash transactions or barter swaps are used to avoid reporting income producing activities.

As tax rates decreased, the conservative argument claimed that people would be more willing to report their wages and pay for goods rather than engage in 'off-the-books' activities. President Reagan's 1981 tax reform programme gained support in Congress partly because the reduced tax rates it established were expected to increase compliance and reduce incentives to search for tax shelters and loopholes. According to the Internal Revenue Service 1986 Trend Analysis, compliance did increase between 1979 and 1982 for taxpayers in 4 of 12 groups, including those with the highest non-farm business income, the highest business partnership income, and the highest salary income. The powerful change in external incentives associated with the 20 per cent tax cut for those in the highest tax brackets apparently *did* make cheating a less profitable activity for some. Noncompliance continued to grow, however, among those in the other eight categories whose tax cut was not as large.

Moreover, after the 1981 legislation reducing all tax brackets was enacted into law, *Business Week* magazine reported massive increases in the use of dubious and illegal tax shelters. An IRS study reported that nonreporting of business income among all taxpayers significantly increased between 1979 and 1982, reducing the amount of taxes paid by $6 billion. The study suggested that this loss was linked to the proliferation of tax shelters.

Conservatives cannot explain why reduced tax rates increased the demand for tax shelters in 1982. If the risks of being caught remain the same and the benefits of noncompliance with lower rates are smaller, then the self-interested should find noncompliance to be less attractive than it was previously.

These facts suggest that continuously cutting taxes on a massive scale is not a viable way to slow the national decline in voluntary tax compliance. If we are trying to buy our way to tax compliance through low tax rates, evidence suggests we are paying too much for what we receive.

The conservative position is that people will not comply with tax laws unless the price is right. People must be rewarded individually to obey the law. Acceptance of this philosophy sends a signal to taxpayers that will directly influence their civic values. If the process of weighing individual costs and benefits of tax compliance is given legitimacy by community leaders espousing conservative philosophy, then a damaging blow is struck against civic values involving taxpayers' duties and social responsibilities which will reverberate for years to come. The civic spirit of a democratic tax system can be vitiated by allowing noncompliance to proliferate unheeded, and by excusing its growth by claiming tax rates are so high that self-interested members of society have reason to avoid taxes. The result will be to steadily erode the credibility upon which the remaining voluntary compliance of the system is based.

NONCOMPLIANCE: HISTORY AND THE SEARCH FOR CAUSES

When Ronald Reagan was elected President, tax compliance at the federal and state levels had been falling for 15 years. The IRS reported that between 1973 and 1981 the amount of annual revenue lost as the result of noncompliance with federal tax law increased by 58 per cent (after adjustment for inflation). According to the conservative estimate of the IRS, $90 billion in revenue was lost in 1982 alone. That enormous sum of money exceeds the amount that the federal government spent that year on Justice, Education, Commerce, the State Department, Housing and Urban Development, Transportation, the Environmental Protection Agency, NASA, and the operations of the House and Senate, the Federal Judiciary, and the White House, all combined.

Table 6.1   Loss of tax revenues by types of noncompliance behaviour 1982

Underreported income	= $52.0 billion (58% of total)
Overstated expenses, deductions, credits	= 13.0 billion (14%)
Nonfilers	= 3.0 billion (3%)
Delinquency	= 7.0 billion (approx.) (8%)
Crime	= 9.0 billion (approx.) (10%)
Corporate noncompliance	= 6.0 billion (7%)
Total	= 90.0 billion

The IRS divides its measurements of types of noncompliance into five categories: underreporting income, misusing deductions and credits, not filing the forms, nonpayment of existing recognized tax liabilities, and all forms of noncompliance due to crime. Table 6.1 shows that in 1982, understatement of income represented the largest drain on tax receipts from noncompliance.

To identify *the causes* of noncompliance, however, it is necessary to go beyond these figures and examine as directly as possible what drives tax-paying behaviour. IRS studies of taxpayer attitudes in 1984 and 1987 used a variety of techniques to elicit truthful answers about taxpaying behaviour. (Some noncompliance is accidental, and can be attributed mostly to errors with tax forms.) The IRS studies focused on intentional noncompliance. The responses of taxpayers were analyzed to find patterns of similar characteristics among noncompliant taxpayers. The only variables substantially correlated with noncompliance were those associated with the social values held by taxpayers.

There is significant empirical evidence that people's attitudes about paying taxes are highly correlated with a certain set of beliefs. It is especially ironic that these particular beliefs are similar to the twisted conservative dialect that has surfaced in the past two decades.

The 1987 IRS report concluded that

cheaters tend to justify overstating deductions and underreporting income as part of a consistent philosophy. For example, those who strongly agree that it's okay to hold back on taxes because 'the government spends too much anyway' are more than twice as likely to overstate deductions as not to do so, and more than three times as likely to underreport income. Those taxpayers who strongly endorse the idea that 'every taxpayer would cheat to some extent if he or she could get away with it' likewise have far higher rates of actual cheating.

The conservative explanation of why people pay taxes is solidly refuted by this study. The IRS found no evidence to suggest that actual tax cheating was related to individual perceptions of the costs and benefits of compliance. Those who believed that the risks of being caught cheating were very small were no more likely to cheat than those who felt the risks were large. Twenty-six per cent of those who cheated by not reporting all the income they earned believed that the IRS is 'always nearby watching', a fear that was significantly less common among honest taxpayers.

The assertion that high tax rates are responsible for low compliance is contradicted by comparing the evidence in Sweden with that in the United States. In Sweden tax rates are very high (55 per cent for a worker earning $10,000) while in the United States the combined rates of federal, state, and social security taxes for a similar worker would be around 15 per cent. Nevertheless, according to figures reported by the I.R.S. and the Swedish National Central Bureau of Statistics, roughly the same proportion of taxpayers cheat in each country. Other countries, such as Italy, have even lower tax rates and yet experience even higher rates of noncompliance. Moreover, a 1969 survey by Professor Burkhard Strumpel of the University of Cologne compared several European nations and concluded that absolute levels of tax rates do not determine compliance. All of these studies show that attributes of different national cultures, which are unrelated to the existing external incentives of marginal tax rates, can shape the level of income tax compliance. The cultural and political history of each national community plays an important role in tax compliance.

Even different regions of the United States historically demonstrate different levels of tax compliance. In a 1993 IRS estimate of tax revenue loss due to tax cheaters, the IRS concluded that the Western United States accounted for higher tax losses than the rest of the country. In western states, the IRS estimates, tax cheaters cost the federal government 10 cents out of every tax dollar owed. In the southeast it is 8 cents, while the southwest estimate is 7 cents. All other regions of the country accounted for approximately 6 cents out of every tax dollar. (Non-American readers should note that the regions with the highest noncompliance rates are those that, in recent decades, have tended to most strongly support conservative political candidates and policies.)

Most of the remaining studies of why people cheat on taxes indicate the importance of social and cultural history. A consistent finding in noncompliance studies over the last twenty years is that younger taxpayers are more cynical about the integrity of their fellow citizens, and are more willing to engage in questionable behaviour and to falsify the amount of income they have earned.

Clearly a realistic appraisal of why citizens pay (or do not pay) taxes must consider both the internal incentives of social norms as well as external incentives. In contrast to the conservative view of taxpaying, the empirical evidence is that noncompliance has strong correlations with the erosion of civilized norms. Furthermore, the IRS's study of tax behaviour indicates that calculations of costs and benefits are not an important determinant of whether or not a taxpayer will pay his taxes. To devise policies to encourage tax compliance therefore we must examine both the calculating behaviour that conservative economists see, as well as internally motivated behaviour. Finally, we must pay particular close attention to the volatile interaction of these internal and external motivations.

INTERNAL AND EXTERNAL INCENTIVES, AND TAXPAYING

In his classic work *The Logic of Collective Action* Professor Mancur Olson accepts the belief that people pay taxes only if they fear getting caught for cheating. He asserts that

> no major state in modern history has been able to support itself through voluntary dues or contributions. . . . Taxes, compulsory payments by definition, are needed.

The weakness in the argument that the fear of sanctions is the only motivator for tax compliance is that, based on the evidence available, any reasonable calculation by self-interested taxpayers of the probability of getting caught and the relevant penalties involved would motivate greater noncompliance than has been experienced historically. Despite a reluctance on practical grounds to admit that tax cheating is a crime that pays, there is a general consensus among tax officials that their power of enforcement is not sufficient to account for the high level of compliance that does occur. Former Commissioner of the IRS, Jerome Kurtz, has argued:

> Our system works best when it works automatically and unobtrusively . . . enforcement activity alone cannot achieve acceptable levels of compliance. Ours is, after all, a voluntary compliance system supplemented by enforcement.

Professor Mark Moore of Harvard suggests that increased enforcement can actually *reduce* voluntary compliance, a conclusion which is logically inconsistent with the philosophy of conservative economics:

[I]f enforcement alone is expanded, the existing norms supporting compliant taxpayers may deteriorate even more quickly. For the expansion of enforcement actions communicates an idea of what is expected of people as well as what is desirable. And if the system is set up on the basis that people will not pay taxes unless forced to do so, taxpayers are granted a license to adopt this attitude for themselves.

This assertion is supported by the 1987 IRS study that indicated that 20 per cent of the tax cheaters who overstated deductions had been previously audited, as compared to 13 per cent of honest taxpayers who have been audited sometime in the past.

This is not to imply that enforcement never plays a role in tax compliance. Declines in compliance have come at a time when enforcement activity has also fallen. The risk of being audited has always been low, and dropped from 3 per cent in 1976 to 2 per cent in 1982. Some small increase in compliance was noted when audit rates doubled to approximately 4 per cent in the late 1980s. Even if caught, however, the prosecution arm of the IRS poses a very limited threat. Of the 25 million cases of tax noncompliance estimated for 1982, less than 2000 were actually prosecuted and only half of these individuals were sentenced to jail. Most cases are settled by payment of interest or penalties.

Internal and external incentives both have a role to play in determining tax compliance. Tax scholar Clara Penniman expresses the relationship between the need for solid enforcement and the development of the civic ethic of voluntary compliance with the tax system:

> [F]eeble administration converts honesty into dishonesty. Unless the income recipient feels (1) that others in a like position are made to discharge their tax liabilities and (2) that the tax-administering agency is making some effort to protect the state's interests by independently checking his income, he will consider it no great misdeed to underreport his income and adopt a 'come and get me' attitude.

Internal and external incentives should be woven together for a successful tax compliance policy. The Franchise Tax Board of California noted in describing their Fair Share programme that enforcement is one important aspect of shaping both current and future norms:

> [E]nforcement programs do have an important role to play, both in terms of providing short-term, limited corrective actions, and in terms of building long-term confidence in the viability of the tax system.

Thus, a viable tax system comes from the effective use of both internal and external incentives.

Enforcement not only plays a large role in directly determining the revenue raised in a given year, but it also shapes civic values – an influence which will be felt in future years. The effect of enforcement on the community can be either reinforcing or corrosive. The problem of selecting the appropriate use of enforcement to maintain and strengthen the community is the same question we raised earlier regarding the proper coordination of internal and external incentives. As we explained in Chapter 3, a choice of this type will depend on the particular traditions and beliefs currently held by American taxpayers.

The actions of a few noncompliant taxpayers can erode the civic value of taxpaying, shifting the balance so that others begin to cheat, eventually leading to actions as a group which were originally preferred by only a few, as reported in Sweden in the 1970s:

> The amount of tax evasion and the compensating additional taxes needed have reached a critical point, and the resultant pressure on honest taxpayers creates a strong tendency to tax evasion even among ... those originally satisfied with the tax system.

Conservatives refuse to recognize that the civic values supporting taxpaying norms can collapse – noncompliance can become, in the conclusion of a 1974 study by East Carolina University Professors Song and Yarborough, 'a favorite sport which taxpayers play unabashedly against their government'. In such a situation the erosion of norms follows the example provided by Professor Schelling's tipping model which we discussed in Chapter 3.

The contagious nature of noncompliance was noted in a study of Ohio residents in 1976 which concluded that 'the more tax evaders a taxpayer knows, the more likely he is to evade taxes himself'. As long as the belief in the integrity of one's fellow taxpayers is strong, compliance is voluntary and cheating is simply not considered an option by most of the population. However, when taxpaying norms decline, compliance becomes more and more based on calculations of the risks and payoffs from cheating.

The task of government in encouraging voluntary compliance is to strengthen the community from which tax paying norms originate. To change social norms it is necessary to operate in the context of the current norms while simultaneously laying the groundwork for a new set of norms. A government cannot appeal to a sense of moral duty if current morals are weak or in disrepute. As Penniman suggests, it is here that strict enforcement can be used to strengthen the legitimacy of the reforming government agency, and to prod individuals out of their current habits towards the new taxpaying regime.

Once social norms have eroded and their influence diminished, we do see a greater applicability of conservative economics. This points to a larger truth regarding conservatism: their paradigm is most applicable where social values are weak, where civilized behaviour has disappeared, and where therefore the external incentives of appetite and fear play a greater role.

The final word on the relationship between enforcement and social norms was made almost 500 years ago by Machiavelli:

Just as good customs require good laws in order to be maintained, so laws require good customs for them to be observed.

REVITALIZING THE CIVIC VALUES OF TAXPAYING

There have been a number of discrete initiatives to increase voluntary compliance. These programmes have both increased enforcement *and* simultaneously attempted to revitalize social norms in order to increase future voluntary compliance.

Actions to strengthen enforcement, taken in isolation, can of course help to maintain and strengthen taxpaying norms – if the tax agency can select those enforcement measures which are perceived to be fair applications of force (that is, in line with current norms). For example, in the 1980s the State of Minnesota pursued 'flashy livers' – boat owners and those with expensive cars and special licence plates – in order to benefit from public support for such 'sting the rich' enforcement.

Norm-setting actions alone can also have a positive effect on compliance if other existing norms can be *refocused* on the noncompliance problem. For example, tax collectors in Massachusetts worked to redirect the values behind the contemporary activism against drunk driving to encompass tax cheating by using similar language and advertising to frame the problem. It has been suggested that the methods and sentiments of anti-smoking activism might be similarly shifted on to the problem of tax cheating.

The most effective policies come from combining the external incentive of increasing risks via more stringent enforcement with the internal incentive pressures from the community values. Civic values ease the pain of government intervention, while enforcement gives credibility to the revitalized norms. Actions in Massachusetts in 1983 illustrate such a process, in four stages:

(1) *Framing the Issue*: The state developed alternative taxpaying norms by building on selected elements existing within current values. In order to establish the attitude that tax evasion is not a victimless crime, the Massachusetts legislature and the media were informed that tax evasion totalled $640 million. After publishing lists of major tax delinquents and identifying uncollected tax bills of $300 million, it was stressed that if noncompliance was eliminated, taxes could be lowered by 10 per cent. Noncompliance was therefore not merely cheating on an abstract 'government', but taking money away from neighbours (which was less acceptable than cheating on an impersonal government). Finally, the state worked to 'emphasize the service aspects [of] a department that cares' in order to establish the theme that enforcement was protecting the honest taxpayer from paying more because of the tax cheats.

(2) *Establishing Credibility*: Massachusetts applied an enforcement 'shock' to get people's attention. A carefully orchestrated seizure drive began in May of 1983 to convey the threat of enforcement. This enforcement drive by itself collected $128.8 million – a 70 per cent increase over the previous year. The state also set out to establish *continuing* media coverage of department enforcement through a series of seizures and other enforcement actions. However, despite these actions, state officials admit privately that this enforcement was too little to change significantly the odds against the tax cheater, instead making more of a real contribution as a means of communicating that the state was getting tough.

(3) *Institutionalize the New Order*: The state established institutional foundations to provide for future maintenance of the new customs being established and to reinforce the perception that a change was occurring.

Legislation in 1983 made tax evasion a felony punishable by up to five years in prison and fines up to $10,000 for individuals. The government was given the power to revoke state and local licences and contracts as well as the authority to contract with private collection agencies (as the federal government already did).

At the same time, the Taxpayer Assistance Bureau was strengthened, a Problem Resolution Office was created, tax forms were simplified, and efforts were made to hasten the refund process – all of these actions supported the view of a fair and socially just tax system for a civilized community.

(4) *Transition*: A transitional mechanism was needed to avoid the injustice of treating past behaviour under the new normative standards, and to allow taxpayers to change their norms while saving face. A three-month amnesty programme from November 1983 to January 1984 allowed tax delinquents, nonfilers, and outright evaders to pay their accumulated

debt without prosecution. The state undertook an ambitious public relations campaign to make clear that 'Amnesty was a one-time, last chance
offer' after which it would be 'No more Mr Nice Guy'.

Massachusetts received immediate increases in revenues from the amnesty (although such increases were not strictly voluntary – they were
received in response to a direct state intervention). Fifty thousand individuals and corporations took advantage of the amnesty programme, adding $80 million to tax revenues as of January 1984. Over three years,
Massachusetts estimates that increases in total voluntary compliance brought
in $564 million. Estimates were that noncompliance had been cut by 25–
30 per cent.

The success is not limited to one year's tax returns. Those who acknowledged their previous noncompliance during the amnesty period have
remained on the tax rolls in the subsequent years. From a broader perspective, the re-establishment of the norms surrounding the important public
duty of taxpaying may have benefits in other spheres of civic life. Increased voluntary compliance with taxpaying responsibilities will help
prevent the erosion of legitimacy of government and law that comes with
the 'sport which taxpayers play unabashedly against their government'.
The positive example set by a tax system which achieves a high level of
compliance may even have some influence on other parts of our lives
where voluntary compliance is important (such as driving).

Conservatives misinterpreted what was going on in Massachusetts, even
after the successful amnesty. *Forbes* described the amnesty with the analogy of child-rearing: 'When you let a bad kid get away without punishment once, how do you ever convince him that you mean what you say?'
Note how the conservative view of human nature leads them towards
treating the public like children as opposed to responsible adults. Since the
public, like children, are assumed to lack any moral character, it is un-
surprising that improvements in compliance cannot be attributed to civic
values. Thus, the *Forbes* article concludes that any increase in compliance
must be due entirely to enforcement – a claim which even Massachusetts's
own tax officials don't make.

Massachusetts' Tax Commissioner Ira Jackson summarized three essential elements in changing taxpayer attitudes:

Why did Amnesty work in Massachusetts? I like to think that for those
who took the offer it was a combination of fear, guilt, and gratitude:
fear of what would happen if they did not settle up, guilt about their past
mistakes and gratitude that we were giving them one last chance to
square things away.

Massachusetts's success cannot be explained by conservative economics alone. Fear came from the state's enforcement efforts, which conservative economics does recognize. Guilt represents the conflict in values when lax taxpaying norms were confronted by the state's framing of the tax cheating issue. Gratitude lays the motivational basis for a shift of attitudes about tax cheating, and the establishment of allegiance to the norms of a renovated ethic of taxpaying. Conservative forces had a role in events, but in this example they were not central.

EVOLUTION OF AN INSTITUTION: TAX AMNESTY

A public policy initiative such as a tax amnesty programme is a fledgling institution – that is, it is a new mechanism that is partially built on existing law and custom, and partially created by the interactions between the politicians and the people. The meaning that people initially attach to this new political initiative is very important. Their understanding of the new policy in their dialect will be the base upon which all future implementation efforts will be grounded.

A particular public policy programme such as tax amnesty will earn its reputation based on experiences reported from where it has been attempted. The initial meaning of any tax amnesty programme may be different after it has already been implemented elsewhere because the recent experience of the earlier programme influences perceptions. Even if successive amnesty initiatives in two very similar states have identical provisions, if the first initiative failed (due to a political scandal or some other event unrelated to taxes), then the second attempt starts off handicapped merely by the negative association with the first effort.

Between 1982 and 1986, nineteen states completed tax amnesty programmes. The appetites of tax officials across the nation has been whetted by the thought of an immediate windfall of new revenues from taxpayers 'coming clean' during the amnesty period. California reaped $144 million, Illinois $154 million, and Massachusetts $80 million. However, if government officials view tax amnesty solely as a quick revenue-raiser, they may miss the important role that tax amnesties can play in helping shape long-range taxpaying behaviour. The opportunity to perpetuate improved tax compliance – and the higher future revenues that this insures – is lost.

Although Massachusetts and California both mobilized comprehensive campaigns to improve tax compliance norms in coordination with their amnesty programmes, other states have been content to take the money and run, with no concern for longer run impacts on social values. Thus the meaning of a tax amnesty – its reputation as a policy tool – can become tainted, as evidenced in the writing of *Washington Post* columnist Hobart Rowan:

> First the slogan was 'privatization' – the sale of government assets. Now it is 'tax amnesty'. An era of oppressive federal deficits always produces innovative gimmickry designed to avoid more painful ways, such as tax increases, to stem the flow of red ink.

If tax amnesties (or other policy initiatives) are used only to attain the limited external incentive benefits that conservative economics identifies the possibility of more civilized use of those programmes is diminished.

Once the importance of civic values is acknowledged in maintaining and strengthening tax compliance, then the noncompliance problem can be addressed by taking advantage of these taxpaying values and by protecting these values from potentially corrupting influences. We can illustrate both of these options with a brief outline of policies which have been proposed to improve compliance in the real world where taxpaying norms are important. These policies are valuable not only in addressing noncompliance, but also in demonstrating how far we have come from the simple view of taxpaying behaviour in conservative economics.

THE DIALECT OF TAX FORMS: SIMPLICITY VS. COMPREHENSION

Tax forms can influence the public context of taxpaying. One of the most publicized goals of the tax reform movement has been to simplify the tax form itself. This desire may seem anomalous in view of the fact that three-quarters of all taxpayers already use simplified 'short' forms. As University of Wisconsin Professor Clara Penniman points out mechanical simplicity is not the same as comprehension. The important question is not whether taxpayers can complete the forms, but whether they understand the law and its purposes.

The process of sitting down and staring at the tax form itself is the primary contact taxpayers have with the tax process. Their interpretation of taxes – the meaning of taxes in the public dialect – is drawn from a history of annual rituals: clearing the kitchen table, sharpening pencils, assembling documents, trying to comprehend strange terms, adding and subtracting numbers, and – increasingly – seeing the bulky forms and immediately handing them to a professional tax consultant.

In recent years several states have modified tax forms not only by making them clear and attractive, but also by providing information as to how the state spends the revenue it collects. Massachusetts has been praised by its citizens for recently including a message of thanks to the citizens for having paid their taxes. Such changes, however, are not enough. Despite the improvements we have seen, most tax forms are still reminiscent of a grade school work-book, carrying with them the connotations of the student–teacher relationship, not the civic relationship between the taxpayer and his or her government.

A tax form can be changed to facilitate the development and maintenance of the community of taxpayers by institutionalizing concern with the duties of taxpaying. For example, some small towns such as Dover, Vermont send out a list of all known tax delinquents to their residents, thus identifying those who are violating taxpaying norms, as well as (by omissions from the list) providing a clean bill of health to all others. It is not hard to imagine what happens the day the tax form arrives in the mail – everybody immediately goes to the list to see if there is anyone on the list that they know. Massachusetts has already put the names of tax-evading businesses in the newspaper. These simple institutions shape an environment in which the issue of compliance is raised in a regular fashion that can support the development of new taxpaying traditions in the community.

NEW INSTITUTIONS FOR PROMOTING TAX COMPLIANCE

There is a thin line between the attitude that tax cheating is acceptable and the actions of that part of the tax return industry whose 'business is to sell "tax savings" to the taxpayers'. As California's Franchise Tax Board notes, 'demand for abusive tax shelters and illegal protest schemes have spawned a tax evasion industry'. Currently, the tax advice industry is organized around the principle of finding the biggest breaks possible for their clients.

It may be possible to change the institutional essence of commercial tax preparers to shape their values so that tax advisors promote compliance rather than evasion. Harvard Professor Mark Moore advocates the licensing of tax advisors, drawing the comparison between tax advisors and electricians, plumbers, and tavern owners (all of whom are licensed), because all are in businesses which have important implications for public safety and order. The intent of licensing is to change the 'business' of the tax return industry into compliance.

Third-party regulators have been used effectively in the past – in the 1930s the Securities and Exchange Commission (SEC) began licensing accountants, and thereby enlisted them to serve public goals of accurate and honest presentation of information. Professor Thomas McGraw of the Harvard Business School attributes the SEC's success to the fact that the existence of the institution of Certified Public Accountants (CPAs) benefited all investors by guaranteeing that every accountant's reports would follow honest and uniform standards and practices. The accountants benefited as their profession became more financially rewarding (since by limited entry into the field they were able to raise their standard salaries). Furthermore, the licensing lead to an increase in the status for the profession of those who had passed this hurdle. Professor McCraw summed up the success of the SEC in creating a new profession as 'the model of public manipulation of private incentives' in creating a self-perpetuating form of business regulation. In a similar way, it may be possible to convert tax advising into a new profession.

Interestingly, the level of compliance for tax returns prepared by Certified Public Accountants was even slightly higher than that of taxpayers who prepared their own returns at more than 94 cents on the dollar. This contrasts quite favourably with attorneys and commercial preparers, who produced less than 90 cents of every dollar owed. By licensing tax advisors in the same way accountants are licensed, we can coopt those who are currently driven to degrade taxpaying norms in their unregulated pursuit of external incentives. Today, tax advisors are ultimately bound within legal constraints, but are without clear and unambiguous licensing laws (which depend in part on a common national dialect) that provide a professional code of ethics. The profit motive will encourage advisors to chip away at the margins of the tax law.

TAX CODE REFORM IN THE 1980s AND 1990s

The 1986 Tax Reform Act represented a significant simplification in terms of conservative economics in that it reduced the number of marginal tax brackets, but it is still largely incomprehensible to those who do not speak the language of tax law. Simplification has not maintained the initial level of public enthusiasm because the sentiments underlying public attitudes towards taxpaying are not based on economic concepts such as the marginal burden of complex taxes. No self-interested person likes to pay taxes – whether there is one tax bracket or twenty. Taxpaying is a public duty which few taxpayers can entirely understand in its current form, and so consequently they find it difficult both to gauge whether they are appropriately fulfilling their role, and to determine whether others are paying their fair share. The problem with most attempts at tax reform is that they have only addressed issues of conservative economic efficiency – they have not been directed at the public alienation and scepticism that eats away at the values that support taxpaying.

Repeated polls have shown that a large majority of Americans believe that politically influential groups and the wealthy get special tax advantages. Moreover, a *Washington Post* poll in 1985 reported that 80 per cent of the population said that they wouldn't complain about the amount they pay in taxes if they thought that the rich were paying their fair share. This mistrust of the rich, however, does not carry over into support for raising upper income tax rates. Instead, the brunt of the animosity against the rich falls on their ability to evade their share of taxes via loopholes uncovered by an army of tax consultants.

The IRS's 1984 survey of taxpayers attitudes indicated that the public consistently overestimates the actual level of tax noncompliance, often by more than double. The emphasis in public attitudes upon loopholes for deductions (as opposed to underreported income, for example, which is four times as great a drain on revenues) indicates how particular forms of noncompliance are suspected far more than their actual incidence merits. According to the IRS, cheating is suspected to occur far more than it actually does. Methods for cheating more available to wealthier taxpayers – such as false deductions and credits, and writing of personal expenses as business costs – were four times more prevalent in public perceptions than in reality.

The political popularity of the idea of broadening the tax base, that is, to eliminate the myriad of deductions and exemptions, comes in part from the belief that the current tax burden is *not* fairly distributed. The problem in mobilizing a broad constituency in favour of an alternative distribution of after-tax income is the same problem present in undertaking the establishment of any new institution. Machiavelli writes:

> There is nothing more difficult to execute, nor more dubious of success, nor more dangerous to administer than to introduce a new system of things: for he who introduces it has all those who profit from the old system as his enemies, and he has only lukewarm allies in all those who might profit from the new system.

A successful coalition for tax simplification and reform must be motivated by more than the goal of receiving a more favourable redistribution of external incentives. This is because redistributions of external incentives are often zero-sum games, leading to the difficult situation that Machiavelli anticipated. Additionally, it is almost impossible to hold together a coalition comprised of individuals who can only calculate their external costs and benefits from their participation. Unifying internal incentives must also be available to hold the coalition support for tax simplification and reform.

The problem with tax reform is that what is touted as 'simplification' still remains so complex and inaccessible to almost all taxpayers that their sentiments for fairness and simplicity seem to be ignored by the legislative debate. Issues in the tax debate have not been argued in the dialect of a civil community, but rather in the language of economics and accounting. Arguments are made not on the basis of duty, but on the bottom line for each individual taxpayer – how each person's after-tax income will be affected by the changes in the tax burdens. In other words, the tax reform we have seen is the tax reform of conservative economics – it can at best achieve only those benefits which come from removing irrational and counterproductive external incentives of the current tax system. Unfortunately, conservative tax reform can not meet the promises claimed by political advocates of tax reform. There can be no windfall benefit for all citizens merely from redistributing external incentives. If we are to raise the same amount of revenue, savings for one group of taxpayers must be paid for by a heavier burden on others.

For tax reform to be viable it must clearly be different from the current system. If the primary issue is who gains and who loses (that is, external incentives only), then Machiavelli's dictum rings true, and the hope of potential beneficiaries will be weaker than the fear of the potential losers. Incremental changes cannot signal a new order of things – they tell taxpayers that the game is the same and only the distribution of rewards is being changed. Only a reform movement aimed at changing underlying social attitudes will allow the possibility that new rewards of a different sort will be reaped.

The virtue that lies behind the public appeal of tax simplification is not merely the desire to reduce the burden of filling out the tax form – three-quarters of the population already use the simple form. The appeal of simplicity is that it permits people to understand the principles on which one of their primary social duties is based. Furthermore, a byzantine tax system makes all those who do not understand its ways feel like outsiders. Since money has the capacity to purchase a reduction in one's duty as a citizen (through the services of tax consultants and lawyers) the internal incentives of tax compliance are particularly vulnerable to erosion. The taxpayer may easily become suspicious that he is being made a fool by his own honest compliance when others profit by legal and illegal loopholes. Simplicity (that is, ease of comprehension) is a necessary first step towards tax code reform that will support improved taxpaying norms.

THE CONSERVATIVE DIALECT OF TAX REFORM

The dialect of conservatism can actually forestall the serious consideration of tax reforms that might work through the use of civic values. The dominance of the self-interested perspective in our public debate insures that the first reaction to any new tax proposal is to calculate the taxes one owes, and determine whether this tax plan makes one a 'winner' or a 'loser'. 'What this policy means to you' will be seen by the news media, the politicians, and the public in terms of what is the bottom line for each taxpayer.

The next conservative comparison to assess the impact of the new plan on the nation is to compare how well others are doing, and to see if the rich and the poor are being treated in accordance with one's preferences for social equity. Eventually, we would even start to look for a way to compare this initiative within the existing political framework. We would consider the reputation of previous tax reform initiatives which had similar external incentive effects to this plan (that is, help the rich, burden families, create disincentives for entrepreneurs, and so forth). But by thinking about tax reform from the perspective of conservative economics, civic values somehow get lost.

The most important discussion is the one that does not naturally occur. What are the principles of a fair tax system? If I pay taxes in accordance with this plan, can I be confident that my fellow citizens are also participating? Are the requirements of this taxpaying duty in line with the beliefs and principles I hold as an American citizen?

In *The Silver Blaze*, it is the dog that does not bark that provides Sherlock Holmes with his key clue to solve a murder. In our public debate on tax reform, it is the questions which are not asked that explain why public sentiment for fair and simple taxation is not being inspired by the plans that have been proposed. In the debate over fair taxation, has anyone yet defined fairness in terms of values and not dollars? The first step in starting real tax reform is to re-establish the dialect of civic responsibility in regard to taxpaying in the sphere of public debate.

The most dangerous aspect of the philosophy of conservative economics is that it encourages us to overlook the civic values which are of crucial importance not only to the vitality of our civilization, but also to the effective operations of our institutions. In looking to our self-interest first, we can miss the choices that benefit ourselves both individually and as a nation.

and flaws of the entrepreneurial system

century ago, Keynes reminded us that the 'outstanding
omic society in which we live are its failure to provide
ment and its arbitrary and inequitable distribution of
society's failure to provide full employment, Keynes
ramme of systematically maintaining healthy entrepre-
ns. This could be accomplished by either (1) government
g its purchases from the private sector whenever business
rim and a slump is expected, or (2) government reducing
private spending, or (3) the Monetary Authority reduc-
o stimulate additional investment spending or some com-
three processes. The resulting additional demand would
otimistic sales expectations for managers and thereby
ss expansion. As the unemployment problem was cured
era devoid of business cycle slumps, Keynes believed
income would naturally become more equitable.

five years following World War II, Keynes's demand
es were not only effective in winning the battle against
nt, but as a side-effect, they also led to a much more
arbitrary income distribution. In recent years, however,
ra shows, industrial societies have regressed in their
e these major flaws of modern economics. Since the
loyment has grown to post-World War II highs for even
ful economies such as Japan and Germany; while in
ncome distribution has become more inequitable both
d within each nation.

g from the civilized solutions already achieved between
the early 1970s may lead some to condemn our system
earch for a more Utopian (socialist?) solution including
ng in the form of industrial policy. Our entrepreneurial
owever, should not be cast off so lightly, for it does
ificant advantages over traditional socialist schemes.

decision-making by individuals in our economy who
ded for 'correct' decisions often makes for better plan-
n in line with consumer desires than centrally planned
economic world where the future is uncertain and can
predicted, a decentralized entrepreneurial system is
to discover what consumers will want in the future,
ners themselves know what they will desire. As we have

7 The Basic Problem of an Entrepreneurial System: Unemployment

We live in an entrepreneurial economic system. Entrepreneurs – the managers of business and government enterprises – are people who make the day-to-day decisions on production schedules, employment hiring and firing, trading activities and investment spending.

The difference between business and government enterprises is that the former are owned by individual investors rather than the community at large.[1] Business managers respond to opportunities for profit to employ workers and create income in the private sector. Managers of government enterprises (for example, the Tennessee Valley Authority, public schools systems, the London Underground, etc.) are civil servants who provide employment and generate income in response to the legislative mandates given to them.

The production decisions of private sector entrepreneurs about the profitability of what they can produce is the primary determinant of whether our free market economy will suffer from unemployment, or whether we will achieve a state of economic bliss where all who want to work can. The ability to earn one's income provides dignity and self-esteem to each individual. As long as there are unemployed people who want to work for a living, a society that requires that some individuals do not have the opportunity to work cannot be called civilized.

If managers of business enterprises believe they cannot profitably hire all who want to work, then there is a role for government in a civilized society to deliberately encourage additional spending, preferably on productivity enhancing capital goods, to create jobs today and to increase capacity to provide more goods for future generations. If today's private demand for new profitable investment is so satiated that it does not produce full employment, then it could be necessary for the central government to embark on projects that may appear to be wasteful when viewed in terms of simple profit maximization by individuals in the private sector.

In a free market economic system, as Keynes noted:

Pyramid-building, earthquakes, even wars may increase wealth. . . . It is curious how common sense, wriggling to escape from absurd conclusions, has been apt to reach a preference for wholly 'wasteful' forms of loan expenditures [government deficits] rather than for partly wasteful forms, which, because they are not wholly wasteful, tend to be judged on strict 'business' principles. For example . . . digging holes in the ground known as gold-mining which not only adds nothing whatever to the real wealth of the world . . . is the most acceptable of all solutions.

If the Treasury were to fill old bottles with banknotes [currency], bury them at suitable depths in disused coal mines, which are then filled to the surface with town rubbish, and then leave it to private enterprise on well-tried principles of laissez-faire to dig up the notes again . . . there need be no more unemployment . . . and the real income of the community and its capital wealth also would probably become a good deal greater than it actually is. It would, indeed, be more sensible to build houses and the like; but, if there are political and practical difficulties in the way of this, the above would be better than nothing.

Conservatives, on the other hand, argue that if only the government would get out of the way – get off the entrepreneur's back – the resulting 'laissez-faire' free enterprise economy will guarantee, at least in the long run, prosperity and full employment.

In the absence of government intervention, however, market economies have had a rather checkered employment history as they have suffered from severe, and sometimes lengthy, bouts of unemployment. The conservative retort to this historical record is that in the short run, unemployment is the necessary price we have to pay to achieve the long run goal of prosperity. As an economics news editor of the *Wall Street Journal*, Alfred Malabre, stated in his book *Beyond Our Means*, 'slumps act to cleanse the economy of strains and distortions that normally mark a peak of the business cycle', thereby drawing an implicit and distasteful analogy to the necessity of taking a laxative to purge the digestive system of the excesses of eating three square meals a day.

But the prosperity peak of a peacetime business cycle is the only time that a market enterprise system comes close to providing full employment and economic well-being for all its citizens. Surely that is a condition to be nurtured rather than purged. A civilized view suggests that the unemployment of business slumps inflicts significant and unnecessary costs on workers and employers alike. Moreover, even if this price is paid, there is no guarantee that prosperity will inevitably follow the slump. Instead there is a perverse sort of Humpty Dumpty economics here – conservatives hope that if they can make the patient sick enough, he is bound to get better. For example, the 8 June 1995 issue of the *New York Times* reported

that Federal Reserve Chairman Ala
States economy was experiencing a
span indicated 'was desirable bec

This bizarre economic philosc
perversity goes almost unnoticed.
the unemployed found jobs and p
the economy. Thus, in the early i
nomenon that with every releas
unemployment and slowing ecor
record highs. As the Great Depr
may be terribly difficult to reco
employment once the malady be

To comprehend more clearly w
not guarantee full employment ir
desirable nor inevitable in the s
the role private sector entrepre

HOW THE PRIVATE SECTC

How does the private sector of
market prices? Why does the
livering the full employment
hope to answer these questio
shortcomings of the private se
and monetary policy acting a
ciency that would otherwise

Business managers may so
for 'non-economic' reasons :
civic responsibility. We will
argument that self-interested
are expected to sell for more
that entrepreneurs in the pr
cash-flow position. Accordi
hiring if they *expect* sales re
involved in increasing prod
expect cash outlays to excee
the profitability of expected
generates the fires of prospe
of the government to make
and nurtured.

The adva

More than
faults of th
for full er
income'. T
advocated
neurial expe
directly incr
expectations
taxes to enc
ing interest
bination of
generate mc
encourage b
and we enter
the distributi

In the twe
augmenting
high unemplo
equitable and
as Table 5.1
efforts to alle
mid-1970s, un
the more suc
recent years t
among nations

This backsli
World War II
and set off an
government pl
market system
possess some
The decentrali
expect to be re
ning and produ
economies. In a
not be statistic
continually seek
often before con

already noted, diversity and the opportunity to exercise personal choice are among the greatest civil assets of a decentralized market system.

It should be the goal of any civil economy to design policies that eliminate, or at least reduce the existing flaw of persistent unemployment in the private sector, while simultaneously striving to maintain the advantages of decentralized decision making. The economic environment should promote personal liberty and freedom of choice without invoking discipline through the fear of unemployment and a poor profit environment. A revitalized and improved economy where unemployment and unnecessary business losses are no longer perpetual threats can provide the basis for evolving the most powerful economic system yet devised on the face of the Earth.

HOW THE PRIVATE SECTOR GENERATES JOB OPPORTUNITIES

Expected future spending creates today's jobs

The production of goods and services takes time – and often considerable time – between the day that workers are hired and the day when there is a product to sell. This means that entrepreneurs have no choice but to be guided in today's production and hiring decisions by the expectations they form regarding what buyers will purchase at some future date.

For example, manufacturers of fashion clothing may have to begin the production of their winter line in March in order to have sufficient quantities in inventory at the start of the autumn shopping season. Yet, at the beginning of spring, most consumers will not have the slightest idea of what articles of clothing they will be purchasing six months hence. Managers, therefore, have no choice but to be guided by the best expectations that one can 'guesstimate' as to what the consumers will be prepared to pay for when they are ready to buy clothes for the following winter.

Money contracts and cash flows

All market-oriented production and trade activities are controlled and limited by contractual arrangements. Once managers are confident enough with their sales expectations, they start the production process by negotiating contracts for hiring the workers and ordering the materials necessary to complete the job. Signing these hire-purchase contracts at fixed money prices puts the enterprise at risk by requiring specified cash payments at specific future dates. Nevertheless these contracts are desirable because they enable management to obtain cost controls over lengthy and complex production processes. In the absence of these fixed contracts, managers of firms that produce goods with long gestation periods would not be able to calculate the total cost of production operations *before* they start up the process. And without the cost control estimates that contracts provide, how could entrepreneurs try to guess whether buyers will pay an amount sufficient to cover the production costs and make the operation worthwhile?

A producer of chocolate bunnies for Easter, for example, will enter into contracts for the purchase of cocoa beans and the hiring of labour in the middle of winter. On the basis of these contractual arrangements, the manager can estimate the cost of producing chocolate rabbits. He or she can then decide how many Easter bunnies the market will buy at prices which will cover these costs and provide a sufficient profit margin.

Without the institution of money contracts, entrepreneurial hiring and purchasing decisions would be impossible and market oriented economic activity would cease. With contracts, managers can estimate costs of these cash flow obligations over time.

Contracts and civilized behaviour

A basic requisite of any civil society is that behaviour is limited by well established laws, shared norms, and commonly understood traditions. A civilized economy is based on the assumption that people will honour their contractual commitments under the *civil law of contracts*. Contracts, therefore, are an essential institution for maintaining civilized behaviour in the production and trading process of an entrepreneurial market system.

Contracts are legal documents which commit the seller to make delivery and the buyer to make a monetary payment at a specific time (either today or at a future date). Under the civil law, the State assures that both parties to a contract comply with its terms. If either party reneges, the state will determine, and enforce, the punitive *monetary* damages to be paid to the aggrieved party by the defaulting party. The State, therefore, acts as a guarantor of contract performance and assures the aggrieved party of 'fair' monetary compensation if the other side fails to meet its commitment. For example, if the cocoa bean seller is unable or unwilling to meet his or her contractual commitment to the chocolate bunny producer, the latter could sue the bean seller and receive a monetary reward equal to the damages suffered because the productive plan for producing chocolate bunnies was interrupted.

Only non-market production and exchange processes, such as those done within a family, monastery, nunnery, kibbutz, etc., can be organized without any money contractual basis. In these non-market situations, the civic spirit is sufficient that all members of the group 'know' that the others will carry out their assigned tasks. In any system where the motivations of the civic culture interact with self-interest, however, enforceable contracts are necessary to provide assurance to each that others will perform as they promise they will.

Cash flow is the 'blood circulation' of enterprise. Sales contracts assure cash inflows to the firm, while hire-purchase contracts indicate the forthcoming cash outflows. When cash inflows exceed cash outflows, i.e., sales exceeds cost, the firm can grow and develop. If, however, cash outflows exceed inflows, costs are exceeding revenues, the firm is being bled white and is on the way to the moribund state of bankruptcy. In this latter case, only a blood transfusion, what people on Wall Street call an infusion of funds, can prevent the inevitable demise of any private sector enterprise. Thus, the maintenance of liquidity, i.e., the ability of the enterprise to meet cash outflows as they come due, is essential to its viability.

Contractual orders, revenue estimates, and employment

Some firms hire workers and produce output only after they have received customers' orders. These firms are known to produce 'custom-made' products. They produce only 'to contract'; tomorrow's sales depends entirely on today's orders. Employment hiring for such firms varies directly with the received commitments (legal promises) of buyers to purchase.[3]

Alternatively, some firms, especially at the retail level, produce without first receiving sales orders. They produce 'to market' or 'on speculation'. Managers in these firms set today's production schedule solely on expectations of future sales without having any legal commitments from buyers. The managers of these 'produce to market' firms can never predict precisely what sales will be. The best they can do is to make an educated guess ('speculate') as to what consumers will be prepared to pay after a lengthy production period. Labour hiring, for these firms, is therefore entirely dependent on managerial expectations that demand will be sufficient to buy the output at profitable prices when the goods are ready to be brought to market.

In sum, then, employment in the private sector depends on entrepreneurial *expectations* of future sales. These expectations are based on (a) existing and expected forthcoming orders of buyers and (b) the managers' guesses as to what future buyers will want. Whenever expectations of future sales fall, managers reduce production schedules and employment decreases.

If, for example, retailers fear a forthcoming slump in sales, then they will not only reduce current labour hiring but they will also reduce orders from suppliers. This change in retail sales expectations will thereby quickly filter back to wholesalers, manufacturers, and subcontractors, causing employment and production to decline in the supplying industries that produce to contract. The resulting increase in unemployment and lost wages feeds back into a further decline in retail sales as the newly unemployed are forced to curtail their retail expenditures. This can induce further cutbacks in orders and employment resulting in recession or depression.[4]

In an entrepreneurial economy only the expectation of spending can create jobs today; a penny spent by a buyer is a penny earned by a seller and/or his suppliers. If these pennies are not spent on the products of industry, the results are lost jobs and profit opportunities, so that 'A penny saved (and therefore not spent) is a penny not earned'.

Contracts, jobs, and an uncertain future

Managers know, however, that 'to err is human' and that their sales expectations may be wrong in both the short run and the long run. In our uncertain world, if human nature does not experience the temptation to take a chance, then entrepreneurial activities would quickly wither away. The managerial virtue of having the courage to meet a challenge when the possibility of success is not as statistically predictable as tossing a coin is why we admire the 'entrepreneur' more than the actuary.

But only a fool would rush in to challenge the unknown without some strategy to protect oneself against unforeseeable and unpredictable deleterious outcomes. The successful entrepreneur is not a fool and therefore does not take on the unknown without some defence in case of disappointment. Long duration money contracts specifying fixed cash obligations limit the downside risks facing entrepreneurs to those that they believe their liquidity position can meet. As long as entrepreneurs believe they have sufficient liquidity to meet the losses limited by their contractual obligations, the allure of potential success (and the possibility of a huge windfall in sales revenue if the market is better than expected) is appealing. For firms that produce to market the possibility of a virtually unlimited gain more than offsets the possible downside loss limitation set by hire and purchase contracts.

In contradistinction to this vision of an entrepreneur protected only through limiting obligations by contract and amassing sufficient liquidity to meet these obligations, conservative economists envision the entrepreneur as a robot decision-maker. Given Samuelson's 'ergodic hypothesis' foundation, this robot-manager is assumed capable of generating 'rational expectations' based solely on a statistical probability analysis of past market data to reliably predict future sales. By possessing these 'rational expectations', these robot-entrepreneurs can never make an incorrect decision regarding future sales.

In the real world that we inhabit, however, the economic future is not statistically predictable. Thus, as Keynes noted:

> Businessmen play a mixed game of skill and chance, the average result of which to the players are not known to those who take a hand. If human nature felt no temptation to take a chance, no satisfaction (profit apart) in constructing a factory, a railway, a mine or a farm, there might not be much investment merely as the result of cold calculation . . . our decisions to do something positive, the full consequences of which will be drawn out over many days to come, can only be taken as a result of animal spirits – of a spontaneous urge to action rather than inaction, and not as the outcome of a weighted average of quantitative benefits multiplied by quantitative probabilities.

Keynes's view of entrepreneurial action spurred by 'animal spirits' is antithetical to the rational manager envisioned by conservative economics. Accordingly, civilized policy proposals developed on Keynes's analysis are diametrically opposite to the laissez-faire programme advocated by most economists who are fundamentally conservatives.

It is these conflicting views of the entrepreneurial decision-making process which lead to different conclusions regarding the likelihood of free markets to automatically generate job opportunities for all, i.e., for full employment. The conservatives's robot entrepreneurial decision-maker is presumed to 'know' with actuarial certainty how much output can *always* be profitably sold just as each apple on a tree 'knows' it will *always* fall to the ground under the inevitable natural law of gravity as soon as it releases itself from the branch. Consequently, conservative economists who assume entrepreneurs have rational expectations about future sales conclude that there is no role for government in providing full employment. The authorities can not fool entrepreneurs into hiring more workers than they would already be doing in a laissez-faire environment.

On the other hand, in a world where the probability of sales revenues cannot be as reliably predicted as a coin toss, that is, in a world where the future is uncertain and statistically unpredictable (a situation that can be technically labeled as nonergodic), the 'robot' manager of conservatives simply would not be able to function. In this uncertain world – our world

– it is Keynes's 'businessmen' who reign supreme. In this world, sales expectations depend on the entrepreneurial spirit of the community – a spirit which depends in large measure on the cultural and economic environment generated by the values of the community. Keynes referred to this entrepreneurial mood as 'animal spirits' in order to distinguish it from the computerized robot decision-maker programmed to maximize profits on the basis of statistical evidence obtained from past outcomes.

The animal spirited business manager is the prime mover of any market economic system. In an uncertain world managers' decisions regarding productive activities are geared towards a mixture of external incentives (the desire for income) and internal incentives (the desire to accomplish something noteworthy, challenging, and respected by the community). The community, via its cultural and civic values, provides the setting for determining the importance of the various elements in the mix of goals entrepreneurs strive for. In a society where expansive entrepreneurial actions are honoured, the use of expansionary governmental fiscal and monetary policy can create additional profit opportunities that can generate a fully employed citizenry.

The prosperity of any entrepreneurial economic system depends on maintaining an ebullient spirit among managers. Expected increases in demand are necessary to induce managers to hire more workers. On the other hand, pessimistic expectations will cause managers to reduce hiring opportunities. If, at any moment in time, realized sales are just meeting entrepreneurial expectations and if managers project current market conditions into the future, employment will remain unchanged. The economic future is precariously hinged on the psychology of the business decision-maker.

Government therefore can and must take action to influence that psychology. If managers become pessimistic (perhaps because they are disappointed in current market performance), then government has the ability, through its taxation, expenditure and monetary policies, to stimulate additional demand that will wake entrepreneurs out of their lethargy and encourage economic activity. As long as there are idle workers and unused capacity, the entrepreneurial system is not delivering the goods. It is wasting available resources which could, if employed, improve the well-being of all the citizens of society. It is the responsibility of a central government of a civilized society to create an environment where the system persistently delivers all the goods it is capable of producing.

The necessary conditions for generating such a full employment environment are that managers must (a) expect sales revenue to be sufficient to profitably cover all the production costs associated with a fully employed system, and (b) expect future demand will continue to grow as rapidly as capacity and the labour force grows. Conservative economic theory *assumes* that these two conditions will always prevail because of a hypothetical economic principle known as Say's Law. The assumption of Say's Law assures that Adam Smith's 'invisible hand' of free markets can always bring about full employment. Keynes, on the other hand, argued that in a market system there is no Say's Law, no invisible hand mechanism to assure a balanced growth between full employment demand and supply. Consequently, only government is strategically located within the free market system to take action *when necessary* to assure that demand keeps up with supply.

To understand the debate between Keynesians on the appropriateness of stimulative fiscal policies (even if these require persistent federal government deficits) and conservatives who argue for an annually balanced budget under all circumstances and regularly proclaim that disaster is looming whenever government deficits occur, one must obtain some understanding of the relevance of a Say's Law assumption to policy analysis.

SAY'S IMMUTABLE SCIENTIFIC LAW AND THE GREAT DEPRESSION

Do people work only to consume? The basis of Say's Law

Conservative economists assert that humans fundamentally dislike working for a living. People bear this gruelling burden of work only because they believe they will earn sufficient income to buy the products of industry necessary to cover the basic necessities of life and, they hope, some luxuries to make life more enjoyable.

In an entrepreneurial society, the fact that one must be gainfully employed in some enterprise to earn income, and therefore survive (and thrive) is generally true. Orthodox economists, however, carry the argument one small – but significant – step further. They insist that the *only* reason people are willing to work is that they *always* want more and more products of industry. The civic value of obtaining social recognition and enjoyment from a job is unrecognized in conservative economic theory. Anytime people earn income, conservatives assume that these people instantly spend their *entire* income on the current products of industry.

Borrowing from banks to spend in excess of one's current income is grudgingly admitted as a possibility. Borrowing, however, is not permitted to alter the generality of the system which not only requires one to earn income today to buy goods today, but insists that as a community we can always work as much as we want to earn a level of income that we entirely spend on the products of industry.

The nineteenth-century French economist, Jean Baptiste Say, argued that since all income was earned by producing things, therefore the production of goods (supply) always created income which, in turn, was always used to buy (demand) all that industry produced. According to Say's Law 'Supply creates it own Demand'. In other words, since production generated enough income to buy everything that was produced *and since all income was spent*, full employment was assured. Everyone who wanted to work would be a potential buyer of everything that could be produced; managers could therefore always expect to profitably sell all they produce.

This practice may have been more common in an earlier century when most workers were barely able to survive on their wages. With such conditions prevalent, the view that people worked to earn income in order to spend it *all – immediately*, on current output, led to the widespread acceptance by economists of Say's Law – where supply creates its own demand.

Say's Law is still held to be a fundamental principle underlying today's conservative economic model in explaining the behaviour of consumers. Students are still taught that buyers have insatiable appetites for products; buyers are constrained in the volume of their purchases only by the size of their income. It follows that whenever one's income rises, the budget constraint is raised and one spends all of this increment in income on the products of industry.

This concept of a budget constraint implies that buyers in general cannot, and do not, ever plan to spend more *or* less than their income on the products of industry.[5] Consequently, classical economists can depend on the natural operation of the immutable Say's Law to guarantee that demand will grow in tandem with the capacity of industry to produce. It therefore follows that in a Say's Law world, managers will never be disappointed by poor sales performance. They can always profitably sell anything they can produce and hence it always pays them to hire all who are willing to work.

Expert opinion and Say's Law

Given the inevitable outcome predicted by Say's Law, conservative economists in the early 1930s could not explain the persistence of the 'Great Depression'. Firms found that their production flows merely glutted the market and that they were unable to sell what they were producing – a situation that was logically inconsistent with conservative theory. It was theoretically impossible and therefore unthinkable by conservative economists that firms would therefore fire workers increasing unemployment and inducing a further drop in sales. The facts of the Great Depression just didn't fit the theory. Massive permanent unemployment is impossible under Say's Law.

The conservative economic experts of the 1930s did grudgingly admit that temporary departures from the full employment that Say's Law promised were possible, just as the swinging pendulum might temporarily move away from its long-run equilibrium position of rest. But the economy like the free-swinging pendulum would, if left alone, quickly right itself. President Hoover, listening to the conservative economic 'experts', whose theories were based on Say's Law, was paralyzed into inaction. He could only promise that if the government remained neutral, 'prosperity was right around the corner' as the economy, like the free swinging pendulum, would soon right itself.

Keynes's rebuff of Say's Law

Keynes attempted to persuade his fellow economists that Say's Law was not valid for entrepreneurial economies. Keynes felt it was necessary to dislodge Say's Law from the minds of economic experts and economics textbooks in order to ultimately influence policy makers to take positive actions rather than to wait upon the 'long-run' free market forces to swing toward a full employment equilibrium.

In a monetary economy, Keynes argued, people are never required to, nor do they necessarily, spend their entire income to purchase currently produced goods. Income earners may wish to protect themselves against what they know is an unpredictable future. People 'know' that it is always possible to find oneself without a job or income in a market economy where economic events can turn hostile without warning. Whenever people became more fearful of the uncertain future, this increased anxiety causes buyers to reduce purchases out of current income and to use their saving to increase their holdings of liquid assets such as cash and other liquid assets readily resalable for cash.

Say's Law and liquidity

To be liquid means that one has the ability to meet one's contractual obligations as they come due. In a market system, contractual commitments of buyers whether they are entrepreneurs or householders result in a stream of cash outflows. All buyers therefore require the liquidity of cash to meet these obligations. As Chapter 8 will explain, money is that thing which by delivery can always discharge a contractual obligation in an entrepreneurial economy. Consequently, the possession of money provides liquidity.[6]

Whenever people's fear of the unknown economic future increases, they will rush to build up liquidity by spending less of their income on the purchase of goods. As people reduce their spending, entrepreneurs will find sales receipts falling. This decline in demand makes managers pessimistic regarding future sales. They will reduce production schedules, hiring, and orders from suppliers, thereby causing the latter to further reduce employment. The economy can therefore collapse into a stagnant state of high unemployment unless, and until, something happens to significantly stimulate total spending. If spending can be revived, then as entrepreneurs realize there is an upswing in demand, they will rehire workers to meet the growing market. In a laissez-faire system in which Say's Law is not applicable, however, there is no 'invisible hand' that automatically ensures the revival of demand. Only the visible hand of the government can provide a recovery of demand when the private sector stops buying.

It is therefore the responsibility of a civilized government to use its powers to make sure total market demand neither declines nor stagnates. Instead, demand must be managed to ensure that it grows in step with increased productive facilities. Increased government purchases and/or tax cuts to increase people's after-tax income and spending are obvious ways to expand total market demand, encouraging managers to expand production and employ idle machinery and workers.

HISTORICAL PARALLELS – BALANCING THE FEDERAL BUDGET

The economic events of the period 1929–33 were dreadful. Between 1929 and 1933, the Gross Domestic Product (GDP), a measure of the total output of industry, declined by almost 50 per cent. GDP reached its low point in 1933 when almost 25 per cent of the labour force was unemployed. The economy seemed unable to turn President Hoover's proverbial corner. In 1932 Roosevelt campaigned on reducing the deficit to balance the budget as the way to end the Depression. After the election, however, Roosevelt's 'brain trust' of advisers informed him that 'prudent' finance would not solve the problem. They looked for a new approach to solve the unemployment problem. Unless some drastic action was undertaken, the existing economic system was unlikely to survive. Keynes's policy suggestions, which did not require balanced governmental budgets, provided some rationalization for the large public work programmes that pragmatists recognized had to be undertaken if jobs were to be created and people's income was to be sustained and increased, thereby reviving the moribund expectations of entrepreneurs.

In his first term in office, President Roosevelt instituted his New Deal legislative programme – a plethora of bills attempting to improve the economic situation. Most of this legislation deliberately stimulated the demand for goods by incurring what was considered at the time huge government deficits (approximately $2 to $6 billion dollars a year – a sum equal to 2–5 per cent of the GDP[7]). Throughout the period, however, Roosevelt's programme was constrained by fears that the large deficits of the New Deal were 'fiscally irresponsible'. If the deficits continued for any number of years the long-run result would be a disaster that would invite national bankruptcy.

The resulting expansion from 1933 to 1936 was, by historical standards, very robust. The 1936 GDP (after adjusting for price changes) was as large as it had been in 1929 before the Great Depression had begun. Employment had risen by almost 15 per cent since 1933 as the unemployment rate fell from 24.9 per cent to 16.9 per cent. In 1936, the annual federal deficit exceeded 5 per cent of the GDP. The total National Debt was approximately equal to 42 per cent of the annual GDP and many conservative economic experts were warning of imminent economic disaster if the government did not end deficit spending and take immediate positive action towards moving to a balanced budget.

In the election year of 1936, Roosevelt recognized this fear of the national debt. Consequently, he promised that if re-elected he would balance the budget. To show his determination to end the horrendous deficits of the federal government, Roosevelt submitted to Congress a budget that significantly curtailed government spending in 1937. The result was to more than halve the deficit from $4.4 billion to $2 billion. This movement towards a balanced budget caused a dramatic plunge of almost 10 per cent in real GDP from the first quarter of 1937 to the first quarter of 1938. The steep decline in GDP ended when this deficit reduction policy was abandoned in 1938 and increased government spending on public works and the beginnings of rearmament for war revived the economy. Consequently, by 1940, after seven years of the New Deal, the GDP was 63 per cent larger than it had been in 1933, GDP per capita had increased by 55 per cent and employment had expanded by 23 per cent. Although the 1940 unemployment rate was still 9.9 per cent, happier economic days had returned to the United States and Roosevelt was re-elected for an unprecedented third term.

During the Second World War, fears of an escalating National Debt were thrown to the winds. The important thing, as in all wars, was to defeat the enemy and not to limit the National Debt. Annual federal budget deficits of between $20 and $55 billion were incurred (equal to 14 to 33 per cent of GDP), while the GDP jumped from $125 to $212 billion. By the end of the war, the National Debt *exceeded* the GDP by 27 per cent[8] while the unemployment rate had fallen to less than 2 per cent.

It took the great deficits of World War II not only to defeat the Axis powers but also to reestablish true prosperity and full employment to the United States. Keynes's policy of deliberate government expansion of total demand, regardless of the size of the national debt, had made full employment an achievable objective for a civilized post-war US economy. Once fears of the size of the debt were put aside, sufficient demand could be generated to bring prosperity to the system. Unfortunately it took a war to prove the effectiveness of Keynes's civilized policy.

Here then is a useful historical parallel between the economic recovery in Roosevelt's Administration and that of the Administrations of President Reagan and his successors. Both Presidents Roosevelt and Reagan took office in the midst of a massive recession. Both extricated the economy by massive (for their time) increases in the federal deficit. Both initially ignored advice from eminent conservative economic experts who publicly proclaimed that these deficits were courting imminent disaster. In the fifth year of the Roosevelt regime, these claims of forthcoming doom led the President to retrench strongly. The result was to plunge the economy into recession. During Reagan's fifth year, the doomsters' warnings brought on the Gramm–Rudman law which mandated small phased-in cuts in government spending until a balanced budget was to be achieved by 1991. The sluggish performance of the economy in 1986 was related to the *modest* first stage of the Gramm–Rudman reductions in government spending (of $11 billion). The economy continued to grow, albeit at a slower rate, as Congress reduced the Gramm–Rudman constraints.

President Bush ran in 1988 on the motto 'Read my lips no new taxes' but the deficits continued to pile up. Finally, in 1990, President Bush bowed to the conventional wisdom and raised taxes substantially to reduce the deficit. By 1991 the economy again slid into a recession.

RONALD REAGAN – THE GREAT KEYNESIAN IN THE WHITE HOUSE

History's greatest deficit spender

Despite his conservative rhetoric, President Ronald Reagan was the first President since Roosevelt to embark, in peacetime, on a huge public works programme (military defence). Although government spending was reduced in some areas, over-all purchases by the federal government continued to rise (in real terms) throughout the first five years of the Reagan Administration. Simultaneously, in 1982, taxes were slashed creating a rapid rise in after tax-income which encouraged consumer spending to rise by 4.6 per cent in 1983 and another 4.7 per cent in 1984. (Consumer spending had fallen in 1980 and shown only minimal increases in 1981 and 1982.)

Reagan's expansive deficit spending policy combined with a lower interest rate policy (between 1982 and 1987) generated additional profit opportunities. Entrepreneurs were encouraged by the rise in sales not only to hire more workers to meet the growing demand but also to increase net investment spending almost four-fold between 1982 and 1984 alone. The unemployment rate in the United States dropped from a high of nearly 11 per cent to 5.5 per cent during the Reagan years.

Professors Barry Bluestone and John Havens of Boston College did a computer simulation study to compare what happened in the first four years of the Reagan Administration compared to what would have happened to the US economy had President Carter been re-elected and had he continued the 'prudent' lower deficit spending priorities he championed in 1977–81.

The comparison is dramatic. According to the Bluestone and Havens simulation the Gross Domestic Product by mid-1985 was 3.1 per cent higher, and an additional 3.4 million additional jobs had been created under Reagan than would have been achieved if the Carter deficit control policies had been continued between 1981 and 1985. This simulation model clearly suggests that if we are not constrained by unwarranted fears of deficits, an active government spending policy can rescue the system from continuing stagnation and recession.

There is a value judgment in our society that additional job opportunities should preferably be in the private sector. This can be accomplished by government placing additional orders with private contractors. Expenditures on schools, highways, bridges, hospitals, public libraries, and parks are desirable. Our world today is clearly enhanced by the legacy of public parks, libraries, and other public facilities built by the Works Progress Administration and the Public Works Administration of the New Deal. As the earlier quote from Keynes on digging for old bank notes illustrated, even wholly wasteful deficit expenditures by government such as employing workers to dig holes and then even fill them up are useful. Besides providing people with a job and the dignity that goes with being an employed member of society, the income earned will buy more useful products of industry.

The failure of the Reagan prosperity to trickle down

The benefits of the Reagan prosperity, were not distributed to all the members of the community. Nevertheless, Bluestone and Havens calculated that the average family disposable income was 7 per cent higher under Reagan than had Carter's policies been continued through 1985. More than 63 per cent of this additional family disposable income went to the richest families in the United States – those in the top twenty per cent of the income distribution. As a direct result of the Reagan expansionist policies between 1982 and 1985, the real income of these richest families increased by 10 per cent over what it would have been under the Carter policies.

On the other hand, families in the lowest fifth of the income distribution – the very poor – actually lost real disposable income under Reagan compared to where they would have been under Carter. Bluestone and Havens note that

> While 413,000 families who were initially below the official poverty line rose above it by reason of the new tax and spending policies, more than 1 million previously non-poor families were forced below the poverty line as a direct consequence of the new fiscal policies. This . . . [increased] the proportion of American families in poverty from 13.5 percent to 14.1 percent. Moreover, those families that were originally below the poverty line (and remained below) actually suffered a further 3.4 percent erosion in their already low disposable incomes.

This evidence provides dramatic proof of the failure of the Trickle Down Theory of economic expansion to permeate throughout the society. In fact, as we have already noted in Chapter 4 *supra*, this redistribution towards the upper income groups and away from the middle and lower income groups has continued into the 1990s. These facts indicate that deliberate expansionist policies increase the national income, and therefore are necessary for a civilized society to sustain itself in the face of potential stagnation. But a truly civilized society should adopt policies which not only assure a continual tilt towards full employment but also provide avenues of opportunity for earning additional income among all members of a society. Only if the goods are widely distributed are the members of society likely to believe that they live in a civil society where the economic system is working for all. If some must lose out so that others gain, winners as well as the losers will think that they are in a zero-sum society which pits members of the community against each other. Existing values are eroded whenever groups in the community are polarized into haves and have-nots.

CONCLUSION ON THE EMPLOYMENT FRONT

For the last half century, those who have comprehended the analysis of Keynes have understood how to ameliorate the unemployment problem which has consistently plagued laissez-faire systems. Government monetary and fiscal policies for expanding demand whenever private spending is otherwise insufficient have always been at our beck and call. Each in his own way, Presidents Roosevelt and Reagan have conclusively demonstrated that job opportunities can be created in the private sector if we have the courage to deficit spend whatever is required whenever unused capacity and unemployed workers are persistent problems. We can control our economic destiny and provide continuous prosperity for our people if we do not let the shibboleths of conservative economics regarding the necessity of not running deficits get in the way.

Of course, perfect balancing of aggregate demand to supply is, in a world of uncertainty, not possible. Some unemployment can still remain – but the history of the last fifty years clearly demonstrates that in those Administrations where either additional government spending, or additional tax cuts, or both were actively and vigorously pursued, employment and output rose rapidly and a feeling of prosperity returned. In those years when a reduction of government spending and increased taxation were legislated solely for the purpose of reducing the deficit and moving towards a balanced budget, unemployment either tended to rise or, at least, did not continue to decline significantly. Even if the economy did not fall into a recession or depression, economic growth tended to stagnate. The facts speak for themselves in justifying Keynes's policies for providing a guiding influence to stimulate aggregate demand at less than full employment.

The reader might ask, if it is so obvious how to eliminate unemployment, why has the United States and other developed countries pursued such a full employment policy so sporadically? The answer lies in the fact that normally as our free market economy approaches full employment, it develops an inflationary bias as sellers of products as well as workers find they can demand higher prices and wages without fear of losing sales or jobs.

Except for periods of war when a specific appeal is made to civic (or patriotic) values, modern entrepreneurial systems have not had the institutional framework to eliminate the problem of continuously rising prices in periods when the economy is close to full employment. In the absence of institutions designed to enlist the cooperative civic spirit required to limit inflationary wage and price increases, the only alternative programme for limiting price level increases has been the barbaric conservative plan to deliberately create unemployment and slack product markets in order to limit inflationary price and wage increases.

We have not progressed further towards a more civilized way of dealing with inflation in large measure because of the many myths regarding the relationship between inflation and the money supply. Accordingly, it is to the question of the role of money and its relationship to unemployment (Chapter 8) and inflation (Chapter 9) in a civilized economy system that we turn to in the following pages.

APPENDIX: A DIGRESSION ON EMPLOYMENT AND
PRODUCTION IN THE PRIVATE SECTOR VS. THE PUBLIC
SECTOR

In basing our analysis on the view that the private sector is the employer of first resort, we are not implying that there is no aspect of the production of goods and services that should (or could) not be produced in the public sector or that public employees can not perform as efficiently and effectively as private sector workers.

In an entrepreneurial system, there are two questions that must be asked about public sector production and employment: (1) Why not permit self-interested market demand determine the total pattern of production, and (2) why not permit profit-maximizing firms to respond to these market demands?

First, the community may believe that certain goods and services must be produced and available to all (or certain specified groups) in a civilized society. Some examples of such products or services include: military defence, police and fire protection, air traffic control, public education, public libraries, statistical information and record keeping, health care, a judicial system both for crimes against individuals and to enforce contracts, a central bank such as the Federal Reserve, the Secret Service to protect public officials, etc.

If individual self-interest can not generate enough market demand to make it profitable for the private sector operating in free markets to provide these goods and services in sufficient quantities to those the public believes should receive them, then there is a role for some form of government intervention to get the job done. If the nature of the task requires that those conducting it be perceived as impartial and removed from private profit concerns, such as with corporate regulation, adjudication, safety testing of new drugs, etc., then a government organization is required.

The remaining question is whether the production and distribution should be done directly by a governmental enterprise with public sector employees or should the government merely provide the necessary financing and managing that makes it profitable for private sector firms to produce the goods and service and deliver them. What criteria is there for choosing between private and government enterprises to produce these products conceived as socially necessary for a civil society? This question is often discussed under the rubric of privatization.

Professor John D. Donahue of the Kennedy School of Government at Harvard University has suggested two principles for deciding whether production of these goods and services should take place in the private sector or in the public sector. Donahue indicates that private sector production is appropriate if (a) the product designed can be *fully* defined in advance, (b) government can choose among at least several competing firms, (c) the product delivered can be evaluated unambiguously and poorly-performing suppliers can be replaced, (d) the cost of poor performance is limited, and (e) the government neither knows nor cares about the methods of producing the product.

Donahue suggests that production is better vested in a public enterprise if (1) product requirements are uncertain or subject to possible revision (e.g., the Manhattan Project to develop the A bomb), (2) competition is difficult to arrange, (3) results are hard to evaluate, (4) costs of failure are high, and (5) the government already knows the best way of producing the product and the public cares about the method of production, i.e., the method of production and employee judgments should be accountable to the public. Thus, for example, when the public cares about an impartial judicial system it appears that providing a government enterprise to produce judicial decisions is preferable to privatization of the judicial system.

Unfortunately, many of these products of a civil society have some aspects that favour privatization while other characteristics favour public sector production. Consequently, there is a public debate regarding whether to privatize the service or to rely on public employees to provide the product to the community. Thus, garbage collection, educational school vouchers, public vs. private colleges and universities, and statistical data collection are merely several examples that fall into this grey area.

There are many activities where government workers perform as well or better than their private sector counterparts, per dollar spent on such activities. Police, fire protection, the national park service, air traffic controllers, are some obvious examples. All residents of a nation are required to obey the civil laws. Government employees, however, are required not only to obey but also to enforce the laws of a civilized society. They are publicly accountable for achieving the objectives of a civilized society. The public accounting for this empowerment responsibility often endows public employees with the civil value of professional honour – a reason why public employees may perform as well or better than private sector employees who have to function under cost minimizing principles.[9]

Perhaps nowhere is this more obvious than in the current controversy involving the provision of health care in the United States. Under tremendous political pressure to reduce deficits by containing the escalating health care costs of an ageing population and a booming technology for extending life, conservatives have turned over the controls of 'managing' health care to private insurance companies and other corporations that organize Health Maintenance Organizations (HMOs). The guiding principle of these private sector organizations is not what is in the patient's best interest but rather cost minimization to improve the bottom line. The result is that hospitals are losing money and to stay afloat financially medical schools are dissociating themselves from these hospitals and thereby losing a valuable teaching tool that will reduce the skills of future doctors.

GOVERNMENT ENTERPRISES: MERELY MAKE-WORK
PROJECTS OR VALUABLE PRODUCING ENTERPRISES?

If government were to hire all of the unemployed in projects where there was a low standard of worker performance, the inefficiencies which surface and attract public attention would sully the reputation of all government service. The problem with direct government employment in activities where it can be demonstrated that performance standards are lower than in the private sector is that such government make-work projects devalue the reputation of government workers in general. The resulting negative public perceptions ultimately render the government as employer of last resort policy untenable. This has been, unfortunately, too often the experience of the United States.

The importance of standards, reputation, pride in one's output, and public perceptions indicate the relevance of internal incentives in any good job creating policy – whether it be in direct job hiring as the employer of last resort, or in the letting of contracts to the private sector to create jobs.

Ronald Moe of the General Accounting Office notes that even with privatization there will still be a need for government employees to manage the letting of contracts. In this process, government employees can assign contractual responsibility to private sector firms (what Moe calls 'third parties'), but public managers are still held accountable for the service performance of the contracting firm. Such third party contracting out processes, however, subtly change the management incentive structure of public programme managers and staff.

Many public managers are originally attracted to public service in general and a particular governmental enterprise because of its mandated mission. When production occurs within the government enterprise, the 'hands on' responsibility for development decisions enhances the internal incentive of professional pride and craftsmanship – as individuals work to secure the best possible outcome for the civilized community and in so doing achieve internal benefits for themselves in obtaining a job well done (for example, President Kennedy's original mandate to NASA of putting a man on the moon in the 1960s).

Reducing the governmental agency function solely to managing a third-party contract letting can, Moe argues, transfer important managerial decision and even much of policy making to the private sector. 'Program managers see that the interesting work is being done by others while they are left with accountability to political leaders for the program and with the routine tasks of contract management.'

With privatization changes in programme management, objectives have to be negotiated with private sector entrepreneurs thereby making corrections in direction more difficult. Thus Moe has argued

> It is critical to the management of third-party contracts that the agency itself retain the capacity to produce goods, perform the research or deliver the services. Only by keeping this capacity will the necessary 'in-house' capability be assured, not only to replace the contractor, if necessary, but also to permit the qualitative evaluation of the product, finding or service from the contractor. If this is not done, the evaluation

process may become simply an auditing process providing information on how well procedures have been followed for expending funds in a legal manner.

If in the letting of contracts, the public perception is one of permissible waste, graft and/or failure to achieve its mission, then the internal incentive that encourages taxpayers' compliance and maintains a pride in citizenship will erode. The challenge facing government is to spend wisely on the goods and services procured for the public, and to insure that the available resources of the economy are not left idle – but are rewarded via both internal and external incentives.

CAN WE PRIVATIZE PROCUREMENT MANAGEMENT?

Government purchases from the private sector involve a number of difficult issues. A key challenge, as Donahue noted, is to fully define the product or service that the government wishes to purchase. Contractors are required to deliver to the letter of their contract and no more. Self-interested private enterprises have no financial incentive to exceed contractual specifications. Unlike the private sector transactions, the government has a rigid procedure for selecting contractors and is prohibited from including factors such as long-term relationships, earned trusts, and past performance that exceeded contract requirements, while these factors are used by private-sector buyers. Consequently it makes it harder to develop mutual internal incentives between government procurement managers and private sector suppliers. To the extent that contractors are motivated only by external incentives, they will tend to cut corners or shirk unless closely monitored or unless the end product can be closely evaluated and the cost of poor performance clearly assessed.

It therefore becomes necessary to have government procurement managers fully specify to the finest detail what is to be delivered and then set up procedures to verify that the delivered product meets all specifications. This processes of specification must be rigorous because contractors have an external incentive to litigate whenever there is the slightest ambiguity in the contract terms. Taken to extremes, this has led to 20-page specifications for a loaf of bread. Recent procurement reforms (instituted by Harvard Professor Steve Kelman who was made head of procurement policy in the Clinton Administration) have eliminated such overspecification processes for small government purchases by allowing government employees to use a credit card for purchases less than $2500. But for larger purchases more scrutiny is still required.

Government is at a serious disadvantage when it engages in disputes over specification and evaluation of delivered products. Any contractor would be willing to pay a significant share of the amount in dispute in order to sway the administrative or legal judgment in its favour (and government procurement contracts often involve very large sums). Thus contractors are willing to engage highly paid lawyers and consultants to provide evidence that they have met the pages of highly detailed specifications.

In contrast, government resources for resolving contract conflicts on product specifications tend to be limited and fixed. Staffing is not based on benefit-cost calculations but rather on existing organizational structure. All but the most senior lawyers working for the federal government earn less than $90,000 per year, many much less. Even if a government lawyer saves the taxpayer $100 million in an product evaluation contract dispute, he or she could not earn a government bonus higher than $2700.

Privatization, however, does offer a benefit to political officials if not the nation as a whole. Business managers are protected from liabilities in a way that government officials are not. First, entrepreneurs in corporations are not normally personally responsible for what their corporations do. On the other hand, nations hold elections to assure that their politicians have a real and personal responsibility for what government does. An entrepreneur can afford to take chances with the assurance that any resulting liabilities can be liquidated with the bankruptcy of a single troubled enterprise. Government does not have the same freedom to acknowledge mistakes, reconstitute another enterprise (often with the same managers) to do the same function, and therefore be absolved from responsibility.

COPS AND ROBBERS: PROCUREMENT OFFICIALS AND PRIVATIZATION

In any successful privatization scheme, government bureaucrats are required to specify fully in advance the product to be delivered, assure competition among suppliers, and completely evaluate the delivered product. These government employees are called procurement officials. They must work diligently to assure that the taxpayer obtains value for every governmental dollar spent on goods and services produced in the private sector.

Government employees who protect hard-working citizens from those self-interested individuals who turn to crime to enhance their incomes are called cops and prison guards. Cops and robbers is a popular theme for television and movies. In political campaigns, the main class of government employees that all conservatives agree we need more of are police and prison guards. A tough-on-crime based political campaign provides an opportunity to enflame the fear and hatred that the conservative philosophy is built on.

No one will ever make a movie where a government procurement official is a hero and the defender of the public. A civil society where procurement managers excel at their job will not be as entertaining as one where a cop fights against barbaric activities. Thus, if our entertainment values provide us with a measure of how we evaluate government service, then it is not surprising that barbaric policies rule the day. We note that government spending on prisons and military defence are very popular among conservatives, even when they are in a budget deficit reduction mode.

If, however, we aspire to the justice, liberty, domestic harmony, and prosperity of a civil society, we must select the less dramatic but more productive view of a society that needs fewer prison guards but more procurement officials operating under civic values that provide recognition for a job well-done. This is the logic of the function of government employees in a civilized society.

Notes

1.   In reality even these lines are blurred, as some government pension funds are invested in businesses, while individual investors hold government debt.

2.   We should not forget that government can also directly create or destroy jobs, as well as produce desirable goods and services either sold in a marketplace (e.g., electricity from the TVA) or distributed to those who need it upon request without charge (e.g., fire fighting services, police protection). The community may believe there are some goods or services that, in a civilized society, the individual must obtain whether the individual wants it or not (e.g., compulsory education, sanitation, vaccination).

3.   For industries that produce primarily 'to contract', statistics collected on the length of the order books, e.g., machine tool orders, are a leading indicator of current employment and economic activity.

4.   This feedback mechanism where an initial change in sales expectations leads to a larger change in actual sales is called the Keynesian multiplier.

5.   In the context of international trading relationships between nations, Say's Law presumes that all the income a nation earns on its exports to other countries will be immediately and completely spent on imports from other countries. If this implication of Say's Law was true, then no nation would ever run a persistent export surplus with all its trading partners and use its unspent export earnings to build up foreign exchange reserves, as Japan has

done in the last decade and a half. For a further discussion of these international trade implications see Chapter 10 *infra*.

6. Other durables, called liquid assets, can also provide this attribute. Liquid assets other than money are any durables which can be readily resold (for money) in well-organized markets, e.g., corporate securities or bonds sold in organized stock and bond markets.

7. In 1994, 2 per cent to 5 per cent of the GDP would involve a deficit between $136 billion and $340 billion. The actual deficit for 1994 was $203.1 billion.

8. For comparison, despite the tremendous dollar deficits of the Reagan Administration which have doubled the total national debt in less than six years, the total national debt was, in 1986, only about half the size of the GDP in that year while the annual deficits between 1982 and 1986 varied between 2.6 and 6.3 per cent of GDP. During the next eight years of the Reagan, Bush and Clinton Administrations, the National debt has doubled again, and in 1994 it was 67 per cent of the GDP. This 67 per cent National Debt to GDP ratio is approximately the same as it was at the end of the Eisenhower Administration in 1959.

9. Unfortunately, the politicians' call for privatization is often merely a subterfuge for engaging in union busting activities to reduce public expenditures. Contracting out to private sector employees who need not be required to provide the same level of benefits as a civilized community does for its public sector workers, can reduce government expenditures and therefore either reduce deficits or permit tax reductions. The quality of the resulting product may be degraded if, in search of private profits and cost minimization, employees are stripped of professional honour.

8 Unemployment Develops because Money doesn't Grow on Trees

A war of words is usually preferable to a real war because it inflicts less suffering on society. In economics, however, controversy generated by confusion and the misuse of language can often produce policies that inflict terrible – and needless – cruelties on many unfortunate members of society. Nowhere is this more obvious than when the subjects are money, unemployment, and inflation.

Conservatives insist that any anti-inflation policy must invoke strict – and predetermined – limits on the growth of the money supply. This Monetarist tenet is held to be inviolable even when conservatives admit that this can cause unemployment and business failures in the short run and a permanent class of unemployed in the long run. Ever since the mid-1970s this monetarist view has dominated policy discussions at the Federal Reserve and in the halls of government. As a result, in the United States there has been more than 6 per cent unemployment in 16 of the 20 years between 1974 and 1994.[1] (By comparison, in the 29 years between World War II and 1974, there was only one year, 1961, when unemployment exceeded 6 per cent.) This high level of persistent unemployment in the past two decades is, according to conservatives, not a cause of policy concern. It is a necessary attribute to contain inflation.

In his 1968 Presidential Address to the American Economics Association, Nobel Prize winning economist Milton Friedman, tried to justify this barbaric infliction of permanent unemployment to fight inflation by labelling it 'the natural rate of unemployment'. The bottom line of this natural rate argument is that no matter how hardworking and skilled the American work force becomes, more than 7 million members of the labour force must be unemployed for the American economic system to function. Any reduction in unemployment below 7 million (or 6 per cent of the work force) is unnatural and therefore undesirable. We object to this misuse of language and the attempt to solve the problem of significant and persistent unemployment by the semantic trick of defining it away as a natural and necessary condition for fighting inflation.

The real problem with this approach lies in the conservative conceptualization that money is equivalent to something that grows on trees. It is a fundamental conservative axiom that anyone who wants to work can get a job at the prevailing wage. One way of visualizing the implication of this axiom is to assume that in every town and city there is an orchard of money trees. When a search for any other employment fails there would be opportunities for all who want to work in the money tree orchard. Anyone who really wants to work can always obtain employment by merely exerting themselves sufficiently to harvest the money trees.

This 'money as a producible commodity' concept, suggesting that anyone can get a job provides a rationale for the conservative argument that those who are counted as unemployed for any length of time simply do not really want to work. The unemployed, therefore, can be stereotyped as indolent and preferring to live off unemployment compensation, food stamps, and other welfare benefits that a civilized society provides as a social safety net. (The fair-minded reader might notice the contradiction between the conservative view that any who want to work can find a job and the conservative requirement that 6 per cent of workers – or seven million currently – are naturally unemployed.)

If conservative economists would explicitly recognize in their theoretical analysis what every three-year-old has been taught, namely that 'money does not grow on trees', then they might realize that it logically follows that it is not because they are lazy that more than 7 million people are persistently unemployed. They are unemployed, not because of some character flaw or because they prefer to live off welfare, but because the conservative economic system requires them as cannon fodder in the never-ending war against inflation.

We will argue that a conceptualization of a money that does not grow on trees is the key to understanding why persistent and significant unemployment can be endemic to a laissez-faire monetary economy. There is nothing natural about unemployment. In a civilized society, it is the primary responsibility of government to provide a guiding influence to expand the total market demand for goods and services whenever unemployment persists. Policies to reduce unemployment must take priority over policies to limit the national debt or to achieve a balanced budget, or to limit the money supply merely to constrain inflationary tendencies. As we will explain, in a civil society it is possible to obtain full employment without inflation by blending self-interest and civic values in a comprehensive macroeconomic policy programme.

If, as conservatives claim, inflation can be curbed only by deliberately maintaining persistent unemployment, then our economic society will never be a civilized one. Fortunately, however, once a correct conceptualization of money and its role is developed, then it will be clear that civilized policies to control inflation can be designed without deliberately imposing job losses on groups in our society.

WHAT IS MONEY?

Although more ink has been spilt by economists in discussions of money than on any other topic, most laypeople are surprised to learn that economists have neither carefully defined the concept of money nor agreed on a single common meaning. The public is most familiar with the conservative Monetarist discussion of money. The flavour of the Monetarist approach is reflected in the simplistic slogan that 'Inflation is always due to too many dollars chasing too few goods'. This dictum argues that if the growth of the money supply increases beyond some fixed rate such as three per cent per annum, then inflationary trends will be exacerbated. The facts, however, are inconsistent with this belief. As noted in Chapter 7, the rate of inflation decreased even though the money supply growth accelerated during the period 1982 to 1986.

DEFINITIONS AND DIALECT

The Monetarist's definition of money

Monetarist economists have combined the basic conservative economic model with their own idiosyncratic approach to money. The Monetarist literature abounds with the use of illustrative examples as 'definitions' of money. For example, a money concept that economists call M_1 is defined as equal to the total (legal tender) currency in circulation plus checkable bank deposits plus travelers' checks. A second money concept, M_2, is equal to M_1 plus some noncheckable bank deposits plus other financial items such as the shares of money market mutual funds, overnight eurodollars and overnight repurchase agreements. Finally, M_3 money is M_2 plus additional items such as large time-deposits, institutional money market funds, etc.

If the distinction between these various categories of money seems confusing to the uninitiated reader, let him take heart in knowing that this Monetarist classification scheme for money is an improvement over earlier published Monetarist 'definitions'. At one time in the late 1970s, the economics literature teemed with seven of these money categories – from M_1 to M_7. In recent years these seven 'definitions' of money have been collapsed into the three categories mentioned above.

Semantic confusion and conflict rather than clarity

Confusion rather than clarity is due to the fact that these M_1, M_2, M_3 concepts are exemplifications. They do not constitute a definition of the money concept. Imagine the confusion and chaos that would occur if astronomers defined the concept of planets by using the name of specific heavenly bodies. Suppose, P_1 planets are Mercury, Venus and Earth; while P_2 planets are P_1 plus Mars, Saturn, Uranus, Neptune, Jupiter and Pluto. (How in this scheme would one know what separates a planet from a moon, a comet, or an asteroid?) Or if some chemists defined molecules in terms of M_1 molecules that consisted solely of inorganic salts, while M_2 molecules are defined as M_1 plus inorganic acids, and M_3 molecules are M_2 plus organic compounds, etc.

Such an obviously bizarre classification scheme for 'defining' planets or molecules is, however, analogous to the status of the existing Monetarist definitions on money. By listing examples rather than defining concepts, Monetarists ignore the critical questions as to what are the attributes of money and what are the essential characteristics that separate money from other things. By avoiding rigorous definitions and instead relying on conceptual fuzziness, however, the Monetarist argument can be reduced to a simplistic dialect that means different things to different people and thus appears to have a universal applicability.

When fundamental concepts, used as the basis for policy discussions, are fuzzy, the resulting conclusions will be muddleheaded. Whenever someone in the financial pages or on television discusses the alleged relationship between the rate of growth of the money supply and inflation, one is never sure whether the reference to money involves M_1, M_2, or M_3. In fact, when discussing the claimed money-inflation nexus, economists often switch between these monetary categories depending on which one provides the better statistics in any time period to back their particular argument.

Why this conservative Monetarist's approach has been able to dominate public discussions may not be at all obvious – especially if one believes that economists are engaged in 'scientific' research devoid of politics and value judgments. In reality, of course, economics and politics are intimately bound together and what is promoted as economic science is often nothing more than the political ideology that is favoured by the economically powerful to conserve their status. Nor is this situation unique to our own time and place. In the 1930s, for example, Keynes explained that the overwhelming consensus of the financial and political community in support of the conservative Monetarist doctrine of his day was due

> to a complex of suitabilities in the doctrine to the environment into which it was projected. . . . That its teaching, translated into practice, was often austere and often unpalatable lent it virtue. That it was adapted to carry a vast and consistent logical superstructure, gave it beauty. That it could explain much social injustice and apparent cruelty as an inevitable incident in the scheme of progress . . . commended it to authority. That it afforded a measure of justification to the free activities of the individual capitalist, attracted to it the dominant social force behind authority.

We suspect that a similar expediency lies behind the mass media's propagation of the Monetarist approach which fundamentally has provided a pseudo-scientific rationalization for the latent anti-labour sentiment that has developed in industrial economies. Years of labour union excesses since World War II created sufficient public inconvenience to loosen the social glue that had bound us into a civilized society of workers, managers, and property owners. The growth in the popularity of Monetarism since the 1970s suggests to us how far developed economies have regressed from the civilized stature they reached in the first quarter century after World War II.

Since Monetarists have not provided a clear definition of money, their analysis of the role of money in controlling inflation and affecting unemployment permits a variety of vague interpretations oriented on the parable of the chase between money and goods. If civilized reasoning rather than appeal to self-interest intuition, emotions, and fears are to become the basis for developing our economic policies then we must insist on a clean, clear, and crisp economic dialect which correctly reflects the world we live in. Only then can progress be made towards understanding the complex relationship between the money supply, the banking and financial systems, employment and inflation.

In this chapter, we will first develop a clear definition of the money concept. This will permit us to explain (a) why the banking and financial industry plays a crucial role in determining the level of employment. In Chapter 9, we will discuss why rising prices (inflation) of the products of industry are primarily related to rising money wage and other production costs rather than directly related to increases in the quantity of money.[2]

DEFINING MONEY

Essential functions and properties

Communication and progress can occur only when, in developing a common dialect, concepts are cast in terms of essential functions and properties. Thus astronomers define stars not by example but as a large mass of incandescent gas powered by nuclear fusion created at its core by gravitational forces. Such a definition, involving critical properties, permits one to distinguish between stars and large planets such as Jupiter for the latter although it has a large mass of gases, it does not have nuclear fusion at its core.

In developing a precise dialect, anything that possesses the essential functions and properties will be an example of the defined concept, no matter how strange it may appear. In the biological dialect, for example, the functional definition of a mammal is anything that gives birth to live offspring and suckles its young. Thus merely looking like a fish, smelling like a fish, and even swimming like a fish is not enough to make a mammalian whale into a fish.

The contractual settlement or claiming function of money

In a civilized society behaviour is governed by well-established laws, shared norms, and commonly understood traditions. One of the most fundamental attributes of civilized economic behaviour in a market system is the belief that people will honour their contractual commitments under the civil law of contracts. In such a system, the essential function of money – the characteristic that sets it apart from everything else – is that money is that thing, which by delivery, settles a contractual obligation. Whatever the community declares is money will possess this essential function of a means of contractual settlement. In a market-oriented system, money and the use of explicit money contracts are fundamental civilizing institutions.

Money as a claim on resources

The resources of any economy are its labour force, its natural resources, and its stock of productive plant and equipment. One of the basic platitudes of economics is that 'everyone has his price!' By this we mean that in an entrepreneurial system, the services or products of any of these ultimate resources can always be purchased from its owner via a contract for a specific sum of money – a money price. This money price is the measure of the external incentive which conservative economists argue is the only factor necessary to motivate people to perform any economic activity.

Whenever we use money to buy goods, or hire workers, or purchase property, we are exercising or using claims upon the ultimate resources of the system. Just as a hat-check ticket allows one to go to the cloak room to claim one's hat and coat, so, in an entrepreneurial system, the green ticket we call money is by law and by custom, the universal claim check on the available goods and services in the economy. Money possesses generalized purchasing (claiming) power – but it does so only in a market economy that utilizes money contracts to organize production and trading activities.

The sources of these claims

There are three ways whereby people come to possess the claim tickets that we call money.[3] First is by the earning of money income through selling one's labour or other services to be used to produce goods. The second way is by borrowing from others who have earned income and do not wish to spend all they have earned.[4] The third way is by borrowing money from the banking system.

In modern market economies, the banking system operates under the rules of the game involving regulation by a central bank such as the US Federal Reserve System. When banks make additional new loans to households or businesses under the rules, the banking system creates new claims that are additions to the existing supply. It is through these regulatory rules that the Central Bank can attempt to control the rate of growth of the money supply created by banks in response to borrowers demand for additional loans.

Liquidity: the time machine function of money

Whenever people plan to save some portion of their currently earned income, it means that they are planning not to exercise all of today's earned claims by buying today's goods and services. Instead the saver wants to defer exercising these currently earned claims, and store this claiming power until some future date. These stored money claims provide the holder with liquidity. To possess sufficient liquidity means being able to meet all one's contractual obligations as they come due.

If savers think that at some future time, they may need to claim a sum of goods and services that exceeds the income that is expected to be earned in that future period, then they may want to build up their liquidity today. For example, a saver might be worried that some unforeseen calamity (e.g., unemployment, sickness, or severe accident) may occur that either reduces future income or requires significant additional unforeseen expenses or both. To store currently earned claims to be available for use at a future date requires the saver to find a time machine to transport liquid purchasing (claiming) power to a future date.

For example, suppose that Ms Jones decides to save $100 out of her January paycheck so that whenever she takes her holiday in June she will be able to buy souvenirs. The saved $100 can be stored in the form of either money (in a bank account or as currency hidden in her mattress or safe deposit box), or other liquid assets (for example, stocks and bonds).

Money and these other liquid assets are stores of value (or time machines) that Ms Jones can use to move today's claiming power to the future. Money is, however, different from all these other liquid assets in that only money can be used to settle contracts. If Ms Jones plans to use any liquid assets besides money as a store of value, then at some future date she will have to resell this liquid asset in a market[5] (like the New York Stock Exchange) to obtain money to pay for her purchases of souvenirs when and if she goes on holiday.

In sum, money is defined as anything that possesses both the contractual settlement function *and* the time machine (liquidity) function of moving claiming-power to the future. Accordingly, currency and checkable bank deposits, including travelers' checks, are money in the current environment for only these are generally acceptable for the settlement of contracts. Other liquid assets (e.g., stocks, bonds, noncheckable deposits, etc.) may possess the time machine function but do not have the claiming function of settling contracts and hence although they are liquid assets they are not money.

MONEY DOES NOT GROW ON TREES

All liquid assets, including money, possess an obvious – but rather peculiar property – they do not grow on trees. The basic conservative theory, however, not only permits, but analytically requires, money to be a producible commodity such as bananas, wheat, peanuts, etc. For the conservative analysis to demonstrate that markets, free from government interference, will automatically generate full employment, however, the money of the economy must be capable of being 'harvested'. (Peanuts – which grow on the roots of bushes if not on trees – are typically used as the example of money as a commodity in some conservative textbooks.)

If money is a producible commodity, then there would never be unemployment. If the money commodity did grow on trees, then unemployed persons, who want to work but are not hired by any business, can always become self-employed entrepreneurs who can harvest money trees in order to earn income. This producible-money concept provides the logical proof for the conservative assertion that in a free market system where people are free to work at whatever they wish, unemployment is impossible. The logic of defining money as a readily producible commodity justifies the conservative stereotype that anyone who wants to work can always be employed and therefore anyone who is unemployed does not want to work for a living. Consequently, it is easy to accept policies that cause persistent unemployment and then treat these unemployed people callously.

If only money did grow on trees, persistent and significant unemployment of those willing to work for a living would be logically impossible. Yet when people become more worried about the possibility of future 'rainy days' and therefore cut their spending on goods, such as autos, in order to build up their liquidity, employment declines in the auto industry. If only money was a producible crop, such as peanuts, the resulting increased demand for time machines (liquidity) instead of space vehicles (autos) would increase the demand for peanuts just as the demand for autos declined. Thus while employment would decline in the auto industry, new jobs would be created in the peanut industry. The unemployed auto workers could be readily re-employed in the peanut industry. In this illustration, where money is peanuts, increased unemployment in Detroit's auto factories would be offset by increased employment on Georgia's peanut farms.

In our world an increase in the public's demand for liquidity, at the expense of the public's spending on producible goods and services, is not translated into job opportunities in the private sector. Business firms can not meet the increased demand for liquidity by hiring workers to harvest more liquidity from trees or to print more money. Entrepreneurs are forced to lay-off good workers, not because they are malevolent, but because the public is buying less of their products.

In an entrepreneurial economy it is the presence of a money that does not grow on trees in combination with the public's desire to hold such money (for liquidity purposes) which refutes Say's Law. (In Chapter 10 we will see the same violation of Say's Law can occur in an international dimension when nations run persistent trade surpluses in order to accumulate ever growing totals of foreign reserves rather than spend all their export earnings on the products of other nations.) The income that is earned by engaging in the production of goods does not assure sufficient demand to sell all the goods produced, as long as each person can voluntarily decide it is in his or her self-interest to put money away for a rainy day, i.e., to hold more money for liquidity purposes instead of spending it. Whenever the buyers decide to reduce their total spending on goods in order to try to enhance their liquidity position, sales will decline causing entrepreneurs to lay off workers.

THE ROLE OF THE BANKING SYSTEM

In a free market economy, full employment occurs only when entrepreneurs believe that there are sufficient profit opportunities to justify offering jobs to all who are willing to work. Managers are willing to provide jobs if they expect that they can sell the resulting output at profitable prices. Unemployment develops, therefore, whenever income earners do not plan to spend their entire full employment income to purchase all the products that industry can produce.

That portion of current income that people do not spend on the products of industry is called savings. The gap between what people earn when the economy is at full employment and what people wish to spend on goods out of this income is called the full employment savings gap. If all spending had to be financed out of current income, then this national savings gap means that people are not spending enough to create profitable opportunities for managers to employ all who are willing to work. To fill this savings gap another source of spending – one which is not dependent on current income – is required. If large enough this second type of spending, when added to current income financed spending, can generate enough sales revenue to encourage managers to produce at full employment.

This second type of spending occurs whenever borrowers' requests for bank loans to buy goods are increasing. The banking system can provide 'new' finance to buy additional goods by creating new checkable deposits (money) for borrowers. This bank created credit finance permits spending to occur that is not financed out of current income. As our condominium construction example *infra* will illustrate, this bank finance is primarily associated with the private sector investment spending and especially construction loans (sometimes called working capital loans) used to pay for the production of capital goods such as plant and equipment. Hence, total spending on investment in any period plays a vital role in determining employment in that period.

Even with new bank financing for all the investment spending that entrepreneurs want to take on in any period, total spending may not be sufficient to completely fill the full employment savings gap if either borrowers can not conceive of enough profitable investment projects, or the cost of borrowing is too high. Whenever such an insufficiency of total market demand occurs, managers whose self-interest is solely related to 'the bottom line' will not hire enough workers to sustain full employment. In this case, there is a role for government either

(a) to borrow in order to finance an increase in deficit spending, and/or
(b) to encourage the private sector to spend more through tax incentives, and/or
(c) to reduce interest rates to encourage additional borrowing for investment spending.

All of these government actions will be designed to augment existing consumption and private investment spending sufficiently to make it profitable for managers to hire all workers who want to work.[6]

Whether banks create new money to finance additional private sector consumption or investment, or to finance government spending to buy more goods and services, the resulting expenditures can fill the full employment savings gap. Our argument so far has required the reader to accept our claim that the expansion of bank credit to borrowers creates new money. It may be desirable, at this point, to explain in some detail why this is so – given our conceptualization of money. To do so it is necessary to discuss the relationship between legal tender currency and bank money (checkable deposits).

LEGAL TENDER VS. BANK MONEY

Legal tender money

Legal tender is defined as that thing which must be accepted for discharging contractual obligations for all debts under the civil law of contracts. Since money is, in our scheme, defined by its contractual settlement feature, then whatever is declared by the State to be legal tender must be money, as long as the values of the national community have not been eroded to the point where no one has faith in the government's ability to enforce contract performance. In the United States, legal tender currency consists primarily of Federal Reserve Notes (IOUs of the Federal Reserve Banks). In 1994, these currency notes amounted to $374 billion, while the total M1 money supply was $1.4 trillion.

Bank deposit money

Other things besides legal tender can be money if they are accepted by law, or by custom, in the discharge of contractual obligations. In fact, most contractual obligations are settled, not with the payment of legal tender currency, but rather with the tendering of a check. Hence, that portion of bank credit which is composed of checkable deposits are part – the major part – of the US money supply.

A checkable deposit represents a contractual obligation of a banker to transfer, on demand, money (and if requested, legal tender currency) to whomever the holder of the deposit designates, as long as the amount on deposit equals or exceeds the sum on the check. Hence the recipient of the check 'knows' that receiving a check is as good as receiving legal tender currency.

Bank deposits can be considered a 'tap issue' of legal tender notes as bankers provide depositors with an 'instant repurchase' clause in which they guarantee the depositor instant convertibility of cheque-book balances into legal tender. Although bank deposits are the liabilities of private banking corporations, bankers can guarantee that they can convert their customers' checkable deposits into legal tender immediately because of the bankers' special relationship with the central bank or monetary authority (the Federal Reserve in the United States) whose IOUs are the legal tender of the country. The Federal Reserve Bank (or Fed) assures all bankers that their checkable deposit liabilities can be converted into legal tender at the immediate option of the banker – as long as the banker is operating under the rules and regulations set down by the Fed. The Fed can always provide these legal tender notes to bankers since these notes are merely its printed IOUs. There is no limit – within the law – as to how much legal tender the central bank can print and provide to bankers.

The liabilities of any other private corporation (other than those of bankers' checkable deposits) do not possess this instant convertibility to legal tender guaranteed by the Federal Reserve. Therefore only the checkable deposit liabilities of bankers are 'as good as' legal tender. Checkable bank deposits and legal tender are equally acceptable to settle contractual obligations. Since payment by cheque is easier and safer than payment by legal tender, checkable deposits have become better than legal tender and are the major form of money in modern economies.

We live in a bank-credit monetary system. Whenever a banker provides a borrower with a loan, the banker does so by creating either a new checkable deposit account, or creating an additional credit to be added to the borrower's original checkable deposit account. Every time the banking system increases its total checkable deposits by making additional loans to the public or to the government, bank credit and therefore the money supply has increased.

Why do firms borrow from banks?

Firms borrow from banks because they want to buy things that they cannot afford to purchase out of current cash inflows. Such loan-financed purchases in the economy permit firms to experience cash outflows in excess of current cash inflows without running into liquidity problems. The bank loan is undertaken to make up the expected cash flow deficiency. The borrower either expects to have sufficient cash inflows at some future date(s) to repay the loan, or else plans to refinance the loan again. Refinancing postpones repayment until some further date in the future.

From an economy wide view, therefore, the use of money contracts and the development of a banking system which can create credit-money have been important institutions for regulating cash flow circulation for the production system. The availability of bank credit on favourable terms can often encourage sufficient private borrowing to provide the proper volume of circulating 'blood' to an entrepreneurial system striving to promote maximum economic activity. If, on the other hand, monetary policy is too 'tight', then the monetary circulation to vital parts of the production system is diminished or even cut off as private borrowing is discouraged. The resultant loss in spending can cause a loss of vitality (unemployment and lower profits) and even mortality (bankruptcies).

MONEY AND THE USE OF CONTRACTS

The institution and evolution of the use of money and contracts to organize complex production processes has contributed significantly to the development of the industrialized world. Contracts permit managers (a) to control costs by fixing the price of labour and materials, (b) to know future cash outflow obligations, and (c) to efficiently organize the proper sequencing of delivery by suppliers.

Toyota became a leader in the auto industry when it implemented its production control system known as the 'just in time' system. In this system, by using contractual arrangements, manufacturing department managers collect goods (from suppliers) in the precise quantity and exact time they need them. The supplier thus had an orderly market and so could adjust his production (using the same approach) accordingly. The use of this 'just in time' contracting system has proved to be so efficient in managing inventories and reducing cost-outflow overages, that today it is adopted by almost all successful managers.

Building a condo: an illustration

The importance of contracts for fixing costs, providing the basis for bank financing, and the efficient carrying out of a complex, lengthy production process can be illustrated with the following example. Suppose a developer is considering building a condominium apartment tower in mid-Manhattan. To decide whether the project will be profitable, the developer will not only have to estimate future demand for apartments, but he or she will also need to 'know' the construction costs involved for the two to three years that it takes to complete the building. To get a handle on these costs the developer will request that the competing construction firms provide bids with written contract offers indicating the costs for construction according to the developer's specification.

For managers of construction firms to be willing to commit themselves to a fixed money sales contract, they will demand fixed money contracts from their workers, suppliers, and subcontractors in order to nail down their own production costs. Similarly, the subcontractors will require fixed contractual commitments from their workers and suppliers. The total monetary costs of this complex project can then be contractually fixed in advance before construction. This permits the various entrepreneurs involved in this project to get a firm grasp on their costs and sales revenue as they produce only when they receive a signed contractual order.

In this simple example, only the condominium developer is willing to sell 'to market'; undertaking a commitment to produce living space before buyers have been lined up to purchase the total output.[7] By fixing cash outflows via contracts for the next two to three years the developer can calculate whether the condo will be a profitable one. The developer must (1) estimate the market prices that can be charged when apartments are ready for sale in order to assure himself or herself that sales revenues will ultimately cover all committed cash outflows, and (2) obtain finance to meet any cash-outflow commitments which will come due before the sales revenue from the apartments are received. The developer typically finances his or her contractual construction cash outflows required via a construction loan from the banker. Armed with this loan commitment, the developer 'knows' he or she has the wherewithal to carry the project to completion. The developer can therefore execute all the construction orders necessary and use the contracts to produce an efficient 'just in time' production process. Clearly, fixed money purchase contracts and bank finance are essential instruments for the developer.

Why are the sellers of labour and materials willing to enter into contracts fixing their future money income payments? These contractual arrangements assure the workers and subcontractors future cash inflows which they can use to meet their contractual cash-outflow obligations.

If the various subcontracting firms do not have sufficient liquidity to meet their payrolls before they receive their sales revenues, they can finance these obligations by borrowing from their bankers. For a fee, bankers will be glad to provide these subcontractors with sufficient bank loans to meet payrolls in the interim before they are paid since the revenues necessary to cover these loans are contractually assured. Thus the uncertainties facing the subcontractors and bankers are reduced. Bankers are therefore willing to create credit to finance the necessary costs to keep the production process going.

Fixed money contracts and a banking system that creates bank money are the best institutions that civilized societies have evolved over the centuries to encourage and permit entrepreneurs to finance and carry out complex, long-duration production. The enforcement of these contracts in terms of fixed money sums protects the cash inflows and incomes of workers, as well as those of the seller-entrepreneurs and their bankers. Simultaneously it limits the liabilities or cash outflows of buyers: thereby protecting both parties to the contract no matter how adversely unpredictable and uninsurable future events may be.

MONEY, BANKS, AND THE PRICE LEVEL

As firms expand production in anticipation of greater future sales, additional production commitments will require an increase in borrowing from the banking system. Only if the total volume of loans is permitted to rise as entrepreneurs desire to expand production can our economy grow. If impediments are placed in the way of the banks responding to entrepreneurial needs, the economy can stagnate and die. As Keynes noted, bank

> credit is the pavement along which production travels, and the bankers
> if they knew their duty, would provide the transport facilities to just the

extent that is required in order that the productive powers of the community can be employed at their full capacity.

This process of having a banking system responsive to the financing
needs of firms that want to expand trade is called the *real bills doctrine* by
economists. This doctrine was the conceptual framework underlying the
development and passage of the Federal Reserve Act of 1913 which set up
the Federal Reserve as the Central Bank of the United States; a monetary
authority to specifically provide for an 'elastic currency' to meet the 'needs
of trade'. Unfortunately, this function of the Fed has been subverted by the
conservative idea that the proper and primary function of any central bank
is to prevent inflation – even if this creates persistent unemployment.

The money supply increases envisioned under this doctrine are called
'real bills' because it was assumed that all bank loan increases would be
used to finance a concurrent growth in the production costs associated
with the needs of managers to expand real output by hiring more resources. The real bills doctrine presumes that the additional bank money
created will be chasing additional goods, not too few goods. Under this
real bills view, therefore, increases in the money supply would never
cause inflation. Monetarists avoid facing this obvious possibility by assuming that (a) in the short run there can be no significant increase in
production so that an increase in the money supply must be 'chasing too
few goods', while (b) in the long run a market economy always produces
the full employment output no matter what the money supply.

Thus, by assertion, assumption, and definition, rather than demonstration, conservatives deny the need for a banking system to provide for
varying needs of trade as changing conditions warrant. Instead, in
Panglossian fashion they suggest that a market economy unfettered by
government will provide the fullest employment possible. All is for the
best in this best of all conservative worlds.

In contrast, our approach has argued that in a money-using entrepreneurial society there is no natural tendency or invisible hand to guide the
system towards the full utilization of all its potential resources. Instead the
economy will only perform up to the level of demand expected to be forthcoming from buyers. This demand will be financed either out of current
income or from accommodating bank credit. A central bank that raises
interest rates before full employment is trying to assure an insufficiency of
borrowing so that total spending is depressed. To the extent that purchases
financed out of current income are less than current income, sufficient
borrowing via additional bank loans is necessary to prevent unemployment
from developing.

If private borrowers do not fill the savings gap, then the government must take the responsibility to assure the gap is somehow filled. The size of the government deficit necessary to promote sufficient demand to achieve full employment, and the resulting expansion of the bank credit money supply, should be of secondary importance. It is of no value for a civilized community to have a government that maintains a balanced budget while its citizens are impoverished. If unemployed resources are available, they should never be idled merely because of a lack of profit and employment opportunities due to an insufficiency of private borrowing and spending. It is of great value to a civilized society to have a government that goes as deeply into debt as necessary to provide for the full employment and prosperity of its citizens when the private sector spending fails to achieve this civilized objective.

Similarly, it is of no value to restrict the growth of the money supply, as Monetarists recommend as a necessary policy to fight inflation. If the government tries to borrow to expand spending while the money supply is strictly constrained under a Monetarist rule, then the banks will be unable to accommodate additional government borrowing without having to raise interest rates (and ration credit) to private sector borrowers. The end result is that the loan market can become congested with borrowers and some private sector entrepreneurs maybe be discouraged from borrowing. In this case increased government borrowing will merely offset some private borrowing, and little or no expansion of total demand or total job opportunities will be possible. Monetarist policy, in these circumstances, merely perpetuates unemployment and recession.

CONCLUSION

An accommodating banking system that has the capacity to change the volume of money with the needs of trade is a necessary – but not sufficient – condition for lifting an economy out of an unemployment morass. If a banking system is permitted to flourish and if the government will act as the borrower of last resort to borrow and spend whatever is necessary to fill the remaining savings gap, then the entrepreneurial system has both the necessary and sufficient conditions to assure its citizens that they will prosper in a full employment civilized economy. Government must always be ready to borrow and spend whenever there is a significant and persistent lack of private sector spending. If we are to keep the government's spending role to a minimum, then the Federal Reserve must accept responsibility for keeping the banking system sufficiently accommodating to provide finance at interest rates which encourage as many private sector borrowers as possible as long as a full employment savings gap exists.

Notes

1. In the years 1988, 1989, and 1990 the unemployment rate was 5.5, 5.3, and 5.5 per cent respectively. The fear that these persistently low unemployment rates were going to trigger accelerating inflation lead the Federal Reserve to increase its discount rate from 5.66 per cent in 1987 to 6.98 per cent in 1990, and President Bush, in 1990, to raise taxes. The effect of these anti-inflation monetary and fiscal policy decisions was to plunge the United States into recession in 1991 and 1992 with the unemployment rate rising to 6.7 and 7.4 per cent respectively.
2. If wage and other costs per unit produced increase, then inflation will occur whether the money supply increases or not. If increases in wages and other costs diminish, then inflation will slow down even if the growth of the money supply speeds up, as, for example, in the period 1982–6.
3. Other methods of obtaining claim tickets involve either stealing money or counterfeiting it. These methods are illegitimate and uncivilized and are ignored in what follows.
4. For purposes of this discussion, we can treat gifts from other income earners as a loan where there is no requirement of repayment.
5. A liquid asset is defined as a durable that does not have significant storage costs while it is readily resaleable in a well-organized and orderly market. The more well-organized and orderly the market, the greater the degree of liquidity of any asset. Assets that cannot be easily resold in a market are basically illiquid.
6. In an economy that engages in foreign trade an alternative source of increasing demand is for foreigners to increase their purchase orders from domestic industry. Thus, many countries look toward exports rising faster than imports, rather than loan expenditures by government, to stimulate demand and provide for their prosperity. As we will explain in Chapter 10, such export-driven growth policies merely tend to export the domestic unemployment problem to another country. These export trade-oriented policies are usually not compatible with full employment of a global civilized community.
7. Of course, if the developer can get buyers to agree contractually to purchase condo apartments before they are built, then the developer is contractually assuring his future sales revenue.

9 Fighting Inflation: Controlling the Money Supply vs. Buffers and Tips

The analysis in Chapter 8 has brought us to the root of the inflation–unemployment dilemma facing a civilized market economy. Government accepts the responsibility for acting as a balance wheel to create and maintain the demand necessary to assure the full employment of all who want to work. In the rare periods of over full employment this may involve reducing total market demands. More commonly this balance wheel function involves either creating incentives for private-sector demand expansion or by direct government purchases of goods and services through contract-letting and/or the expansion of public enterprises such as the National Park Service, the Post Office, etc.

A necessary requirement for any successful governmental demand stimulus process is a banking system that provides the necessary financing (real bills) as required. Unfortunately, a banking system that can provide finance for managers to expand output, is also capable of providing finance for managers to meet inflating wage and other raw material costs even if output is not expanding. The problem of inflation involves resolving the dilemma of how to allow bankers to finance real economic expansion of the GDP without simultaneously financing inflationary demands for higher wages and prices.

In the face of increasing market demand, businesses and workers may respond in several ways. They may, in their own self-interest, raise the prices of the things they sell without producing any more goods and services. Alternatively, they may increase production by employing some previously unemployed resources instead of raising prices. If the major response to demand increases are price rises (or even if price increases occur within the context of a stagnating market demand), the result is inflationary. If output expansion is the major response, on the other hand, the community experiences growing prosperity without significant inflation.

For conservatives there is only one way to combat inflation that is consistent with their view of maintaining liberty in a society where people are motivated solely by self-interest. In a 'free' society, workers and entrepreneurs should be free to demand any price for their services, even if such demands are inflationary. As the former Prime Minister of the United Kingdom, Mrs Thatcher, was often quoted as saying, 'One of the rights of a free society is the right to price oneself out of the market.'

If the government guarantees full employment, then each self-interested worker, union, and business will have little fear that their higher price will result in lost sales and unemployment. Full employment assures that there would no longer exist what Marx called 'the industrial reserve army of the unemployed'. Only when the central bank adamantly refuses to increase the money supply to finance inflationary demands, will the resultant slack demand in the market place discipline *all* workers and firms with the fear of loss of income. The conservative hope is that this fear will keep wage and price increases in check. To make this fear credible, all firms and workers must be threatened. Nothing closely approaching full employment prosperity can be tolerated.

Conservatives, therefore, deplore any governmental fiscal effort to pay long-term unemployment benefits or other income supports (entitlements) to those inevitably caught in the natural unemployment rate web. Conservatives fear that a permanent social safety net will mollycoddle casualties in the war against inflation so that others may think there is little to fear if they join the ranks of the unemployed. A ubiquitous and overwhelming fear instilled in all members of society is a necessary condition for the barbarous conservative anti-inflation programme to work. The result is inevitably that the civil society is the first casualty.

Responsibility for the fate of the more than 7 million individuals and business firms that will be priced out of the market is not directly traceable to the specific actions of the central bankers. The individual or political action responsible for creating misery and destroying the stability of the family life for millions of workers and business men can be avoided by the aloof policy makers just as in warfare, where it is easier for one's conscience to drop a bomb from a high altitude on thousands of impersonal civilians that one does not see, than to kill a single enemy in hand-to-hand combat.

As long as there is an obdurate, pre-announced limit to the growth of the money supply designed to achieve a natural unemployment rate target, banks can not provide sufficient funds for full employment prosperity. The resultant weakened demand – a persistent departure from full employment – forces managers to lay-off workers. It is only through the employed observing the misery of those trapped in the natural unemployment rate quagmire that, according to conservative doctrine, we can appeal to the self-interest of the remaining employed to curb their future wage and price demands. If they do not behave in a non-inflationary manner, the big stick of the central bank will force some to join the ranks of the unemployed. Since which ones will become casualties are not obvious, then the entire population must fear the possibility of unemployment.

We challenge this conservative view that it is necessary to perpetuate an underclass of unemployed to keep demands of the remaining employed at non-inflationary levels. It is wrong to engage in such policies in a civil society for it involves a philosophy based on fear. Persistent unemployment is not something required by natural law. Abandonment of a full employment goal should not be worthy of consideration for any society claiming to be civilized. To understand the basis of our challenge to this uncivilized belief in the natural rate of unemployment, it is necessary to examine the complex relationship between inflation, income, and employment.

INFLATION AND INCOME

Inflation occurs when the prices of the many produced things that we buy are rising so that it takes more dollars to buy the same volume of goods. There are various statistical price indices that attempt to measure inflation. The Consumer Price Index (CPI) is the index most familiar to the general public. It is a measure of changes in the average price of goods that urban consumers buy. The GDP price index is a broader and more comprehensive price statistic measuring changes in the prices of all the goods and services produced in a nation, that is, the Gross Domestic Product (GDP).

GDP includes all domestically produced goods including those bought (a) by consumers, (b) by businesses for investment purposes, (c) by government, and (d) by foreigners (exports). Since the National Accounting System that is used to measure GDP is based on a system of double-entry bookkeeping, the 'double-entry' offsetting the value of gross domestic production is the value of the total gross *income* earned by those who contribute to the production of GDP. Any increase in the prices of the components of GDP must be accounted for by an identical increase in the prices paid to income earners (that is, wages, rents, interest, profits). Consequently, the key to comprehending the direct cause of inflation is to understand that *every increase in the price of things produced is simultaneously an increase in someone's income.*

The annual gross income of the nation can be thought of as a huge pie (see Figure 9.1) 'baked' or produced by the combined efforts of workers,

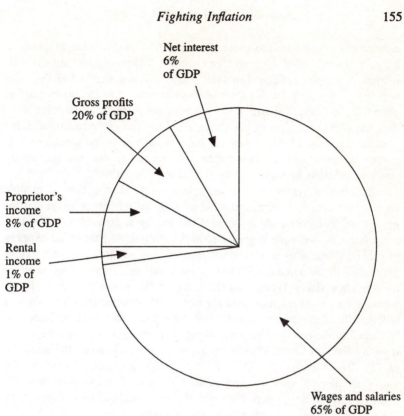

Net interest
6%
of GDP

Gross profits
20% of GDP

Proprietor's
income
8% of GDP

Rental
income
1% of
GDP

Wages and salaries
65% of GDP

Figure 9.1   Income shares of US GDP (1994)

property owners, and entrepreneurs. Each contributor to the production of
this pie receives, in payment for his efforts, a sum of money income. This
income gives the recipient a claim to a slice of this income pie. The size
of the slice claimed depends on the price of the productive services the
contributor has provided. Figure 9.1 shows that, in 1994, workers received
65 per cent of the total income earned in producing GDP in the United
States, while interest going to income recipients was 8 per cent, propri-
etary plus rental income was 9 per cent, and gross corporate profits (including depreciation) were 20 per cent.

Anyone whose services are highly priced in the marketplace earns a
claim to a large piece of the pie. Those whose services have a lesser
monetary value in the market place will earn claims to a smaller slice. The
unemployed earn no claims at all and if they have no savings will require
private charity, government unemployment compensation, and/or other

entitlement to purchase any piece of the pie. Obviously, either as individuals or as members of a group (for example, labour unions, cartels) self-interested people can improve their relative living standard if they can negotiate a higher price for their services compared to the prices paid to others. If, however, the size of the pie does not increase at the same time, then the gain in the slice of pie obtained by any one group raising its price is at the expense of the rest of the income earners in the community. If money incomes increase faster than the real pie grows, the accounting result is inflation as measured by the GDP price index.

Inflation is a symptom of a struggle over the distribution of income among members of a community. Inflation occurs whenever individuals or groups try to increase their share of the pie by contriving to raise their price faster than the pie is growing. In the struggle to gain at the expense of others, those who receive the largest price increases for the services they sell will be winners able to buy more pie; the prices of the services they sell are rising faster than the price of the goods they buy. Those whose prices have not increased (or have increased less than the average) will find that their money incomes fail to keep up with inflation. They will be forced to claim a smaller piece of pie. This struggle over income shares is what Professor Lester Thurow means when he characterizes the economy as *The Zero-Sum Society*. The winners' inflationary gain is offset by the losers' smaller pie slice, as long as the total size of the pie is unchanged.

Obviously, in any inflationary period, the losers will be unhappy with the outcome. Even the winners in this uncivilized struggle may be disappointed, however, since their increases in money income will not buy as many additional goods (more pie) as they might have expected, due to the ensuing rising price of goods. Therefore, inflation is politically unpopular among all groups, even the winners who often do not regard their own 'hard earned' and 'deserved' money income increases as causing inflation. To the extent that the authorities use planned unemployment to fight inflation by creating weak markets for products and therefore workers, then the 'zero sum' for society becomes a negative one as the size of the pie is reduced from what it would be if we maintained a fully employed society.

THE POSTWAR INFLATION AND UNEMPLOYMENT HISTORICAL RECORD

In the absence of community-held values as to the acceptable distribution of income, a free market economy with full employment cannot harmonize the conflicting income demands of people motivated solely by self-interest.

Indeed in a world devoid of civic constraints on income demands, conservatives have recognized that the only way to fight inflation requires income losses, unemployment, the destruction of potential profit opportunities, and a resulting reduction in the total size of the pie to keep people's total money income demands in their place.

The postwar historical record shows that only during the period 1961 to 1968, and again briefly in 1972 to 1973, was the US economy able to approach full employment without suffering any threat of inflation. In these years, when the government implemented a policy that appealed either completely or at least partly to civic values to directly constrain money income growth to the real growth in the GDP pie (so-called 'incomes policies'), the US economy was able to approach full employment without suffering any threat of inflation.

During the Kennedy–Johnson years of 1961 to 1968, prices were held in check by a wage-price 'guideline' policy which urged limiting money wage increases to the growth in the average productivity of labour. These guidelines were entirely voluntary. There were no external incentives, no monetary rewards or punishments to enforce labour to accept these restrictions on their wage demands. The guidelines relied solely on the civic values in support of the community's interest. The spark of these civic values was captured in President Kennedy's inaugural address where he challenged the many self-interested individuals and groups in the country to 'ask not what the country can do for you, ask what you can do for the country'.

For almost seven years, these voluntary wage guidelines worked. The unemployment rate declined from 6.7 per cent in 1961 to 3.6 per cent in 1968. Over this entire period, the price level increased by only 16 per cent while the money supply increased by 70 per cent[1] and the size of the real GDP pie grew by almost 40 per cent. This rapid non-inflationary expansion was the result of increased government deficit spending resulting from a military buildup and a tax cut.

With the growth of the unpopular Vietnam war under President Johnson, however, the civic cohesion generated by the Kennedy charisma was shattered and support for voluntary compliance with the wage-price guidelines disappeared. In 1968, employees in the airline industry demanded and obtained wage increases that were significantly larger than the guidelines. Wage settlements in other industries quickly followed the same patterns as voluntary compliance to the guidelines ended. The price index rose 4.2 per cent in 1968. As self-interest wage demands were rekindled, a change in government fiscal policy that increased taxes and restricted government spending was put in place. The result was that the government budget swung from a deficit of $13.2 billion in 1967 and $6 billion in 1968 to a surplus of $8.4 billion in 1969. The swing from deficit to government surplus reduced total market demand and the economy fell into recession in 1970–1. Unemployment rose to 5.9 per cent.

During the entire decade of the 1970s, part of the civil agenda was a continuing search for an acceptable incomes policy to replace the Kennedy–Johnson voluntary 'guidelines' to control inflation and to provide for an equitable sharing of the economic largess of a fully employed society. Conservatives, on the other hand, using economist Milton Friedman's Monetarist analysis that 'proved' that only a natural rate of unemployment could achieve a non-inflationary environment, developed a political rhetoric that emphasized that restrictive Federal Reserve monetary policies were the prime guardian against inflation.

Despite his conservative credentials, President Nixon abandoned the conservative call for persistence in pursuing a natural rate of unemployment. In August 1971, President Nixon successfully instituted a direct incomes limitation policy by putting wage and price controls in place. This approach was, of course, in direct conflict with the expressed conservative philosophy of his Administration. It was seen as a pragmatic solution to win the 1972 Presidential election.

Nixon's version of an incomes policy freed the Federal Reserve of responsibility for controlling inflation. The Fed immediately eased monetary policy. The result was a vigorously non-inflationary economy where real GDP grew at a rate in excess of 5 per cent during 1972 and 1973, while inflation dropped from 4.5 per cent to 3.3 per cent. This vigorous recovery with less inflation contributed to the Nixon landslide victory. Almost immediately after his re-election, Nixon dismantled his incomes policy. Prices climbed by 6.2 per cent in 1973 and by 11 per cent in 1974. Inflation was again the principle economic problem on the public agenda.

By 1975, President Ford felt the necessity to hold a 'White House Conference on Inflation' where approximately 700 leading US economists engaged in a two-day discussion of what to do about inflation. The only tangible result from this meeting was President Ford's WIN (Whip Inflation Now) Campaign that tried to emulate Kennedy's example of appealing to civic values. The public saw the WIN campaign as a stunt, not a policy. President Ford did not have the leadership qualities to create a new community of civic values. After the erosion of civic values under Johnson and Nixon and the Watergate scandal, the environment was not receptive to 'catchy' advertising slogans to whip up public support.[2]

Unemployment increased from 4.9 to 8.2 per cent between 1972 and the planned recession of 1974–5. Inflation dropped to 5.8 per cent by 1976. With a recovery in the early years of the Carter Administration, however, the inflation rate again rose to 6.5 per cent in 1977 and 7.7 per cent in

1978. Inflation was getting out-of-hand. President Carter therefore proposed a direct incomes policy – a 'real wage insurance' scheme – which would use the external incentive of reducing taxes for those who limited wage increases to a socially acceptable level. The Carter proposal, however, was abandoned by the President even before Congress could act.

Thus after Nixon's successful 1971–3 incomes policy, any suggestions for adopting an incomes policy were hesitatingly proposed and quickly abandoned. Restrictive monetary policy became the 'only game in town' to fight inflation. When inflation reached 11.3 per cent in 1979, the Federal Reserve – under a new chairman, Paul Volker – invoked a brutally restrictive monetary policy. Interest rates were pushed to unprecedented high levels, finance dried up, and loan defaults proliferated.

The result was to create a severe worldwide recession, the worst since the Great Depression of the 1930s. Unemployment soared from 5.8 per cent in 1979 to a peak of 10.8 per cent in mid-1982. The rate of inflation dropped from 13.5 per cent in 1979 to approximately 4 per cent in the last few months of 1982. In August 1982 as Mexico briefly defaulted on its international loans and thereby threatened the viability of the major banks in the United States, the Fed relented to avoid a precipitous financial crash.

Simultaneously, President Reagan pushed through Congress, a massive tax cut in tandem with increased government spending. The result was to expand dramatically the total demand for the products of industry just when the Federal Reserve's August 1982 change in monetary policy allowed the banking system to create the additional bank credit necessary to finance the resulting economic expansion. The economy quickly revived from the 1979–81 recession, the greatest recession since the Great Depression of the 1930s. By 1986, the federal government was running annual deficits of over $200 billion while, since the Mexican loan problem, the Federal Reserve pursued a very accommodating easy money policy. Inflation was not a problem as consumer price increases reached a low of 1.1 per cent. The unemployment rate had only fallen to 7 per cent,[3] higher than it had been in for any year during the first quarter century since World War II. Nevertheless, the economy was in better shape than it had been in most of the 1970s.

Although there were still almost 8.2 million unemployed workers in the United States, on March 1, 1987 'liberal' economist and Nobel Prize winner Franco Modigliani supported the natural rate argument when he wrote in the *New York Times* that

we are now relatively close to the minimum level of unemployment that can be reached and maintained without a serious risk of rekindling inflation.

Modigliani unabashedly claimed that there is broad agreement among economists that not more than 1 million additional jobs could be filled (reducing the unemployment rate by less than 1 per cent) without inflationary repercussions. Apparently the conservative rhetoric had so permeated the economics profession that even economists who viewed themselves as political 'liberals' were willing to sacrifice the economic lives of the 7 million jobless to constrain inflation. Conservative barbarism had become the collective conventional wisdom of most economists.

Despite President Reagan's rhetoric in support of a balanced budget, the Reagan Administration continued to run up gigantic budget deficits and prosperity reigned. Consequently, between 1986 and 1989, 8 million new jobs were created and the number of unemployed fell to 6.5 million. In 1989, inflation had increased to 4.6 per cent. President Bush and the Federal Reserve became worried again about inflation. In the fall of 1990, President Bush introduced a tax increase to reduce the deficit at the same time the Federal Reserve tightened its monetary policy. The result was the recession of 1991–2 where the unemployment rate rose to 7.4 per cent while inflation subsided to approximately 3 per cent.

At the outset of the Clinton Administration, the government apparently made an informal deal with Federal Reserve Chairman Greenspan that it would substantially reduce the annual deficit over five years (with most of the reduction in the later part of the period) if the Federal Reserve eased its monetary policy. In 1993 with the annual Federal deficits still exceeding $250 billion (but declining), the Federal Reserve eased monetary interest rates significantly. The economy expanded. Unemployment for the entire year was 6.1 per cent while inflation was 2.4 per cent.

By February 1994, however, Federal Reserve Chairman Greenspan indicated that the decline in unemployment had stirred his fear of possible inflation in the future. Monetary policy was reversed and by a series of small steps monetary policy became more restrictive throughout 1994. The effect was a drastic slowing of the economy in 1995 with unemployment rising. By late spring 1995, the Federal Reserve again reversed its policy to avoid drifting into another recession.

THE LESSONS OF THIS HISTORY

What lessons can we learn from this postwar history?

First, the only successful anti-inflation policies that were associated with vigorous growth and a rapid expansion to full employment occurred when members of the community accepted an incomes policy – either the voluntary guidelines of 1961–8 or the wage and price controls of 1971–3.

Second, compared to the period between 1972 and 1980, the conservative monetarist policy of the 1980s and 1990s has been moderately successful at constraining inflation, but only at great cost in terms of persistent high unemployment and significant unused industrial capacity.

We therefore conclude that if we want to live in a civil society that strives to control inflation and achieve full employment for all its citizens, then we need an incomes policy that is seen as just by the American electorate.

Anti-unionism as an anti-inflationary incomes policy

The anti-inflationary incomes policies adopted by the Reagan Administration were different both in degree and in kind from those of his predecessors. Early in his Administration, President Reagan made union-breaking respectable when, in 1981, he destroyed the Air Traffic Controllers' Union by firing all striking controllers (who were government employees).

Reagan's anti-union stance was legal. For the prior half-century, however (since Calvin Coolidge broke the Boston Police Strike in the 1920s), government officials had been extremely reluctant to use legal measures to cause the demise of a workers' union. The vigorous anti-union action by President Reagan altered the public perception of the permissible relationship towards unions, severely weakening the power of all unions and thereby significantly lowering inflationary wage demand pressures. In an assessment of the economic policies of the 1980s, former Federal Reserve Chairman Paul Volker has stated that 'the most important single action of the [Reagan] administration in helping the anti-inflation fight was defeating the air traffic controllers strike'.

Second, Ronald Reagan unlike most politicians in the 1970s stayed the course with the Federal Reserve Chairman Volker's single-minded restrictive Monetarist policy. The result was to make politically acceptable the conventional wisdom that a tight monetary policy should be designed to maintain a buffer of unemployed workers. While we endorse a policy of maintaining buffer stocks of raw materials and commodities to fight inflation, as we will discuss later in this chapter, we reject this buffer approach when dealing with people. The conservative use of human buffer stocks has tipped the economy into a more barbaric stance regarding the existence of unemployment and poverty in our midst.

THE MONETARIST VIEW – BLEEDING THE ECONOMY TO CURE THE PATIENT

Milton Friedman, the world's foremost Monetarist economist, is usually credited with coining the statement that 'Inflation is always and everywhere a monetary phenomenon'. Friedman asserts that there is a *fixed* long-run relationship between increases in the quantity of money and the rate of inflation. This Monetarist argument is ultimately based on the old homily that inflation is merely 'too many dollars chasing too few goods'.

This 'too many dollars' cliché is usually illustrated by employing a two-island parable. Imagine a hypothetical island where the only available goods are 10 apples and the money supply consists of, say, ten $1 bills. If all the dollars are used to purchase the apples, the price per apple will be $1. For comparison assume on a second island there are twenty $1 bills and only 10 apples. All other things being equal, the price will be $2 per apple. Ergo, inflation occurs whenever the money supply is excessive relative to the available goods. Conservative economists conclude that had the second island limited its money supply to $10, no inflation of apple prices would have occurred.

The flaw in this parable comes from what is not discussed. Why was the money supply greater on the second island? That 'why' matters. If the increase in the money supply is the result of entrepreneurs borrowing from banks to finance an investment (for example to hire additional workers necessary to harvest 30 additional apples) then the result will be that the $20 chases forty apples, and the apple price will be only $0.50. The moral of this paradigm is that if additional bank money is used to hire additional workers and install other productive investments, then an increase in the money supply need not be associated with higher prices but with greater output.

Restrictive monetary policy increases bankers' costs of borrowing funds. Bankers then charge higher interest on loans to borrowers. These higher finance charges increase business operating costs thereby reducing profit opportunities. Consequently, entrepreneurs will be less willing to borrow to finance current production and employment. Management's inclination to fire workers may be exacerbated if they interpret the higher interest costs as a warning signal that a restrictive monetary policy-induced recession is on the way.

If the resulting weakened market environment forces workers contract demands or even reduces existing wages and benefits (so-called 'give-backs'), then the rise in production costs can be halted. In the interim there may be a painful 'stagflation' – a stagnating production of goods with some rising prices as some earlier inflationary cost agreements work their way through the system.

If, on the other hand, the Fed does not develop a restrictive monetary policy when labour is demanding inflationary wage increases, then bankers can expand their loan operations. Accordingly, if a community vigorously pursues a full employment goal, while simultaneously having no societal limitations on people's inflationary income demands, then the economy has a built-in inflationary bias. Since conservatives do not believe that civic forces can affect either people's behaviour or the real economy, this has led them to argue that an anti-inflationary restrictive monetary policy is the 'only game in town' as a government pursuit of full employment creates continuous income demands that are inflationary.

By creating unemployment, income losses, and weak markets for goods, conservatives expect to make most members of the society fearful and too weak economically to fight over the distribution of income. In puritanical terms, Monetarists often suggest that such monetary discipline 'is good for the system' – comparable to the curative blood letting practices of fifteenth-century physicians. Conservatives acknowledge that unemployment and recessions may inflict pain and suffering but, they claim, that a stiff dose of monetarist medicine is needed to purge the system of those who would otherwise try to extort inflationary money income demands on the rest of society.

In the long run, in true Social Darwinistic philosophy, conservatives argue that this monetarist cathartic prescription necessarily punishes the lazy and makes industry leaner and more efficient. To prevent the cries of those who are hurt by such polices from being addressed in public forums, conservatives argue that the Federal Reserve must be independent of any political pressures. In other words, central bankers must not take account of the civil values of the community that require everyone to be able to find a job. Instead the central bank must single-mindedly eliminate inflationary pressures by creating a persistent underclass of unemployed workers and failing entrepreneurs among the members of society. Conservatives advertise the apparent virtues of a policy of deliberate, persistent unemployment as good for the system in that it 'loosens up labour and goods markets'. Again, we see conservatives resorting to the barbarism of a Leviathan independent central bank to govern by inflicting a purgative pain on the public.

This conservative policy of deliberately hurting members of society should never be a first choice solution for a civilized society. Austere and unpalatable policies are not necessarily virtuous. Planned unemployment is the last resort of a community that has failed to develop a civilized economic policy. Once we understand the relationship of money to the production processes in a market economy, we can develop a civilized solution to the apparent full employment vs. inflation dilemma.

CONTRACTS, PRICES, AND INFLATION

It is possible to build on our earlier discussion of the role of money and contracts to design civilized policies to fight inflation without intentionally keeping people out of work. Previously, we argued that business firms could either produce inventories so that they can instantly respond to spot market demands or they can respond to contractual orders for delivery at a specified date in the future. This means that there are two types of prices in a market system; the prices of goods in spot markets and the prices of goods that are contractually ordered in advance of delivery. Conceptually, therefore an economy can suffer from (a) spot (or commodity) price inflation, and/or (b) contract price (or incomes) inflation. Accordingly we must develop policies to deal with each kind of inflation.

Spot price inflation

Spot prices require immediate delivery. Since production takes time, only goods that already have been produced and are currently being stored as shelf inventory can literally be sold in spot markets. Any sudden increase in demand for immediate delivery (or decline in shelf-inventory supplies) will cause a *spot market inflation.*[4] Any increase in spot commodity prices can be viewed as a windfall change in the income (or wealth) of those possessing the existing commodities before the price rise occurred. The homily of the two islands so dear to Monetarists' hearts, each with a fixed inventory of 10 apples and (sudden) different demands (assumed to be related to differing money supplies), is a simple illustration of such a spot-price inflation.

Buffer stocks as a solution for spot price inflation

A spot or commodity price inflation occurs whenever there is a sudden and unforeseen change in demand or available supply *for immediate delivery.* This type of inflation can be avoided, if there is some institution that is motivated, not by self-interest, but rather by the civic value of protecting the community from wild spot price movements in basic commodities. This agency must maintain a buffer stock of these essential goods. Buffer stock management involves maintaining a commodity shelf-inventory that can be moved into and out of the spot market to absorb shocks to the spot market coming from market disruptions. If, for example, there is an unforeseen shortage of a commodity that might cause the spot market price to change dramatically, some of the buffer stock can be sold in the market to augment supply. Similarly if there is a sudden drop in demand, the buffer stock institution can purchase from the market and prevent the glut from unduly depressing prices.[5]

For example, since the oil price shocks of the 1970s, the United States has developed a 'strategic petroleum reserve' stored in underground salt domes on the coast of the Gulf of Mexico. These oil reserves are designed to provide emergency market supplies to buffer the US oil market if it is suddenly cut off from foreign supply sources. In such a situation, the spot price of oil would not increase as much as it otherwise would; a spot oil price inflation could be avoided as long as the buffer stock remained available. Thus, during the 100-hour Desert Storm war of 1991, government officials made strategic petroleum reserves available to the market to offset the possibility of disruptions (actual or expected) from affecting the spot price of crude oil. The Department of Energy estimated that this use of a buffer stock prevented the price of gasoline at the pump from rising about 30 cents per gallon during the brief Desert Storm period.

Similarly, if the United States had increased its purchases for the strategic oil reserves during the first half of 1986 when spot oil prices dropped from $20 to almost $10 per barrel as the result of worldwide excessive inventories of crude, the resulting oil price deflation and its devastating impact on the income of domestic oil producers in the oil patch of the Southwestern States could have been mitigated. In this case, however, the large existing federal deficits prevented the government from spending additional sums to buy oil as its price fell.

In the absence of such buffer stocks of commodities, every unexpected change in spot demand or available supply will produce an immediate change in spot prices. In times of great uncertainty about the future use and/or availability of important commodities, for example, oil, metals, agricultural crops, etc., the spot price can fluctuate dramatically in short periods of time – as they did during brief periods in the 1970s and 1980s.

Rising spot prices signal an inventory shortage that encourages managers to expand output. The resulting rebuilt inventories will end the spot-price inflation. Falling spot prices signal producers that inventories are excessive. Managers will cut back future production to work off the existing inventories, thereby stopping the price decline. Spot-price inflation (or deflation) should subside, provided it does not induce change in the future costs of production. To the extent that the spot prices of commodities are rising, however, it may take too long for new supplies to come to market. Buyers may not be able to wait for a return to more normal supply–demand conditions, or they may be stampeded by fears of an uncertain future into thinking that the current spot-price inflation will permanently affect future costs of production, thereby encouraging producers to raise their supply contract prices.

Use of buffer stocks as a public policy solution to spot-price inflation is as old as the biblical story of Joseph and the Pharaoh's dream of seven fat cows followed by seven lean cows. Joseph – the economic forecaster of his day – interpreted the Pharaoh's dream as portending seven good harvests where production would be much above normal followed by seven lean harvests where annual production would not provide enough food to go around. Joseph's civilized policy proposal was for the government to store up a *buffer stock* of grain during the good years and release the grain to market, without profit, during the bad years. This would maintain a stable price over the fourteen harvests and avoid inflation in the bad years while protecting farmer's incomes in the good harvest years. The Bible records that this civilized buffer stock policy was a resounding economic success.

Obviously the idea of using buffer stocks to stabilize commodity prices is not new. It was used briefly by the United States during World War I. It was revived as part of the agricultural policy of the New Deal to maintain farm income. In the period from the end of the Second World War until the 1970s, an explicit US government policy was to maintain significant buffer stocks of agricultural products and other strategic raw materials to support prices that adequately rewarded producers for efficiently organizing the production process. This US policy helped stabilize commodity prices worldwide even as world demand for foodstuffs and other basic commodities exploded under the stimulus of global economic growth and rising populations.

The other side of the coin of stable commodity prices was stable incomes for farmers and other commodity producers. The result was (a) prosperity for raw material producers, (b) encouragement of continuing productivity enhancing investment in these areas, and (c) a non-inflationary price trend for the food and basic commodity component of the consumer's budget despite a soaring global population and rapid worldwide economic growth. From hindsight, clearly, the stability of commodity prices was an essential aspect of the unprecedented prosperous economic growth of the world's economy over the quarter of a century since World War II.

The success of this postwar buffer stock programme over several decades, however, was its ultimate undoing. As productivity in food and other primary products increased (encouraged by a guaranteed price), some tax-payers began to object to the cost of carrying the buffer stock. Objections were also raised to the idea that the income of farmers and other commodity producers was being guaranteed at what appeared to be consumers' expense. After all, if the existing surplus buffer stock was dumped on to the market, spot prices would fall, providing the consumer with a 'bargain' – at the expense of producers.

Public attention was not drawn to the fact that the urban taxpayer, as a consumer, received the benefit of a plentiful food supply at stable non-inflationary prices. Furthermore, as workers and entrepreneurs in the industrial sector, urban taxpayers had plenty of job opportunities producing the many industrial products that only prosperous raw material producers could demand.

In its first years, the Nixon Administration dismantled these buffer stock programmes to save warehousing costs and to use these savings to reduce the deficit while financing the war in Vietnam. World spot commodity markets were left to the mercy of unforeseen and unforeseeable events. The result was the violent commodity price fluctuations that occurred in the 1970s and 1980s. In the early 1970s – even before the first oil shock in 1973 – world spot food prices began to soar as a result of some natural disasters that reduced harvests and fishing catches. Since world commodity supplies were no longer buffered, those prices moved widely in response to these unforeseen disasters.

As the government held buffer stocks disappeared, any cartel of producers that existed, or could be formed, had the freedom to raise prices by restricting supplies. Cost-of-living escalator clauses in many wage contracts were triggered by this 1970s spot inflation in foodstuff and other raw materials that went into the production of consumer goods. The resulting cost-of-living wage increases meant that this spot-price inflation spilled over into production costs (incomes) inflation for many industrial goods. This process was already well under way in 1973 even before the OPEC oil cartel's embargo drove oil prices through the roof, and exacerbated the situation of a spot-commodity inflation spilling over into an incomes inflation.

As a result of the 1970s spot-commodity inflation in food and petro-leum, many foreign nations who were net importers of agricultural products and oil were especially hard hit. In the absence of any significant international buffer stock, each nation attempted to become more self-sufficient in any of these basic commodities that they could produce rather than pay the cartel supported 'exorbitant' prices of many traditional foreign producers. This self-sufficiency movement was further fanned by the Carter grain embargo in 1979 that signalled foreign grain importers that, for political reasons, they could no longer count on United States production to feed their population at any price.

The politically motivated actions by the Nixon and Carter Administrations eliminated the United States as the world's major buffer stock operator who had, for decades, maintained international spot commodity price stability. When the US publicly abandoned the role of the world's non-profit buffer stock operator, commodity producers and consumers were given a clear signal that their future prosperity could no longer be secured by the civilized post-World War II international trading relationships. Between 1945 and 1970, the United States acceptance of the role of buffer stock coordinator in many internationally traded raw materials had contributed dramatically to the development of an international community that had guaranteed profitable prices for basic commodity producers and the promise of especially good profits for those who searched out the most efficient production methods. In return the consumer received plentiful supplies without inflation. Under this social regime, the global production and consumption of basic commodities involved a positive-sum game. Both producer and consumer groups shared in the resulting economic gains.

When this economic community collapsed, producers' prosperity began to depend on their ability to form coalitions against consumers to extract income from them – at best, a zero-sum game. As the postwar international civil economic community broke down, many of the efficiencies of a civilized world were lost. To counter soaring basic commodity prices, many nations subsidized inefficient domestic producers. The result was that the world's production for many basic food commodities expanded and excesses came on to world markets just when the United States and then most of the rest of the industrial world was plunged into the Great Recession of 1979–82.

The collapse of demand in this Great Recession led to a startling commodity spot-price deflation in the early 1980s. Consequently, agricultural and energy prices fell dramatically. The agricultural and petroleum sectors in the United States were brought to the brink of disaster as were many commodity producers around the world. The Reagan economic revival, induced by tremendous increases in the government deficits expanding domestic demand for imports as well as domestic production, reversed this worldwide decline. This Reagan demand-stimulating reversal set the stage for the economic miracle of some nations, especially the Pacific Rim nations of Japan, Hong Kong, Taiwan, Korea, and Singapore, who were well-situated to take advantage of the sudden surge in demand for imports by the United States.

If we have learned anything from this history of commodity price gyrations, it is that wild commodity spot-price swings in free markets create havoc, inefficiencies and misery – sometimes among producers and sometimes among buyers. At any point of time these volatile spot-price movements produce some winners and offsetting losers between producer and consumer groups, giving the impression that it is the zero-sum game described by Professor Thurow. From a longer prospective, the whole world has been a loser as a result of the unbuffering of commodity prices under the Nixon presidency compared to the world's economic performance from 1945 to 1969 when spot-price stabilization was an explicit policy goal.

INCOMES INFLATION

Rises in money wages, salaries and other material costs in production contracts always imply an increase in someone's money income. As we have seen earlier, the costs of production of a firm are the other side of the coin of the income of people who provide labour or property for use by the firm in the production process.

With slavery illegal in civilized societies, the money-wage contract for hiring labour is the most universal of all production costs. Labour costs account for the vast majority of production contract costs in the economy, even for such high-technology products as NASA spacecraft. That is why inflation associated with production prices is usually associated with money-wage inflation.

Wage contracts specify a certain money-wage per unit of time. For example, a secretary may earn $10 per hour. If during the hour, the secretary types 20 letters then the unit labour cost of each letter is $0.50 (20 letters divided by $10). If she demands and obtains a wage increase to $15 per hour and still types 20 letters per hour, the cost of each letter has been inflated to $0.75. This labour cost plus a profit margin or mark-up to cover material costs, overheads, and profit on the investment become the basis for managerial decisions as to the prices they must receive on a sales contract to make the undertaking worthwhile.

If money-wages rise relative to the productivity of labour, then the labour costs of producing output must increase. Consequently firms must raise their sales contract price if they are to maintain profitability and viability. When any production costs and therefore contract prices for

orders are rising throughout the economy, we are suffering an order contract or *incomes inflation*.

A PROPOSAL FOR A TAX-BASED INCOMES POLICY (TIP)

To prevent an incomes inflation requires some method of limiting money-
wage rate increases (and gross profit margin). In 1970, Professor Sidney
Weintraub of the University of Pennsylvania laid out a simple but clever
anti-inflation incomes policy that he called TIP or a *Tax-based Incomes
Policy*. TIP made use of both civic values and self-interest, although the
latter was more prominently displayed in the proposal. TIP is designed to
counter inflation by placing a penalty – an external disincentive – on those
companies that grant wage increases in excess of a socially acceptable
non-inflationary wage-growth norm based on average labour productivity
increases.[6]

The basic philosophy of TIP is that wage increases in excess of productivity growth will harm all members of society. Inflationary money wage
increases violate a basic civic value. Firms that give in to inflationary wage
demands are inflicting a cost on the entire society, similar to what polluters
do when they discharge wastes into the air or public waterways. Weintraub's
penalty TIP charges enterprises for the 'inflation pollution' that granting
inflationary wage increases produces downstream in the economy.

How would this affect the competitive strategy of individual firms? TIP
can be considered as a more flexible version of the team salary cap system
used by the National Football League (NFL) where each team has the
same number of players and the total salary payments for each team is
fixed. Club owners can vary the salary of individual players as long as the
average pay per player is unchanged. The TIP calculation would be based
on the setting limits on the average compensation (salary, wages, bonuses
and fringe benefits) per full-time employee in business firms. As average
productivity grows in the economy, this average compensation would
increase at the same pace.

In the NFL no matter how a team does, they cannot exceed the payroll
cap for each year. Nevertheless, entrepreneurial creativity and individual
player initiative would not be stifled as managers can still reward their best
players with the best salaries within the overall constraint. A similar compensation constraint would be on firms under TIP but individual workers
and managers can still receive the highest pecuniary rewards.

Just as some teams in the NFL outperform others, so some firms will
outperform others in improving their productivity. With TIP these firms

will pass a smaller share of the rewards of this above average growth in productivity to their current employees. The rest will be passed on to buyers in terms of either improved quality or lower prices making this firm more competitive and able to obtain a greater market share. Thus, firms with above-average productivity increases will grow faster than their competitors. As their market share grows, hiring will be greater in these more efficient firms. Over time, the composition of the work force will be continually shifted towards high productivity growth firms and economy-wide productivity growth should increase. As the output of such high productivity firms increase, total profits and therefore return to its shareholders will also increase.

Under TIP, those business firms that accede to inflationary wage demands at the bargaining table would be punished for their indiscretion. TIP involves external disincentives (higher taxes) levied directly on those whose behaviour fosters inflation. This TIP punishment is limited to those who permit inflation to pollute the economy while the Monetarist natural unemployment rate anti-inflation policy inflicts punishment indiscriminately on the entire community. All business firms find their markets are less profitable than they would be at full employment while many workers are denied job opportunities whether their individual behaviour was inflationary or not.

Once instituted, TIP would have to be a permanent policy institution if the inflationary dragon is to be permanently tamed. There must always remain on the books a civic statement of what is an acceptable non-inflationary behaviour as a constant reminder that inflating one's income at the expense of others is always contrary to civil behaviour.

If a specific future date for the end of TIP was to be announced, its effectiveness would diminish as that date approached. Everyone would be told, in effect, that soon social constraints on inflationary income behaviour will disappear. The existing civil value would erode as each member of society could no longer rely on the civilized behaviour of others to forgo inflationary money-earnings demands. Self-interest alone would encourage each person to try to increase their own money income *before* others did so first. The struggle over the distribution of income would be reignited – and could be dampened only by the dousing waters of a planned recession and persistent unemployment.

Credibility and compliance with TIP

TIP is based primarily on the external incentive of paying a prohibitive fee or tax for engaging in anti-social behaviour. It, however, also mixes education and internal incentives in a manner similar to the way road regulations govern driving behaviour on the nation's highways. Speed limits, for example, are permanent but the magnitude of the speed limit can change depending on driving conditions, the need for energy conservation, etc. – factors whose *raison d'être* in achieving society's goals are clear to an educated driving public. Similarly TIP would be a permanent institution but the magnitude of the allowable wage increase could vary depending on economic conditions. Public education would be necessary to explain the factors affecting the magnitudes involved in TIP.

Obeying speed limits, paying taxes, and similar civic behaviour, depends to a considerable extent on voluntary compliance working in tandem with fines levied on those who excessively violate the rules. Governments never reward good drivers who stay within the speed limit, or taxpayers for paying their proper taxes. Such actions are the expected social behaviour of all citizens, even if it is not in their own self-interest. Similarly, those whose wages and income increases are non-inflationary need not be provided an external reward – civil behaviour would be expected and would be a reward in itself.

Civilized governance relies on a coordination of enforcement with social norms. Sanctions work best when their primary function is to guarantee that social norms will not be taken lightly. This provides social norms with the credibility to develop, and it prevents the erosion of the norms by scofflaws.

The institution of TIP would violate the current norms of both unions and business firms who believe in 'free collective bargaining' that is, wage negotiations without government interference – just as a pollution tax can violate the norms of environmentalists who believe that polluting is an absolute evil and therefore no one should be permitted to pollute the air or waters merely because the polluter can afford the charge. Consequently the implementation of TIP must be accompanied by a strong effort to earn credibility in the eyes of both entrepreneurs and labour. Four broad areas are involved in earning credibility.

Framing the issue

Entrepreneurial fears of massive government regulation and burdensome additional record-keeping requirements must be eliminated. Weintraub's TIP proposal was to be applied to only the top 2000 firms in the United States. These firms produce approximately half of the GDP and are key to the general wage level and profit margins set in the rest of the economy. Managerial control of such large enterprises already requires extensive record keeping. TIP would not add to this burden as compliance could be calculated from existing records and shown on an additional three or four lines on corporate income tax forms. The record keeping of smaller businesses – and especially start-up enterprises on which the vitality of the entrepreneurial system depends – would not be affected at all.

The public must be educated to understand that TIP will be inexorably linked to a set of expansionary fiscal and monetary policies. Social acceptance of TIP is part of a strategy to achieve full employment production and the highest standard of living possible for the community. The context must be established that the only alternative to a permanent incomes policy is either permanent high rates of unemployment (to limit inflation) or high inflation (which creates turmoil and destroys the civilized economic community). TIP is the tool that allows society to unleash its full economic potential without having to fear either of these consequences.

TIP must possess a simple structure so that the public can comprehend what is being implemented. Business, labour, and the general public must be convinced that TIP represents a ubiquitous social norm in the sense that:

(a) TIP will not be vulnerable to political manipulation. TIP will not create a new arena where individuals and groups compete for higher incomes through political pressure or backroom deals.

(b) TIP will not be vulnerable to noncompliance resulting from accounting gimmicks and other misrepresentations that hide excessive wage increases of dishonest firms while penalizing workers and entrepreneurs of honest companies.

(c) TIP will not grossly distort the economy by creating a new set of strange incentives.

TIP must be recognized as a permanent part of the economic landscape.

Transitional problems in installing TIP

Those whose money-income status is caught in the transition from the current situation to a TIP relation must be treated fairly. This suggests that it will be easier to institute TIP during a period when inflationary forces are not strong (as in the late 1980s or early 1990s). With inflation low it may appear that there is less need for a TIP policy. If, however, we are to avoid a permanent state of slow growth or stagnation, then a direct incomes policy is essential to restoring a full employment prosperity to our economy. The United States as well as the rest of the industrial world has an especially attractive window of opportunity for instituting TIP during the mid-1990s (as compared to the 1970s when it was clearly needed – but the transition would have been especially difficult).

It is always difficult to change values and institutions, especially as they have developed in our market economy in recent decades. If we are to be able to achieve an economy where all who want to work can find employment and earn the dignity of being a contributing member to society, then it is necessary to develop a core of civic values around the need to stop inflationary income demands that might otherwise emerge. It would be foolish to rely solely on civic values without any external incentives to keep inflation in check, as the breakdown of the Kennedy–Johnson incomes policy demonstrated. A successful permanent incomes policy such as TIP will have to rely on external incentives as well.

This is not a fatal problem. Societies often develop institutions that draw significant support for their existence and acceptance from related – but separated – civic values. For example, there is no self-interest involved in simply donating money to charity. As Dickens' self-interested entrepreneur Ebenezer Scrooge recognized, the more one gives to charity the less one has for oneself. Even a tax deduction for charitable contributions (as long as the tax rate is less than 100 per cent) involves a loss of self-interest as the contribution means less after-tax income than not giving at all. On the other hand, charitable tax deductions within a larger framework of a civil community that values highly charitable contributions combines external and internal incentives that can make philanthropy a very rewarding activity for the giver.

IMPORTED INFLATION

Until this point, the discussion of inflation has implicitly assumed that inflation was always due to a rise in prices of domestically produced goods. Yet with nations that trade with other nations, rising prices of goods brought from abroad can result in an imported inflation (as the oil price shocks of the 1970s clearly demonstrated). Although a complete discussion of the ramifications of international transactions must wait until the next chapter, it is useful at this point to briefly summarize how inflation can be imported.

Imported inflation occurs when the price of imported goods in terms of the domestic currency, rises. If there is a fixed exchange rate where the amount of domestic currency paid for a unit of foreign currency does not change, then as inflation occurs in a foreign economy, the cost of imports in terms of money is rising. The rising cost of imports is due to either a foreign commodity and/or incomes inflation.

Between 1945 and 1972, the world operated under a fixed exchange rate system developed at meetings in Bretton Woods, New Hampshire, in 1944. One of the major conservative arguments that ultimately led President Nixon to withdraw the United States from the Bretton Woods system was that it permitted the transmission of inflationary forces across national boundaries. Conservatives argued that under a flexible exchange rate system (where the amount of domestic currency paid for a unit of foreign currency can vary daily), any inflationary tendency in another country cannot be imported. Instead any inflation in the price of goods produced in another nation will lead to a *pari passu* drop in the amount of domestic currency paid for a unit of foreign money thereby insulating domestic markets from importing inflation. Recent history has shown, however, that the post-1972 flexible exchange rate system *per se* has not insulated the domestic economy from importing inflation. Any time there is any reduction in the exchange rate of domestic currency vis-à-vis the foreign currency, there can be an imported inflation – even if there is no change in the foreign production costs and foreign prices charged by foreign suppliers. This problem of importing inflation due to the price of the domestic currency falling relative to foreign currencies will be discussed in the next chapter.

CONCLUSION ON A CIVILIZED ANTI-INFLATION POLICY

To paraphrase that old sage, Benjamin Franklin, if as a community we don't all hang together to fight inflation, then we will all hang separately by accepting the barbarous conservative anti-inflationary policy.

Civilized policies to handle inflation rely on us acting as a community. One of the most important functions of government in any anti-inflationary struggle is to educate the public that any on-going income distribution struggle is ultimately costly for all. It is a mug's game – a no-win, everyone loses negative-sum game – although at any point of time there may appear to some winners.

In the absence of a sensible policy about a civilized resolution to the income distribution question, the result is not a zero-sum game, but a real loss in total income as governments pursue restrictive monetary and fiscal policies that feed back depressionary forces on each other.

ARE DECLINING PRICES A GOOD THING?

The decade of the 1970s was a period of almost continuous feedback between spot and incomes inflation. The mid-1980s, on the other hand, was a period of modest income inflation in the industrial sector partially offset by some sectoral commodity and incomes deflation (notably in agriculture and oil). As a consequence of falling energy and food prices partly offsetting modest wage and price increases in other sectors, inflation in the United States fell to a negligible 1.1 per cent in 1986. The substantial decline in energy and food prices meant that many small producers who could make a profit if these prices were stable were forced out of business. With the reduction of these marginal producers, these sectoral prices rose again and the inflation rate began to rise substantially until the recession of 1991 slowed the inflation rate.

After suffering through the pain of inflation and the planned recessions of the 1970s, many conservative economic commentators look favourably upon the sectoral price deflation that occurred in the 1980s. Piqued by the 1970s bumper stickers in the oil producing regions of the US that proclaimed 'Drive at more than 55 mph; and freeze a Yankee', people in the northern energy consuming states in the 1980s might take relish in the income deflation being suffered in the oil patch region of our country. Taking pleasure in the economic misery of others in the community, however, is clear evidence of the breakdown of civilized behaviour.

A civilized society must accept the responsibility of not only containing inflationary surges in the income demands of groups in our community at the expense of others, but it must also act to limit *sharp* declines in the income of others. In the 1970s, the real income loss of energy consumers towards domestic energy producers was moderated by oil and natural gas price controls and a windfall oil profit tax. In 1991, the use of the strategic petroleum reserve during Desert Storm again shielded energy consumers against a loss of income to energy producers. It therefore seems equitable that the government should have borne some responsibility to provide relief for the loss of income oil producers suffered from the capricious drop in oil prices in the 1980s. One possible policy has already been suggested in the accelerating of purchases of a strategic petroleum reserve as a buffer stock in the period of falling crude oil prices.

More important than policies to deal with specific sectoral price changes (all deflationary and inflationary price movements start off as sectoral changes), there is an important civic principle involved. We cannot govern a civilized economy by encouraging or even permitting open conflict among members of the community. The recent resurgence in the popularity of the idea that it is proper to look out for one's own income without any thought of social responsibility has produced dreadfully detrimental economic effects. Just as civilized people, in this age of advanced technology and massive destructive weapons, have realized that 'war is too important to be left to the generals', so in this age of complex, interdependent economies, we should realize that 'income distribution is too important to be left solely to the capricious forces of the market'. If we have not learned this principle yet, then we are destined to continue to suffer the terrible economic and social costs of an independent Federal Reserve's pursuit of a persistent significant rate of unemployment to fight the threat of inflation.

In the past few years, we have been lulled into a false sense of security by the deliberate slowing of economic growth and prosperity that has contributed to the reduction of OPEC's market power and the reduction in militancy of unions. The free market external incentives that create income distribution conflict have been weakened by running the economy at slow throttle. When and if the economic pendulum inevitable swings back, the important question is whether we will be ready.

Sixty years ago, Keynes warned that 'the outstanding faults of the economic society in which we live are its failure to provide full employment and its arbitrary and inequitable distribution of income'. In the last half century, modern economies have learned how they can, if they desire, avoid the great unemployment problems of the past, but in so doing they may have exacerbated the income distribution faults in our system. This lesson was learned the hard way, first by creating the economic conditions for the inflation of the 1970s without having a civilized incomes policy in position, and then by relying on conservative restrictive policies to subdue income distribution conflicts by inflicting unemployment and thereby causing rates of economic growth that, as we will demonstrate in the next chapter, are far below what a civilized economy is capable of delivering to its members.

Notes

1. Again these facts conflict with the conservative monetarist doctrine regarding the relationship between money supply growth and inflation.
2. President Carter experienced a similar disappointment when he tried to enlist public support for energy conservation by declaring it the 'Moral Equivalent of War' without any positive leadership actions. The cynical public labelled the Carter moral equivalent policy 'MEOW'.

3.   Inflation in Europe had also subsided but unemployment remained at a post-war high.
4.   Spot-price inflation can easily be associated with prices of commodities (for example, wheat, pork-bellies, crude oil, etc.) that are traded on well organized, spot markets. The concept can also be associated with the price of second-hand houses, collectibles, etc.
5.   This interference with spot market prices is well-established in most security markets. For example, in the New York Stock Exchange there is a 'specialist' who function as a market-maker in specific securities by holding a buffer stock. The market-maker is required by the rules of the exchange to maintain an orderly market by selling securities from inventory when the price is rising in too rapidly (in a disorderly manner) and buy securities if the price is falling precipitously. If the price movements swamp even the buffering attempts of the market-maker, then 'circuit breaker' rules are applied that suspend trading until a more orderly market can be established.
6.   Between the end of Second World War and the oil and other commodity price shocks in the 1970s, the major inflation problem experienced by the United States was primarily due to money-wages increasing at a more rapid rate than productivity increases. Studies made during the Kennedy Administration indicated that labour productivity increased on average by approximately 3.2 per cent per annum since World War II. If average money wages rose by say 5.2 per cent then the economy would experience a 2 per cent rate of inflation. Thus the Kennedy–Johnson guidelines called for annual money-wage increases that did not exceed 3.2 per cent. Since the early 1970s, however, profit margins have tended to rise substantially even as the rise in money-wage rates increases slowed. A TIP proposal today would probably require some explicit method for constraining profit margin increases (but not total profits which could still grow as output expanded to meet demand growth).

10 Policy for a Civilized Global Economy: Whose International Debt and Currency Crisis is it Anyway?

Near the end of World War II, economists representing the Allied nations met in Bretton Woods, New Hampshire to plan a postwar international monetary community. Basic to the civilized scheme developed at Bretton Woods was a belief that the nations of the world should be united via a fixed exchange rate system where the value of one nation's currency in terms of another rarely changed. For example, if one could be assured of always being able to exchange one US dollar for 90 Japanese yen, we would have a fixed exchange rate between dollars and yen.

This Bretton Woods fixed rate system lasted over a quarter of a century until, in August of 1971, President Nixon began the unilateral withdrawal of the United States. By 1973, the Bretton Woods system was replaced with a system of flexible (sometimes referred to as floating) exchange rates. In this floating system the amount of foreign currency exchanged for a unit of domestic currency may change continuously.

Neither flexible nor fixed exchange rate systems are new to international trade. A flexible exchange rate system operated for much of the period between the two world wars. Before World War I, under the international gold standard and between 1947 and 1973, under the Bretton Woods Agreement, the world traded under a fixed exchange rate system where governments cooperatively accepted responsibility for stabilizing the costs of foreign currencies.

THE GOLDEN AGE OF ECONOMIC DEVELOPMENT

The Bretton Woods years were an era of unsurpassed economic global prosperity. Economist Irma Adelman of the University of California has characterized the Bretton Woods period as a 'Golden Age of Economic

179

Table 10.1   Real GDP (annualized growth rate)

Years	Real GDP per Capita OECD Nations		
1700–1820	0.2 per cent		
1820–1913	1.2 per cent		
1919–1940	1.9 per cent		
1950–1973	4.9 per cent		
1973–1981	1.3 per cent		
	Major Industrial Nations	*New Industrializing Nations*	*Developing Nations*
1973–1990	2.5 per cent	3.5 per cent	−0.1 per cent
	Total Real GDP		
	OECD Nations		*Developing Nations*
1950–1973	5.9 per cent		5.5 per cent
	Real GDP per Capita		
	OECD Nations		*Developing Nations*
1950–1973	4.9 per cent		3.3 per cent

Development . . . an era of unprecedented sustained economic growth in both developed and developing countries'. Table 10.1 provides the statistical evidence that Adelman used in reaching her conclusion about our economic golden age.

Although we do not possess reliable statistics on GDP per capita before 1700, it is probably true that from biblical times until the Renaissance the average standard of living in the world showed little improvement from year to year or even generation to generation. Improvement in global economic living standards began with the development of merchant capitalism during the Renaissance period in Europe. Between 1700 and 1820 (see Table 10.1) the per capita slice of the economic pie was increasing an average annual rate of 0.2 per cent. Thus, if the average person lived approximately 45 years, the person's standard of living increased less than 10 per cent from the time of birth to death.

Living standards started to increase substantially early in the nineteenth-century. The Industrial Revolution period was truly revolutionary. During the years 1820–1913, annual living standards improved ten times faster than in the previous century as annual growth rate of 1.2 per cent compounded year after year. The average increase in labour productivity was almost 7 times greater than during the previous 100 years. The per capita income of the advanced nations of the world more than trebled in less than 100 years. No wonder this period is often portrayed in Western literature as the era of growth of the common man.

During this 1820–1913 period the volume of world exports grew thirty fold as a global economy and financial system were created with a fixed exchange rate under a gold sterling standard. The growth rate during the Golden Age of Bretton Woods, however, was almost double the previous peak annual growth rate of the industrializing nations during the Industrial Revolution (from 1820 to 1913). Annual labour productivity growth between 1950 and 1973 was more than triple that of the Industrial Revolution. Moreover, between 1950 and 1973, real GDP per capita in the developed (or OECD) nations grew 2.6 times faster than between the wars.

The resulting prosperity of the industrialized world was transmitted to the less developed nations through world trade, aid, and direct foreign investment. From 1950–73, annual growth in per capita GDP for *all* developing nations was 3.3 per cent, almost triple the growth experienced by the industrializing nations during the Industrial Revolution. The total GDP pie of the less developed countries (LDCs) increased at almost the same rate as that of the developed nations, 5.5 per cent and 5.9 per cent respectively, but the higher population growth of the LDCs caused the lower per capita income growth.

By comparison, the economic record of the flexible rate systems between the world wars and since 1973 is dismal. The growth rate of the major developed nations since 1973 is approximately half of what it was during Bretton Woods, not much better than the experience of the nineteenth- and early twentieth-century. Moreover the OECD nations have suffered through persistently higher rates of unemployment and, especially during the 1970s, recurrent bouts of inflation. The contrast for the LDCs since 1973 is even more startling with annual real income per capita declining. The best performances since 1973 have been turned in by the newly developing nations along the Pacific rim, but even with their 'economic miracle', their per capita improvements are significantly lower than those experienced by the industrial nations between 1950 and 1973.

Finally, it should be noted that during the Bretton Woods period there was a better overall record of price level stability than either during the post-1973 period, or between the wars, or even under the international gold standard.

THE LESSON THAT SHOULD HAVE BEEN LEARNED

What can we conclude from these facts? First, fixed exchange rate systems are associated with better global economic performance than flexible systems. Second, during the postwar period until 1973 global economic performance was nothing short of spectacular. It exceeded the remarkable performance of the industrial revolution and the gold standard fixed exchange rate system. This unparalleled 'golden age' experience required combining a fixed exchange rate system with another civilizing principle, namely that the creditor nations must accept a major share of the responsibility for solving persistent international payments imbalances that may develop. Third, the Bretton Woods period was a remarkably crisis-free economic era.

Since the breakdown of Bretton Woods, on the other hand, the global economy has stumbled from one global economic crisis to another. Economic growth around the world has slowed significantly while the growing global population threatens to reduce standards of living. The number of mouths to be fed are threatening to increase at a faster rate than global GDP. Economics has once more become the dismal science with its Malthusian overtones.

Instead of bringing the utopian benefits promised by conservative economics, the post-Bretton Woods system has generated a growing international monetary crisis. As early as 1986 *New York Times* columnist Flora Lewis noted that government and business leaders recognize that 'the issues of trade, debt, and currency exchange rates are intertwined'. Lewis warned that the world is on a course leading to an economic calamity, yet 'nobody wants to speak out and be accused of setting off a panic ... the most sober judgment is that the best thing that can be done now is to buy more time for adjustments to head off a crash. ... decision makers aren't going to take sensible measures until they are forced to by crisis'.

The current international payments system does not serve the emerging global economy well. The *Financial Times* of London and *The Economist*, both previously strong advocates of today's floating rate system, have acknowledged that this system is a failure and was sold to the public and the politicians under false advertising claims.[1] Yet no leader is calling for a complete overhaul of a system that is far worse than the one we abandoned in 1973. No one has the courage to speak out in public forums and suggest that the conservative philosophy that has governed our economic affairs in recent decades is a formula for economic disaster.

THE CONSERVATIVE PRESCRIPTION FOR INTERNATIONAL TRADE PROBLEMS

Whenever a nation sells exports the nation earns income that is a claim on whatever foreigners produce for sale. When a nation buys imports it either

Table 10.2   United States current account balance (in $ billions)

Year	Current Account Balance
1980	1.2
1981	7.0
1982	−11.4
1983	−44.5
1984	−99.8
1985	−125.4
1986	−151.2
1987	−167.1
1988	−128.2
1989	−102.8
1990	−91.7
1991	−7.0
1992	−67.9
1993	−103.9
1994	−155.7

spends previously earned (through export sales) claims on foreigners or borrows from foreigners to pay for these imports. The payments for exports and other activities that earn income from sales to foreigners minus the purchase of imports is called the nation's *current account balance*. If this balance of payments between a nation and the rest of the world is positive, we say the nation is running a current account or trade surplus and it can store all these extra earned claims into assets called *foreign reserves*. If a country is running a current account deficit, then it is spending more abroad than it is earning selling things to foreigners. The trade deficit can be financed by either running down formerly accumulated foreign reserves (if any) or by borrowing from foreigners.

Table 10.2 presents the current account balances for the United States from 1980 to 1994. In 1994, for example, US exports and other earnings from foreign transactions totalled $698 billion. Imports and other spending abroad equalled $804 billion. The resulting current account deficit was $156 billion which was financed primarily by borrowing from Japan and other nations who were running export surpluses.

It is an economic truism that if a nation is importing more than it is exporting, then other nations must be exporting more than they are importing. In other words, if any nation is running an international balance of payments deficit, other nations must be in surplus. Conservative economic doctrine teaches that the deficit nation, by buying more than it is selling in international markets, is temporarily 'living beyond its means'. It therefore follows in the conservative creed that such prodigal nations *must* take action to reduce spending on imports by 'tightening its belt' that is, by adopting deflationary policies to reign in the spending of their citizens. Conservatives believe that surplus nations have no responsibility for initiating any adjustments to reduce the payments imbalance.[2]

This conservative belief dominates the practices of institutions such as the International Monetary Fund (IMF) that were designed to help nations experiencing chronic current account deficits. Consequently the IMF always advises trade deficit nations that they have only two policy choices.

The first policy option, 'tightening one's belt' requires the nation's government to increase taxes to reduce consumer spending *and* to reduce government spending, thereby reducing the services provided to its citizens. Belt-tightening is designed to lower the income of the nation so that it spends less on everything *including imports*.

A belt-tightening policy aggravates depressionary tendencies in these nations, and creates widespread unemployment and economic hardship. This does not matter to the IMF advisors. Creating income loss, unemployment, and increased poverty is 'the *necessary* price you have to pay' for the nation's prodigal ways, as any high-paid IMF economist will tell the deficit nation's policy makers – usually over a sumptuous state dinner.

Warming to his topic, this conservative economist will explain, as he puffs on his cigar over an after-dinner cognac, that the second policy that should be implemented (usually as a supplement to the first) is to encourage the exchange rate to decline so that an 'impersonal' market force reduces the nation's standard of living by making imports more expensive. With the resulting price of imported goods relatively higher, the nation's domestic industries become 'more competitive' in both overseas markets and at home. It is rarely explained that the home market for products will be depressed as the result of government belt-tightening policy. Consequently, there will be a net job increase only if there is a very substantial increase in employment in export industries to more than offset the loss of jobs due to the weakened home markets.

Our conservative economic expert does not explain that this policy of encouraging a falling dollar (or pesos, or lira, and so forth) will, if successful in increasing sales abroad, merely export the nation's unemployment to foreign workers whose bosses will find their companies suddenly becoming less competitive. Encouraging a fall in one's exchange rate to make one's industries more competitive is a barbaric conservative policy that can improve one's own job position only by exporting unemployment.

The ultimate effect of these policies is to reduce the standard of living of *both* deficit and surplus nations. The deficit nation's living standard declines as its gross domestic product pie shrinks under a belt-tightening policy. Under declining exchange rates, the real income of the deficit nation declines as its people pay a higher price for the goods they buy. The surplus nation's living standard declines as these policies lead to a decline in its export markets and it suffers from increasing unemployment.[3]

Adoption of conservative policies does not improve the world's economy. Unemployment and idle capacity are, at best, merely shifted from one nation to another. More likely global employment and real output will fall as conservative belt-tightening policies unleash depressionary forces. Furthermore, if these conservative policies are aggressively pursued by a large economic entity, then, as the history of the Great Depression demonstrated, the surplus nations will not stand idly by when their industries lose significant foreign markets. Instead they will retaliate with like policies in an attempt to re-export the unemployment to others. The resulting trade wars can only make all nations worse off.

THE RESPONSIBILITY FOR RESOLVING INTERNATIONAL TRADE IMBALANCES IN A CIVIL GLOBAL COMMUNITY: THE MARSHALL PLAN EXAMPLE

During World War II, Europe's productive capacity was ravaged. Immediately after the war, Europeans required huge quantities of imports to feed themselves and to rebuild their factories and cities. During 1946 and 1947 European nations used up almost all of their prewar savings (their foreign reserves) to pay for imports from the United States, the only nation that had available productive capacity.

Under any conventional conservative international monetary system, once their reserves were exhausted the Europeans would have to either accept the burden of adjustment by 'tightening their belts', that is by reducing demand for imports to what the negligible amount they could earn from exports or to borrow dollars to pay for imports. The Catch-22 of these alternatives were:

(1) Europeans could not produce enough to feed their population. To tell a starving person to tighten one's belt is not only an uncivilized suggestion but it imposes an impossible condition. Had the necessary 'belt-tightening' been undertaken, the result would have been to depress further the war-torn standard of living of Western Europeans. This would have induced political revolutions in Europe, not to mention recession in America's export industries.

(2) During the Great Depression, European export earnings were so

low that they defaulted on most of their international debts. Given
this experience and the fact that their postwar industries were in
shambles and could not produce enough in exports to service their
debt, American banks would not make the massive loans needed
by Europeans. It was also obvious that any direct US government
loans could not be repaid.

As a civilized strategy to avoid the political and economic chaos that
would probably have occurred in Europe, the United States offered to pay
for the European potential trade deficits (of imports over exports) necessary
to rebuild Europe through the Marshall Plan and other aid programmes. In
essence, the Marshall Plan permitted foreigners to buy United States exports
without either drawing down their last pennies of foreign reserve savings
or by going into debt that could not be repaid in the foreseeable future.
Through the Marshall plan and other aid programmes, the United States
was demonstrating a civilized attitude to the entire global community.[4]

If the United States left the deficit nations to adjust to the vast looming
trade imbalance by reducing imports, then (a) the standard of living of
Europeans and Asian residents would have been substantially lower *and*
(b) the United States would have slipped into a great recession as there
would have been too little international demand for the products of her
surplus industrial capacity.

The Marshall Plan and large-scale foreign military and economic aid
programs *gave* foreigners large sums of American dollars, *as a gift*, so that
they could buy American products. The result was that:

(1)   huge benefits accrued to both foreigners and US citizens. Foreigners
      used these gifts to buy the American goods necessary to rebuild
      their economies and to feed their people. Americans obtained
      additional jobs and earned more income by selling exports to these
      foreigners; and,

(2)   by its generosity the United States invigorated, enriched and
      strengthened the international community to the immense economic
      gain of all nations outside the Iron Curtain.

The Marshall Plan gave away a total of $13 billion in four years. (In
1994 dollars this is equivalent to $139 billion.) This 'giveaway' repre-
sented 2 per cent *per annum* of the United States' GDP. Nevertheless,
American consumers experienced no real pain. During the first year of the
Marshall Plan, US real GDP per capita was 25 per cent greater than in
1940 (the last peacetime year). Employment and per capita GDP grew

continuously between 1947 and 1957 as these foreign aid funds financed additional demand for US exports. These were exports produced by employing what otherwise would have been idle American workers and factories creating jobs and incomes for millions of Americans. For the first time in its history, the United States did not suffer from a severe recession immediately after the cessation of a major war.

The entire free world experienced an economic 'free lunch' as both the debtors and the creditor nation gained from this United States 'giveaway'. The Bretton Woods system in tandem with the Marshall Plan, where the United States took deliberate steps to prevent others from depleting their foreign reserves and becoming overindebted internationally, resulted in a global golden age of economic development.

By 1958, however, the US international position of being able to export more than it imported was coming to an end. Foreign aid grants exceeded the United States' trade surplus of demand for US exports over US imports. Unfortunately, the Bretton Woods system had no mechanism for automatically encouraging emerging trade surplus (creditor) nations to step into the civilizing adjustment role the US had been playing since 1947. Instead these creditor nations converted a portion of their annual dollar export earnings into calls on the gold reserves of the United States. In 1958 alone, the US lost over $2 billion of its gold reserves. In the 1960s, increased US military and financial aid responses to the Berlin Wall and Vietnam accelerated this trend.

The seeds of destruction of the Bretton Woods system were sown and the golden age of global economic development ended as the trade surplus nations continually drained gold reserves from the United States. When the US closed the gold window in 1971 in order to avoid a continuing reduction in its foreign reserves and then in 1973 unilaterally withdrew from Bretton Woods, the last vestige of a potentially enlightened international monetary approach was lost – apparently without regret or regard as to how well it had served the global economy.

COMPARING THE MARSHALL PLAN AND THE TREATY OF VERSAILLES

This civilized historical episode enhancing a postwar international civil community can be compared to the barbaric policy and the resulting fragmented international system that followed the First World War. Under the 1919 Treaty of Versailles, the victorious Allies imposed a harsh settlement on the defeated nations. Massive reparations were imposed on Germany as the European Allies attempted to obtain compensation for the costs of the war that they had incurred.

In his book *Economic Consequences of the Peace*, John Maynard Keynes spoke out against the uncivilized policy of imposing reparations on these wartorn nations. Perhaps the victorious European nations whose citizens had suffered through years of war cannot be blamed for mistrusting Keynes's civilized economic arguments or the political ideals of President Woodrow Wilson. The evils of waging war may have eroded the civilized values of the European Allies to the point where they felt compelled to demand a barbaric financial retribution.

The result of this Allied barbarism may have been initially satisfying to the warlike passion for revenge by humiliating a former enemy. But barbaric treatment can breed more barbarism, as the evils imposed by the oppressor shape the values of the oppressed. Although the primary responsibility for Nazi Germany does not lie with the British and French economic policies after the war, to the extent that they helped shape German society's values of the 1920s and 30s, the harsh Allied terms for peace did have a significant role in the outcome that occurred in the 1930s and 40s in Europe.

The United States was the only victorious nation that pursued a civilized policy of not claiming reparations. The United States developed a loan plan (the Dawes Plan) for aiding the Germans to meet the Allied claims. Unlike the other victorious Allies, the United States enjoyed an economic boom in the 1920s as the Allies bought American goods with these Dawes plan dollars. The European victors, even with the boost of war reparations, experienced much tougher economic times.

TODAY'S INTERNATIONAL DEBT CRISIS

The spectre of several international debt problems haunts global capital markets. One problem is associated with the liabilities of the countries of Latin America, Africa, and the former communist countries of Eastern Europe. The other involves the international debt of the world's largest debtor, the United States.

The large growth of Latin American and African debts (of both oil producing and oil consuming nations) essentially had its origins in the OPEC oil price explosions of the 1970s. The growth of the Eastern European debt had its origin with the crumbling of the Soviet Union in the 1980s that forced these Soviet-dependent Eastern European nations to turn to the West for more imports. The growth of the United States debt had its origins in the Reagan recovery from the Great Recession of 1979–82.

In a fundamental sense, these international debt problems are inextricably tied together in that (a) they threaten the very viability of the international financial community and (b) their resolution will involve innovative and unorthodox policies.

The Latin, African and East European Debt

The fundamental fact that must be faced is that, in essence, most of the international debt of the Latin American and African nations will never be fully repaid, while repayment of most of the Eastern European debt is only slightly less questionable. The repayment of the debt is not possible in the foreseeable future – and given the magic of compound interest, most of the debt servicing will fall into default when, and if, the next serious global economic recession occurs.[5] Moreover, even if these debtor nations continue to service their international debt obligations, these debtor countries will be potential targets of currency speculation attacks that could destabilize the economies of the developed world.

The United States debt

In the early 1980s, with large tax reductions and increased federal government spending, the Reagan Administration created the largest peacetime dose of 'Keynesian' demand stimulation in history. Reagan's Keynesianism induced an economic recovery from the worst global recession in half a century. Much of the induced demand stimulus spilled over into a US demand for imports thereby causing additional employment in the export industries of other nations. The United States acted as the 'engine of growth' pulling the other industrialized nations out of the global recession by a rapid increase in US demand for imports and the resultant growth in US current account deficits to a peak of $167 billion in 1987.

The resulting US trade deficits meant that Americans were spending more on foreign goods then they were earning from selling goods and services abroad. As Table 10.2 shows, the US current account balance swung from a small surplus of $7 billion in 1981 to large and persistent deficits under the demand stimulating policies of Reagan and his successors. After peaking in 1987, the US current account deficit started to decline. It bottomed out at $7 billion in 1991 – a year of recession and the Gulf War. With the recovery from the 1991 recession the US current account balance has again increased to over $150 billion per year.

Conservatives see this persistent United States trade deficit as indicating that Americans are consuming beyond their means. Conservatives add, with a tone of moral righteousness, that Americans are not saving enough[6] – they are using foreign savings to finance a sinful splurge of wanton consumption. Japan and other beneficiaries of this increased US import demand obstinately run current account surpluses as a result of the growth of their exports more rapidly than their imports.

These surplus nations have not reciprocated either by directly respending their dollar earnings on additional imports or by further stimulating their own domestic economies so that their residents can buy more of everything including imports. If they had, the surplus nations would have set up a backflow of orders for United States' goods that would have helped redress the imbalance between US imports and exports since 1981. Instead, these surplus nations enjoyed this fast export growth that encouraged employment expansion in their export industries while they saved a significant portion of their export earnings in the form of foreign reserves. For example, in 1995, Japan's foreign reserves were $156 billion, almost double the $79.5 billion reserves of the United States while Japan's GDP is much smaller than that of the US.

Operating under the assumption of Say's Law, conservative economic theory argues that no nation will continually export goods unless they want to buy foreign products with their export earnings. Conservatives would argue that it would not be in one's self-interest to work hard to produce goods to be sold abroad and to receive only sterile gold, or foreign IOUs rather than goods and services in return. This continuing accumulation of foreign reserves by countries such as Japan, Taiwan, Singapore, since the 1981, however, refutes the application of Say's Law on an international scale.

To finance the huge trade deficits since 1981, the United States has had to sell assets and increase its international indebtedness to foreigners. The Japanese, West Germans, Taiwanese and others were only too happy to finance US imports over exports by holding the amounts of US debt they held on their international account.

CURRENCY SPECULATION PROBLEMS AND THE INTERNATIONAL MONEY SYSTEM

Since the 1970s, total international debt has grown substantially while economic growth has slowed down. If a nation's debt rises relative to its foreign earnings in today's floating rate system, worries about the nation's ability to meet its debt obligations increase. At some point fears of possible default can cause many foreign investors to simultaneously pull their liquid investments out of the debtor nation. The result is a speculative run on the nation's currency as its market value precipitously sinks with a potentially devastating effect on all concerned.

Conventional economic analysis has not been able to suggest how to resolve this complex relationship between the international debt level and currency speculation problems except to claim that, in the long run, a free market will solve all problems. But in the long run, 'we will all be dead'. There is, therefore, an urgent need for an innovative approach that will permanently remove the threat of nations amassing large and persistent international trade deficits and thereby encouraging disorderly currency speculations that can cause irreparable harm to the economy of many nations. In order to develop a basis for such an innovative programme, we must first understand more fully how the international financial markets operate.

Money in an international trade setting

There is no universally agreed upon international money that settles contracts between residents of different nations. Crossing national boundaries, traders must agree on which nation's laws and money will govern their contractual agreement. Those engaged in the international trade of goods and services are continually entering into contracts calling for future payments or receipts in terms of foreign currencies. To reduce uncertainties about the costs of these future commitments, traders need some assurance of the meaning of the future money values of these international contractual commitments. One or both of the parties to an international contract will be using a different currency to settle their domestic transactions than the one required for the international commitment. Either the buyer will have to obtain foreign money to meet the commitment or the seller will receive a foreign currency in payment. In some cases, both buyer and seller may be dealing in foreign money as, for example, when a French refiner buys crude oil for US dollars from the Kuwaiti government.

The monies of other nations are called *foreign exchange* and these various currencies are bought and sold in the *exchange market* at a price called the *exchange rate*. Cooperation between governments is an important factor governing the ease and the terms upon which foreign exchange may be purchased. Depending on the degree of cooperation between the governments, the exchange rate may be either fixed or flexible.

Fixed vs. flexible exchange rate systems

In a fixed exchange rate system, the central bank or, as in the case of Argentina, a currency board, acts as a 'market-maker' for foreign currencies. In this market-maker role the Authorities fix the exchange rate by posting the price that they stand ready to buy or sell unlimited quantities of the foreign currency. If the Authorities announce that they will maintain an unchanging exchange rate, and if the 'maker' has sufficient reserves of both the foreign and domestic monies to back this announcement, the exchange rate between the currencies will remain fixed as the foreign reserves are used to buffer the exchange rate market.

For example, the Central Bank of South Korea can maintain a fixed exchange rate by agreeing to sell 690 Korean won for each US \$1 offered, or to sell US dollars at the equivalent rate of 0.00145 dollars for each Korean won. In order to back this offer, the Central Bank of Korea has to have an inventory of US dollars (or other liquid assets readily resalable for US dollars) sufficient to meet all the demands of those who wish to sell won for dollars. This inventory of dollar assets is called the foreign exchange reserve of Korea. To have a global fixed rate system requires the monetary authority in each nation to announce fixed buy/sell prices for all the major countries of the world.

Under a fixed exchange rate system, domestic bankers, who deal directly with the public, are assured by their central bank or currency board of a fixed price for buying or selling various foreign monies. A small service charge is added to this price whenever a banker buys foreign monies from, or sells to, the public. In turn the public is thereby assured of a fixed price for any foreign currency it has to buy or sell.

In a flexible exchange rate system, on the other hand, there is no government 'market-maker' institution which guarantees an unchanging price for foreign money. Hence, if people increase the demand for imports they will need more foreign currencies to settle their international obligations. This will increase the demand for foreign exchange and the free market price of foreign money will rise in terms of domestic currency. As one has to give up more units of the domestic currency to get a unit of foreign currency, the domestic currency will depreciate in value. If, on the other hand, the demand for the foreign currency declines, the market price will fall and the domestic currency will appreciate.

In a flexible rate system the Monetary Authority may still 'intervene' to affect the price by buying or selling currencies in the market. This type of central bank intervention, however, is neither pre-announced nor automatic. Rather all that is announced is that any interventions that may occur will be limited to preventing the free market from becoming what the Authorities call 'disorderly'. By 'disorderly' the Authorities mean that the 'free market' exchange rate is moving, in their judgment, too rapidly in either an upward or downward direction. Such disorderly movement is usually associated with 'undue' speculation about the future value of the exchange rate.

For example, on 4 September 1986, the Federal Reserve Bank of New York issued a public statement that to limit the fall of the US dollar, 'foreign central banks intervened to slow the decline in the dollar by making sizable purchases of the currency between May and the end of July, but the Federal Reserve Bank stayed out of the currency markets'. In this case, the foreign Authorities intervened to prevent the dollar exchange market from becoming disorderly, but neither the Federal Reserve nor other major central banks tried to fix the dollar exchange rate at any specific level. Despite this intervention the dollar fell by 9 per cent against the Japanese yen and 5 per cent against the German mark during this period.

Another illustration of intervention occurred in the spring of 1995. The Mexican peso crisis had adversely affected speculators' view of the future value of the US dollar causing the dollar to decline rapidly from over 95 yen to the dollar to approximately 81 yen to the dollar. The Federal Reserve led a coordinated intervention by all the G7 central banks to stabilize the dollar's value at approximately 83 yen to the dollar. This intervention was successful. Further intervention by the Bank of Japan over the following months increase the dollar to 88 yen by July 1995.

The dialect of exchange rates

A fixed exchange rate system provides the international production and trading community with a Rosetta Stone for precisely translating values from one national money to another over the life of the contract. As such it forms the basis of a common or shared dialect of worth – of financial values – which is an essential element in avoiding inefficient economic activity. In effect, a fixed exchange rate system reduces all the world's various monies to a single common denominator. Everyone can then understand the value of the sums involved in any contract whether they be denominated in dollars, yen, marks, pounds, francs, or pesos.

A stable civilized system with interacting groups, each with its own (money) language, requires that the dialect of one group possesses a clear correspondence with the dialects of the others so that all of the separate dialects form an easily comprehensible whole. A fixed exchange rate system, by assuring a precise translation of international money values over time, strengthens the foundations of the international civil community. The unprecedented growth of the world's economy under the fixed exchange rate system of Bretton Woods, as well as the rapid growth under the old gold standard, provides clear evidence of the tremendous payoff that can be obtained from such a civilized trading system.

In a flexible exchange rate system, on the other hand, the common value dialect among traders is either defective or absent. Good decisions can yield bad results if exchange rate changes are unforeseen. Suppose that, in 1983, when the dollar equalled approximately 250 yen, the management of a large US firm decided that it would be very profitable to build a factory in Japan to produce goods for the American market. At that exchange rate, managers could estimate that the dollar cost of hiring Japanese workers when the plant became operational would be significantly less than hiring US workers to operate a similar 'state of the art' plant in America. When this Japanese factory came on stream several years later, however, the dollar was equal to 140 yen. Management found that this new engineering-efficient plant was economically inefficient and could be operated only at a terrible dollar loss. What was a 'good' investment decision in 1983 turned out to be a calamity when the investment came into operation. As the dollar fell further this profitable investment became a disaster.

Whenever changes in the exchange rate occur (or are suspected but not accurately predictable), the value of an international commitment in terms of domestic money at the time of the agreement can differ in an unforeseen way from the value at the date of settlement. The more uncertain the economic future appears to be, the more managers will hesitate to make commitments and the greater will be their desire to stay liquid in order to be able to meet any unforeseen economic contingency.

Floating exchange rates, inherently engender more uncertainty about the meaning of international values over time. International contractual commitments are much more dangerous than undertaking the same activity under a fixed exchange rate system. The lack of a common dialect of economic values with flexible rates means that the demand for international liquidity will be greater than with a fixed exchange rate system. Since, as we noted in Chapter 8, any increase in the demand for liquidity reduces the total demand for producible goods, a flexible exchange rate system is an additional unemployment-provoking force in the global economy.

A conceptual illustration

People's eyes often glaze over when economists try to explain the international deficit problem. Complications multiply when the participants are located in different countries using different currencies. In what follows we hope to provide a stimulating, but simple, illustration comparing international financial transactions with interregional ones within a single country, for the latter, with its use of single currency, is easier to comprehend.

An international payments deficit is merely a special case of unbalanced trade between two geographical regions (say Mountaintop and Coastal-land) where the value of Mountaintop's export earnings from sales to Coastal-land does not equal the value of Mountaintop's import purchases from Coastal-land. In this circumstance, Mountaintop is running a trade deficit with Coastal-land and is under pressure to raise sufficient money to settle this payment imbalance by either borrowing funds or selling assets. Coastal-land's residents, on the other hand, are not under any immediate economic pressure. They can either buy assets of, or make loans to, the Mountaineers. Alternatively, the Coast residents can stop selling to the Mountaineers as the latter experience difficulties in meeting their payments.

If Mountaintop and Coastal-land are in separate nations, conservative economists insist that the only permanent remedy for this trade imbalance is for some belt-tightening policy by the Mountaineers in tandem with a reduction in the exchange rates so that Mountaintop's money is worth less in terms of Coastal-land's currency. With a depreciated currency, the competitive position of Mountaintop's industries will improved and they will be able to sell more to buyers on the Coast (at the expense of the Coast's firms). Simultaneously, Coastal-land's goods become more expensive to the Mountaineers who will therefore reduce their import spending. Export sales will grow and imports fall, conservatives argue, until the export–import imbalance disappears.

If, however, Mountaintop and Coastal-land are both regions within the United States, then there is never a question of a change in the exchange rate between the money used in the Mountain region vis-à-vis the money used at the Coast. For example, if people in the Rocky Mountains imported more from New England than they exported this would create a trade imbalance between these regions of the United States. No one would claim that the solution required that the dollars used in Denver should be worth less than the dollars of New York. Nor would conservative economists recommend such a policy.

Why does the fact that regions with trade imbalances within the same national boundary make a difference? This can best be explained by conceiving of what would happen if various regions in the United States were in separate nations.

Envision the United States divided up into 12 separate nations – one for each Federal Reserve Bank District.[7] In each District there is a Central

Bank that issues its own legal tender currency. (This is, in fact, the situation in the United States.[8]) Yet the exchange rate between a five dollar Federal Reserve Note issued by the San Francisco Federal Reserve Bank and one issued by any of the other 11 banks is always fixed (for example, $5 San Francisco = $5 Boston).[9]

Let us start our hypothetical illustration during a period when no trade imbalance exists between the San Francisco region and the Boston region. Payments for each region's imports are offsetting. The demand for money by New Englanders to pay Californians equals the demand for money by the latter to pay the former. If, however, Bostonians suddenly decide to import more California oranges, there will be a net western flow of dollars to pay for the additional oranges. As cheques clear through the banking system to pay for these oranges, banks in the Boston area will experience an outflow of dollars while banks in California will see their depositors' dollar balances grow.

To be consistent, the conservative economist should invoke the law of supply and demand to argue that this trade payment imbalance should result in Californian dollars rising in terms of Boston dollars until the trade imbalance is eliminated. In fact, however, we never experience such an exchange rate change occurring within the US because (1) the Federal Reserve System maintains a fixed exchange rate by acting as the clearing house to assure that San Francisco and Boston dollars always exchange at a rate of one for one, while (2) the federal government's regional taxation and spending policy can be used as a longer-term transfer device to induce a reverse eastward flow of dollars.

As income of the orange producers increases in California, government's tax revenues will rise. The government can draw off these additional tax revenue dollars from California and spend the dollars (and more) in Boston, where income and liquidity is being lost (and therefore recessionary pressures are building up). The result of this regional fiscal policy will be to set off a new flow of bank clearings from California to Boston – a reverse direction compared to the original regional export–import spending pattern in the private sector. The government is, in essence, helping to finance Boston's continuing orange imports.

In the three decades following World War II *non-conservative* governments, whether Republican or Democratic, recognized that regional trade imbalance will not only initially depress the deficit region's economy but will, if unchecked, in the end adversely affect sales and income of the surplus region. Government, therefore, did not hesitate to use such fiscal policy to shore up employment in both regions by regional redistribution fiscal policies.

The civilized result of this enlightened policy of a civilized society is that *both* regions benefit and better economic growth is experienced throughout the nation. In our hypothetical example, Californians are able to continue earning higher incomes through a strong continuing demand for orange exports and New Englanders, with the help of sufficient government spending, can still earn sufficient income to maintain their standard of living including buying California oranges.

In the absence of such regional fiscal policies, Californians would end up losing their additional income earned from the increased sale of oranges as Bostonians run out of funds to buy oranges. Boston's economy would become more depressed as its banks, losing funds to California's banks, are no longer able to finance local entrepreneurs even to the extent of maintaining payroll and employment levels.

The moral of this story is that in the absence of an active government policy to offset this regional cash-flow imbalance problem both regions are ultimately worse off. In a world of laissez-faire, the Californians would find their Bostonian customers becoming so impoverished that they would not be able to buy oranges unless the Californians either (a) continually 'lend' them funds to maintain purchases or (b) bought more products from Bostonians so they could afford to buy the additional oranges. It is unlikely that Californians, motivated solely by self-interest, would be so accommodating to reach a civilized solution. Instead, the free market result will be detrimental to all in the private sector of both regions.

Unfortunately, in the last two decades as the conservative view became dominant, the US government has not used its regional fiscal powers to resolve regional payments imbalances and thereby promote economic growth everywhere. The result has been a mug's game with a decline in overall national economic growth and a competition among each region to obtain gains at the expense of other regions.

In the case of international trade deficits there does not exist a global taxing and spending authority, or any other institutional arrangement to redress persistent trade imbalances that occur and that can unleash global recessionary forces. Yet the benefits of such an arrangement to residents of both deficit *and* surplus nations should be obvious from our Mountaintop and Coastal-land illustration.

Our analysis is not merely an interesting hypothetical illustration. Rather, as we have already explained, its message is supported by the facts of the Marshall Plan where both deficit and surplus nations benefited because a large trade surplus nation actively worked to prevent the build up of its claims on foreigners.

Unless the surplus nations buy additional imports, the trade deficit nations can not earn enough to pay for all it imports. Under the current floating rate system, those nations that currently run large export surpluses, for example, Japan and other Pacific rim nations, are unwilling to expand their purchases of US made goods *at the expense of their domestic industries*. For those nations to do so would mean that they would permit US job growth at the expense of creating unemployment in their own countries as their firms lose domestic sales to imported products. These lost sales mean lower profits and more unemployment at home – just when these nations are already experiencing significant profit disappointments and higher unemployment associated with either slow growth or recession. Under the current international system, nations that can achieve growth by policies that deliberately encourage exports to grow more rapidly than their demand for imports are rewarded by being able to maintain substantial job growth in their domestic industries. The 'economic miracle' of these nations is that their export markets are growing while their domestic industries are assured of dominant positions in the market at home.

Under the current international trading system, export surplus nations have no external or internal incentives to accept any responsibility to increase purchases of imports relative to export sales. The current system fails to produce a prosperous global environment because it resolves any persistent trade deficit problem by following the conservative wisdom of using external incentives to force a deficit nation to depress its economy in order to lower its citizens' income so that they cannot afford to buy as many goods (including imports) as before. This spreads contractionary forces *globally* by lowering employment and income in other nations' export industries. The result is that there are more than 38 million workers unemployed in all the OECD countries and 120 million globally.

WHAT CAN BE DONE TO ACHIEVE A CIVILIZED SOLUTION TO THE INTERNATIONAL PAYMENTS PROBLEM?

What is required are measures that encourage the major surplus nations to accept their *global* civic responsibilities by directly *spending* their export surplus on either more imports, direct new foreign investment, or grants to less developed nations (foreign aid).[10] In the best interests of international civilization, nations that run persistent trade surpluses must be educated to understand that by simply continuing to build up liquid claims against the rest of the world they endanger the progress of the entire global economic community. If we adopt a different international system those surplus nations will be able to exercise their civic responsibilities without fear that they may be punished by the market imposing external disincentives on their industries.

Unfortunately conservative economic analysis has provided a rationalization that asserts the entire fault of an international trade imbalance can be blamed on the deficit nation. One hopes that, in the longer run, public discussion of civilized economic policies will educate the decision-makers of all nations of the error of these conservative ways. Then, surplus nations will recognize that in the self-interest of the *global* community, excessive accumulation of foreign reserves must be prevented.

A civilized, cooperative, international policy of limiting reserve accumulations due to trade surpluses will generate a new economic golden age that can improve the economic well being of all nations. It will also stabilize the political basis for democratic modern capitalist development around the world. The conservative approach, on the other hand, will promote only dissention and political unrest as 'free' economies fail to deliver all the goods they are capable of producing.

To encourage surplus trade nations to meet the civil challenges of our global economy, the Marshall Plan should be held up as an historical illustration of how a civil international community gains when surplus nations meet their civil responsibilities. All nations should cooperate with the United States in this endeavour not because we threaten them, but because they, like us, value a civilized global economy.

As *New York Times* columnist Flora Lewis has noted many in high places recognize that we are heading for an economic crisis. Government and business leaders, however, prefer to try and muddle through as today's conservative rhetoric gives Panglossian platitudes the status of all-knowing wisdom. Unless forced by a crisis, these leaders will not take innovative actions. Of course, reform by crisis is better than no reform at all, but there is still time to avoid the crisis and to abandon the barbaric path that conservative policy has forced us on. We can steer a more civilized course if the United States is willing to take on a courageous leadership role in proposing a permanent international resolution of these global economic problems.

People must be educated to realize that a civilized international monetary system can be designed (as suggested at the end of this chapter). Such a system encourages trade surplus nations to initiate adjustment policies (as the US did under the Marshall Plan). Internal incentives have to be reinstituted that encourage the cooperation of all nations in the spirit of the Marshall Plan for improving global well being and, simultaneously, external incentives should be developed to make it costly not to cooperate.

Because the United States is still the world's strongest economy and biggest market, it must take the lead in fostering such a civilized approach.

RECURRING INTERNATIONAL CURRENCY CRISES

In a free market economy, whenever a debtor builds up a substantial debt relative to its current income receipts, creditors and other interested parties always worry whether the debtor will have enough liquidity to meet the next contractual obligation. This is true whether the debtor is a person, a business firm, or a nation. For example, in October 1994, Mexico's reserves totalled $17 billion. In December 1994, a Mexican government official announced that the country's reserves had dropped to $6 billion and to conserve its remaining reserves the government would permit the peso to fall by 53 centavos (or approximately 14 per cent).

This news caused many foreign holders of the $30 billion outstanding short-term Mexican government debt to worry whether Mexico would have sufficient international liquidity to meet its debt commitments. Fear of a further fall in the value of the peso and a default mounted. Many fund managers who held peso denominated assets felt it would be prudent to sell pesos and profitable to sell the peso short. The result was a disorderly decline in the value of the peso by 54 per cent as foreign reserves dropped to $2 billion by January 1995.

A complete collapse of the peso was prevented when the Clinton Administration provided an immediate $20 billion in direct US loans, and $10 billion more promised. International agencies such as the IMF promised another $20 billion in credits.[11] The purpose of this financial package was to convince fund managers that the Mexican government could defend the a lower peso value and it would not default on its short-term debt obligations. By assuring that all who wanted to sell their peso-denominated portfolio holdings they could do so at the current market price, the Clinton Administration hoped to convince most fund managers not to sell any of their peso assets.

The immediate impact of the Clinton rescue package was that many Wall Street fund managers took advantage of this peso to dollar guarantee and liquidated their peso holdings without any further loss. In the first two weeks after the loan package was announced, over $10 billion of the loan was spent redeeming pesos for dollars. In the absence of this emergency relief financial guarantee, the fund managers who unloaded their Mexican holdings would have suffered substantial additional dollar losses in liquidating their holdings in a declining peso market. Accordingly, this arrangement was characterized by many in the mass media as a 'bailout of Wall Street investors'.

By the end of May 1995, the Mexican government had already spent almost $23 billion. Over $15 billion of the borrowed funds were spent redeeming foreign holdings of short-term government debt. Another $4 billion went to help Mexican companies redeem their foreign debt. Almost $4 billion was used to permit depositors in Mexican banks to move their funds abroad (capital flight). Little of this emergency financing went to restore some of the loss in real income suffered by the Mexican population.

At the G7 summit in Canada in June 1995, the United States obtained tentative support for the principle of establishing a permanent 'emergency reserve fund' to be operated by the International Monetary Fund (IMF). The purpose of this G7 sponsored fund would be to permit the IMF to provide credits to any nations that suffer speculative attacks similar to the peso's experience in the winter of 1994–5. This emergency reserve fund policy for dealing with currency speculation crises in a flexible exchange rate system is merely a more organized form of the ad hoc interventions of central banks that have occurred between 1973 and 1994. In principle, it is neither innovative nor likely to end currency speculations from breaking out in the future.

Although the fall of the peso relative to the dollar was stopped by these loans, the peso crisis quickly led to a disorderly fall of the dollar relative to the yen and the deutsche mark. By March 1995, the *New York Times* noted that in global financial markets 'where image is often more important than reality . . . the dollar is being dragged down by the peso' while the German mark and Japanese yen appear to be the only 'safe harbors' to portfolio fund managers. By April, the dollar's plunge against the yen had gotten so severe that Japanese Finance Minister Takemura was quoted as questioning whether the system of free-floating exchange rates adopted in 1973 should be reconsidered so that governments had more influence over their currency.

Under the post-Bretton Woods floating rate system, foreign currencies are objects of speculation. In free global financial markets, any significant change in the exchange rate can create the opportunity to earn enormous profits (or suffer enormous losses) for people who manage large portfolios of liquid assets. Any whiff of a possible currency weakness can become a conflagration spread along the information highway as fund managers and multinational controllers, in search of speculative yields or safe harbours, move funds from one country to another in nanoseconds with a few clicks on a computer keyboard.

In Congressional testimony in March 1995, Federal Reserve Chairman Alan Greenspan stated that 'Mexico became the first casualty . . . of the new international financial system' that permits hot portfolio money to slosh around the world 'much more quickly'. Greenspan was explicitly recognizing that the 'new [conservative] international financial system' rewards self-interest oriented fund managers in plush offices who can slash the real income of the Mexican population almost in half as a result of their computer-generated moving of funds. There is no room for remorse in this 'new' system that will punish severely any fund managers, with a social conscience, who might hesitate to sell the peso if they knew the devastating impact this would have on the real income of the Mexican population.[12]

Finally, the possibility that other nations in Latin America or elsewhere can become additional casualties of the 'new international financial system', is implied in Chairman Greenspan's testimony. To prevent this dismal global scenario we must develop a permanent policy to prevent persistent international deficits and large-scale currency fires.

FIGHTING CURRENCY FIRES IN INTERNATIONAL CAPITAL MARKETS

Since 1973, the only acceptable defence against speculative excesses in the free exchange rate market is for the central banks of the major developed (G7) nations to intervene by buying the currency that is sinking. If the intervention is successful, the speculators will be convinced that there are no further profits to be made by betting on additional weakness in the currency. If not successful, the result will only further enrich the speculators who transfer claims to foreign reserves from the central banks to the accounts of the speculators. (This might be called the Soros Effect, in honour of fabled speculator George Soros who claims to have made billions speculating against the success of central bank interventions.)

Our experience with the peso and other currency crisis in recent years as well as the history of the sluggish growth of the post-Bretton Wood era should suggest, even to advocates of free international capital markets, that 'hot money' portfolio flows can have massive disruptive real effects. What is required in this global economy with computer linked financial markets is not a system of 'ad hoc' central bank interventions or even IMF emergency funds interventions. During the time between when the speculative crises breaks out and the international institution(s) decide that the free market can not extinguish the currency fire and therefore intervenes with sufficient firefighting funds, the 'new international financial system' can severely burn the real economy. What is necessary is to build permanent fireproofing rules and structures that prevent imagery-induced speculative currency fires. Crisis prevention rather than crisis rescues must be the primary long-term objective of a civilized global economic system.

Conservatives, on the other hand, argue that any attempt to limit financial speculation in today's free global capital markets is a violation of the civil liberty of free self-interested individuals to choose what they want to do with their funds. (Relying on phrases that indicate 'freedom of choice' and 'civil liberties', this argument indicates how language matters in public discussions and how conservatives have captured and twisted the civil dialect to their own political ends.)

In a civilized society, however, it is not a violation of civil liberties to prohibit people from boarding an airplane with a gun. Moreover, no one would think we are impinging on individual rights if the society prohibits entering a movie theatre with a Molotov cocktail in one hand and a book of matches in the other – even if the person indicates they have no desire to burn down the theatre. Yet, in the name of free markets, we permit fund managers to imagine an exploding Molotov cocktail and then yell 'fire' in the crowded international financial markets any time the 'image' of a possible profitable fire moves them.

More than a half-century ago, Keynes recognized the danger inherent in free international capital markets that permit self-interested individuals to speculate on foreign currencies or to seek safe harbours whenever the fear of currency weakness moves them. Keynes wrote:

> there is not a country which can . . . safely allow the flight of funds [hot money]. . . . Equally there is no country that can safely receive . . . [these portfolio] funds which cannot be used for fixed investment [to build plant and equipment].

In other words, a civilized global economy should not permit people to move funds to other nations simply to make short-term speculative exchange rate profits (or avoid losses). If fund managers are not willing to make long-term commitments to leave international funds invested in illiquid but productive plant and equipment (whose economic value can not be readily repatriated), then it may be necessary to develop institutions that create internal and external incentives that prevent these international hot money flows from occurring.

Permitting self-interested individuals to move funds in search of speculative exchange rate profits or to avoid losses can create economic catastrophes for both the receiving nation and the nation from which the funds are departing. Just as civilized society has an absolute prohibition on yelling fire in a crowded auditorium, so must a civilized economic system institute laws that make the movement of large speculative funds impossible.

REFORMING THE WORLD'S MONEY TO RESTORE THE GOLDEN AGE

There is an urgent need to reform the international payments system to prevent future debt problems and currency crises. If we do not, the global economy might easily collapse into another Great Depression similar to the 1930s. Even if a major collapse does not occur in the near future, international monetary reform is needed if we are not to perpetuate the poor global economic performance of the post-1973 flexible rate era. The only question is with what do we replace the current system.

To restore the conditions of the 1950–73 global golden age, we must design a new civilized international monetary system around an institution for settling international payments (a clearing house) which has pre-agreed upon rules for (1) an orderly method of fixing the values of national currencies and (2) a mechanism for encouraging nations that pile up 'excessive' credits at the clearing house as a result of running persistent large trade surpluses to put these credits to work to create jobs around the world. To gain international cooperation, this clearing house should be designed so that it does not require any nation to surrender control of its domestic banking system or its fiscal policy.

To accomplish this we propose that the major nations of the world reach agreement on a clearing house that obeys the following five principles:

1.   The unit of account for measuring account balances at the clearing house and hence the ultimate reserve asset for international transactions is the International Money Clearing Unit (IMCU). IMCU's are held *only* by the central banks of each nation (and not the public) as deposits at the clearing house. Consequently, all major private international transactions must clear between central banks' deposit accounts in the books of the clearing house.

2.   Each nation's central bank guarantees one-way convertibility in terms of providing a specific number of units of domestic currency for any IMCU units offered to it by other central banks. Thus, for example, a US importer requiring French francs to pay for imported Bordeaux wine would pay dollars to his or her bank. The importer's banker would then send

these dollars (less commission) to the Federal Reserve. The Federal Reserve would settle the importer's debt by transferring IMCUs from its account at the clearing house to the Bank of France's account. Upon receipt of the IMCUs, the Bank of France would deposit the required francs in the French wine exporter's bank in Paris.

3.   The exchange rate between each nation's currency and the IMCU is set *initially* by each nation – just as it would be under an international gold standard. Once set, this rate will remain unchanged except for conditions discussed in proviso 5 below.

4.   A trigger mechanism would be in place that encourages any creditor nation to spend what is deemed (in advance) by agreement of the international community to be *'excessive' credit balances* at the clearing house. This trigger mechanism would prevent a nation from persistently piling up credits (international liquidity) at the clearing house by selling more to other nations than it buys from others.

At the option of the creditor, these excessive credits can be spent in any combination of three ways: (a) on the exports of any other nation member of the clearing house, (b) on direct foreign investment projects, and (c) to provide a Marshall Plan form of foreign aid to deficit members.

In the unlikely event that the surplus nation does not exercise its civil responsibility and spend or give away all these excessive credits within a specified time, then an external incentive will be imposed to encourage such actions. This external incentive will be a continuing tax that would be assessed by the clearing agency and paid out of the excessive credit balances until the remainder of the excess credits were exhausted.

The revenues from this tax could be used in a number of ways. For example, the credits could be used to provide relief for nations suffering from natural disasters or wars. In particular, efforts could be made to competitively procure necessary supplies from businesses in deficit nations when possible. If no other spending projects are possible, then the revenues could be distributed among the deficit nations according to a pre-agreed formula based on need.

This last resort tax action by the managers of the clearing house represents an external incentive for the nation to spend its excessive credits. Since any surplus nation can always spend its excessive reserves to buy things, invest in productive plant and equipment, or give gifts to others, it is not likely that the clearing house managers would ever have to tax such balances.

Proviso 4 recognizes that those nations that persistently run trade surpluses are earning income which they refuse to spend and in so doing are creating unemployment in the export industries of their trading partners.

Proviso 4 creates the civil guidelines and incentives for all nations to behave as if Say's Law was operative to achieve the global full employment result that conservatives merely presume will occur naturally in a laissez-faire market system.

Our trigger mechanism produces a different remedy than the belt-tightening proposal of conservatives. We provide debtor nations the opportunity to work harder and produce more that can be sold as exports abroad and thereby earn additional income. In essence, we create incentives to encourage debtors to work their way out of debt while simultaneously residents of surplus nations have the opportunity to obtain more goods and services without having to work harder. Belt-tightening conservative policies, on the other hand, try to remedy persistent trade deficits by depressing the economy of both the deficit and the surplus trading nations. The conservative remedy is a recipe for making the average citizen of both nations worse off.

The hoarded excessive credits provide the necessary wherewithal for the trade surplus nation to take action to show its civic responsibility to the global community. By disgorging these excessive credits, the responsible creditor nation solves the current account imbalance problem by promoting global economic expansion and prosperity. Yet, the surplus country has considerable discretion in deciding what combination of the three ways of accepting the onus of adjustment is in its citizens' best interests. Under our trigger mechanism, excessive credits become the Black Queen in an international game of Old Maid and must be passed on to others who can make better use of her. In this international game, however, there are no losers. As in all civilized games, all participants are winners who reap benefits.

5. The initially fixed exchange rates between the local currency and the IMCU would be devalued only to reflect inflationary increases in the domestic costs of producing goods. If, for example, Canada is experiencing 5 per cent inflation, then Canada's central bank would have to provide 5 per cent more units of domestic currency for each IMCU offered to it. Thus, every central bank is assured that its holdings of IMCUs at the clearing house will never lose purchasing power in terms of buying foreign produced goods, even if a foreign government permits inflation within its borders. Consequently this proviso prevents any nation from passing the inflation malady to others. Each nation must cure its own inflation disease in the civilized manner discussed in Chapter 9.

One beneficial effect of fixing exchange rates in terms of provisos 3 and 5 is that this eliminates the possibility that a specific industry in any nation can be put at a competitive disadvantage (or secure a competitive advantage) against foreign producers solely because the exchange rate changes independently of inflationary changes in domestic production costs. In other words, exchange rate variability *per se* can no longer create the problem of a domestic industry losing (or gaining) its global competitiveness simply because its currency is overvalued (or undervalued). For example, during the period 1982–5 the US dollar appreciated dramatically and became overvalued. As a result important manufacturing industries in the American 'rust belt' lost their competitiveness and were forced to retrench or shut down completely. The impact on the workers in the area was devastating. By the end of the 1980s, the dollar had fallen dramatically and the skeletal remains of these rust belt industries were again competitive. Unfortunately in the interim some plants were permanently closed and scrapped so that the competitive reversal could not revive the communities or restore the dignity of workers devastated by plant closings.

Under our five-point proposal, there will be some self-interest incentives for surplus nations to cooperate with the deficit nations in working out the adjustment processes utilized. The existence of this international arrangement assures the surplus nation that there will be similar cooperative measures in the future should the tables be turned. One reason that many nations currently hoard their surpluses as reserves instead of spending them is that they fear that the trade pattern may change against them in the future, as they have in the past. Under the current conservative philosophy, the only protection against such an adverse change of events is to use current trade surpluses to build up the nation's liquidity reserves[13] to protect oneself against such unforeseen calamities.

A cooperative international economic community that promotes expansionary tendencies can result in increased productivity and greater economic well being for all. The resulting mixed capitalist system, where the community encourages the conditions for an overall expansionary growth environment while permitting private production and marketing decisions can only reinvigorate the tremendous potential of the existing resources of all nations.

Some will complain that this five-point proposal is too innovative, too utopian. The problems facing the global economy are resolvable, but not easily resolved. If we start with the defeatist attitude that it is too difficult to change the awkward international system that we are enmeshed in, then no progress will be made. We will doom future generations of workers to stagnant employment opportunities where in many nations the people with jobs will work harder just to stay even while more people join the ranks of the persistently unemployed.

Indeed such defeatist views must be rejected. We must explore proposals that promote global growth to provide work and income for workers and residents of all nations. We are proposing international cooperation in an endeavour to make a global civilized society. Unless progress is made on this issue, the dismal science of economics will be condemning the global capitalist economy of the twenty-first century to a bleak future just at the time when it has won the war against the communistic economic system.

Notes

1. *The Economist* magazine (6 January 1990) indicated that the decade of he 1980s will be noted as one in which 'the experiment with floating currencies failed'. Almost two years earlier (17 February 1987), the *Financial Times* admitted that 'floating exchange rates, it is now clear, were sold on a false prospectus ... they held out a quite illusory promise of greater national autonomy ... [but] when macropolicies are inconsistent and when capital is globally mobile, floating rates cannot be relied upon to keep the current accounts roughly in balance'.

2. In its international trade version, Say's Law implies that the only permanent demand for imports from foreigners is obtained by supplying goods to foreigners, that is, supply for exports produces its own demand for imports. Thus, in the long run, persistent deficits in the balance of payments are impossible.

3. The 1993 North American Free Trade Agreement (NAFTA) was promoted to the American people by the Clinton Administration on the promise that it would deliver an expansion of high paying jobs in export industries selling goods to Mexicans without increasing the inflationary tendencies in the US. With the plunge of the peso during the winter of 1994–5, Mexico was forced to depress its economy as a requirement for IMF loans (see footnote 11). America's trade surplus with Mexico turned to a deficit estimated to be $12 billion in 1995. Not only has the promised net increase in jobs for Americans because of NAFTA expected expansion of exports to Mexico vanished in a puff of exchange rate smoke, but more than 700,000 export related jobs in the United States have been put in jeopardy by the peso collapse.

4. The Marshall Plan was even offered to the Soviet Union who refused it.

5. Mexico and Brazil have defaulted or threatened default several times since 1979. To lighten their intolerable international debt burden, partial debt forgiveness has been provided for many nations including the former French colonies in Africa, Egypt and Mexico.

6. The 1994 current account balance has risen substantially and the 1995 current account balance is expected to rise further despite the fact that the personal savings ratio of Americans have been rising from less than 3.5 per cent in the 1980s to 4 per cent in 1994 and a projected 5.5 per cent in 1995.

7. This regional division is the result of regional fears that existed when the Federal Reserve System was set up in 1913. The country was divided into

12 Federal Reserve Districts with a separate Federal Reserve Bank in each district (for example, Boston, New York, Philadelphia, Cleveland, Richmond, Atlanta, Chicago, St Louis, Minneapolis, Kansas City, Dallas, San Francisco).

8. If the reader doubts this, he or she should look at the US currency in his or her pocket. To the left of the portrait on the face of each bill is a seal indicating which of the 12 Federal Reserve Banks issued that particular piece of currency. Most people will find they have currency from more than one of the District Banks – but that they treat each Bank's issue interchangeably – because the exchange rate between the currencies is always fixed. Yet it was not too many years ago, that each District Federal Reserve Bank would send currency issued by other District Banks found circulating in its region back to the issuing bank for redemption.

9. Just as the Authorities always assure that the exchange rate between dimes and dollars is ten to one.

10. In the analytical dialect of conservative economics, whenever there is a 'market failure' there is a role for government institutions to fill the gap. When peoples or nations behaviour violates Say's Law, then, analytically honest conservatives, must admit there is a market failure on a grand scale.

11. Sarah Kerr has quoted Michael Camdessus, the Director of the IMF, as endorsing these Mexican loans 'since Mexico has been an exemplar of the approach . . . recommended by the international community'. Camdessus indicated that the 'IMF had a responsibility' to support Mexico since it had accepted the IMF's advice for 'a market based approach [that] forces its economy to contract'.

12. Mexico's Secretary of Labor, Santiago Onate Laborde, estimates that approximately 6 million Mexicans, almost 19 per cent of the labour force, were unemployed six months after the peso crisis.

13. For example, after the first oil price shock of 1973, Japan ran huge payments deficits. No nation came to assist her. Only by running down previously built up foreign reserves was Japan able to weather the storm of the mid-1970s.

11 A Final Summing Up

A civilized society encourages its citizens to excel in all the endeavours they undertake. The motto of a civilized society is 'if a thing is worth doing it is worth doing well'. A civilized society encourages the maintenance of love and loyalty to the community, sensitivity and compassion to the needs of others, open and honest dealing with others, and all actions necessary to perpetuate and strengthen the civil order of the community. To motivate all its citizens to behave in a civil manner while achieving these objectives, a prosperous civil society adopts a set of rules (or laws) that combine *self-interest* and *civic values* so that its citizens may enjoy the benefits of each.

During the last forty years in the public debate over economic policy, self-interest and civic values have been offered as incompatible alternative guiding principles for the government of our nation. Conservatives have pursued prosperity through self-interested individuals acting in a market system free of any government interference. Liberals have sought justice and compassion in the society at all costs. One camp strives solely for competitiveness and the survival of the fittest, while the other focuses primarily on fairness in dealing with others and the sharing of our national product. The tragedy is that neither side recognizes that humans can be motivated both by self-interest and civic values to produce a prosperous and civil society. Self-interest and civic values are both part of the American national character and our heritage. Both can be preserved and strengthened by the rules that make a prosperous nation and a civil global community.

The single-minded pursuit of conservative policies which we have witnessed in recent years does not free individuals from the intervention of its national institutions. Instead, through the natural rate of unemployment philosophy conservatives perpetuate a barbaric role for government, and uncivilized treatment of the weak in our society. This does not necessarily imply that conservatives are intentionally malicious and mean-spirited. Honest and well-meaning attempts to devise public policy in strict accordance with conservative philosophy inevitably erodes the civic values that support effective government.

The effects of years of conservative policies that motivate solely through appeals to fear and appetite (greed) have been witnessed across the nation. Since Ronald Reagan's supply-side tax cuts in early 1980s, in order to achieve better compliance with the tax laws government has tried bribing taxpayers (particularly the wealthier ones) by cutting their tax rates. At the same time government has encouraged an aggressive Internal Revenue Service to create terror in the hearts of all citizens through its auditing procedures. The result is that many of our citizens see the IRS and other governmental employees, who have taken an oath to obey and enforce the laws of the nation, as the enemy who should be lied to, castigated, and even shot at. Taxes are perceived not as the responsibility that citizens must make towards maintaining a civil society, but as simply an attempt to reduce the self-interest activity of every taxpayer by taking away their income.

To resolve any trade imbalance between nations, conservatives have argued that the weaker of the two nations should be the one to make adjustments by 'tightening their belts', that is, the trade deficit nation should deliberately lower the living standards of its people. Not surprisingly, over time the people who have suffered under the rule of these policies have learned to hate and despise their governments and the international agencies such as the International Monetary Fund that are required to support such barbaric policies. Despite the pain and grief caused by these conservative policy recommendations, the basic problems these policies were intended to address remain not only unresolved but continually festering.

The last 25 years of American economic history have been unduly shaped by the barbaric conservative policy of planned recession. To fight inflation, the government has intentionally depressed the economy so that workers will be so fearful of losing their jobs that they will not demand inflationary wage increases. Those who follow the conservative philosophy have been dominant in both political parties. It is in opposition to those who blindly follow the conservative dictums that we largely direct this book. As the political pendulum continues it swing to conservatism, we are being governed by a generation of political leaders and an electorate that has forgotten (or never learned) the tragic history of the Great Depression and its barbaric impact on most of the families in America. They have forgotten the grim situation President Roosevelt faced when one third of our nation was ill-fed and ill-housed despite the fact that the economy had sufficient resources to provide a comfortable standard of living for all its citizens. Roosevelt noted that 'the only thing we have to fear is fear itself'. In removing fear (the main weapon of conservative economics) Roosevelt and his successors through the 1960s adopted elements of an economic revolution that first made the United States and then ultimately most of the free world a more civil and prosperous place.

A swing to any extreme, as we have experienced with conservatism in recent decades, tends to bring forth the outstanding flaws of the system. As we noted in Chapter 5, the planned economies of Eastern Europe and China, with their preoccupation with full employment and equitable income distribution, lost the ability to motivate people to work hard, innovate, and produce excellence in all its endeavours. The result was a collapse of the planned state economic system and a swing to the other extreme where there are massive inequalities in income and many who would be willing to work cannot find a job. The democratic mix of markets and civil values enabled the capitalist system to win the war with communism. In the last quarter century, however, there has been a·slow erosion of the civilized economic base and a slippage towards the barbaric laissez-faire system that required a significant number of people to be relegated to a perpetual underclass to maintain an inflation free environment.

We want to modify the picture presented by the conservative cult of the entrepreneur, but there are better and worse ways to make this change. To abandon the fuel of self-interest which drives us towards entrepreneurial excellence would be an incredible waste. Instead, we must work quickly to develop an ideology and a set of policies which will enable us to enjoy the benefits of both self-interest and civic values.

WHERE DO WE START?

Our understanding of economics can drastically alter the world in which we live, as demonstrated by the story of Arthur Laffer and his supply-side cocktail napkin. The power of the people to discuss and debate the real economic issues of our nation and the emerging global economic community face is all too often underestimated. People discuss economics all of the time; on the shop floor, in the board room, in the cafeteria, at the bar, on the softball field, in the kitchen, and on radio and television talk-shows. Since economics, as we see it, is built not only on the self-interest of the people, but also on their civic values, then our national economic debates must necessarily take place in part among the people who will be governed (and will govern themselves!) in accordance with national economic policy.

The use of an impenetrable analytical dialect by economic experts can sometimes be a bit overwhelming, but the secret behind the jargon is that the basic issues are normally quite simple. Although we want the excellence of experts in implementing our economic policies, it is our duty as citizens to formulate the goals America should pursue. This duty is combined with self-interest through the institution known as democracy – the election process enlists the self-interest of the candidates to listen to the citizens and to address their concerns. Even if one vote seems small in a nation of millions, to cast a vote properly, after using one's judgment and consideration, is to achieve the civic excellence which the Founding Fathers had hoped for in the American people.

Our understanding of economics must also be shaped in the forum of debate in our academic institutions and think-tanks. Unfortunately, by gaining control of the economic budgets of these institutions, conservatives have controlled the dialogue that is permitted in their halls. Despite their professed belief in the open and free market for goods and services, conservatives have not encouraged an open and free debate on economics in the intellectual marketplace of academia and think-tanks. By gaining control of what is acceptable thought in economics, the intellectual fortress of conservative economics has not had to weather critical analysis by what they perceive as their peers.

In order to look towards harvesting our resources of civic values as well as those of self-interest, we must establish a common language of analysis in which to discuss both of these forces in the public debate. It is necessary to place the generalized sentiments of civic values into a more analytically rigorous structure, and at the same time, the rigid technical analysis of self-interest provided by conservative economics must be unwound, so that we can examine the general philosophical premises upon which it is built.

We have identified the force behind civic values in terms of internal incentives, which motivate behavior to do a task 'for its own sake' in accordance with a set of ideals established within a community. This is in contrast to the external incentives of self-interest in conservative economics, which motivates people to do things only by fear and appetite.

We saw how a society based solely on self-interest would eventually lose the institutions that support civilized behavior. We also showed how a careless combination of internal and external incentives could render one or both useless in motivating desirable economic behaviour. By carefully utilizing existing institutions of family, community, and nation, we can safely combine self-interest and civic values to achieve civilized outcomes.

Since we were presenting a view quite at odds with the picture given in conventional economics, we turned to the obvious question of what's wrong with economists? In general, the answer is that the profession of economics has bound itself inexorably to an analytic structure known as the classical model. This model focuses solely on self-interest, and thus not only blinds most economists to the influences and importance of civic values in motivating behaviour; but it also reveals an incomplete and unrealistic view of the role of self-interest itself. Consequently, even complicated and sophisticated computer simulations based on this classical model retain these basic flaws and hence are faulty in both their ability to explain and to predict behaviour. Thus, even an economist with civilized intentions is left facing the same problem as a pacifist who works in a gun shop – he can't use his professional skills to pursue his ethical principles.

We have developed four major concepts that are essential to a civilized economic analysis but are absent from conservative economics:

Civic values are not the same as the conservative concept of individual preferences. When conservatives refer to preferences for love, duty, honour, justice, and excellence, they can, at most, be describing deteriorated forms of civic values. In a healthy civil community, civic values can not be exchanged for money, nor do they exhibit the other aspects of self-interest which conservatives attribute to all goods. On the other hand, these civic values can provide a positive-sum for society, delivering benefits without a compensating cost being inflicted elsewhere.

Civic values come from the civil community. Ideals and standards exist only within a community. People develop their individuality and sense of self *from* their membership in one or more communities. A community provides internal incentives to its members, and as the resulting civil society evolves, so do those internal incentives.

Civilized Government is the process by which we combine self-interest and civic values into institutions. These institutions, when properly designed, protect civic values from the corrosive effects of self-interest. At the same time, institutions make use of productive forms of self-interest, enabling people to enjoy the products of both. Effective government must change with the times, adapting old principles and institutions to emerging conditions.

Civic values can be enjoyed only when there is civic virtue. Self-interest is relatively straight forward; effort and cleverness are all that are needed for individuals to reap its rewards by following its dictates. Civic values are equally important, but more complex. For people to enjoy civic values, they must be constantly vigilant in order to protect and maintain the institutions of their civilization from the erosion of barbaric self-interest tendencies.

Civic virtue is necessary for society to enjoy the benefits of civilization. This virtue *cannot* be pursued solely by each person calculating his own self-interest in terms of costs and benefits. For those who subscribe to a conservative philosophy, the rewards associated with civilization must seem unattainable.

CIVILIZED ECONOMIC POLICIES

Our argument has shown that civilized economic policies require an effort to create a shared dialect of purpose and responsibilities in establishing any new economic institution to meet the evolving economic changes. Civic values provide an additional resource to strengthen civilized economic policies. If government is to make use of internal incentives, then the civic values of the public are of critical importance. This places our economic debate back where all of our important national debates should be held: in the forum of concepts and ideals which make up our nation.

In this book we have discussed a number of major initiatives which can make beneficial use of the unique role government must play in a modern economy. Not only does government have the capacity to combine both internal and external incentives in strengthening our interdependent economy, but government's vantage as a major economic actor not driven by self interests permits government to take actions on behalf of the economy as a whole.

Our conclusions regarding specific civilized economic policies can be summarized as follows:

Reviving the post World War II International Civil Community. We must create a more civilized approach to international debt and balance of payments problems so that the world's trade surplus nations recognize that it is not only in their self-interest, but also their global civic responsibility to avoid excessive surplus by living up to their means. Such a change in international attitudes would benefit all nations. It would be best to create institutions which operate similarly to the civilized institutions that we urge for controlling domestic money and inflation problems. We have, however, momentarily lost the opportunity to build on the sound foundation laid at Bretton Woods, an international monetary authority similar to a civilized central bank.

Under President Nixon we permitted the potential foundations for an international civilized economic system to begin to erode. The erosion has continued under Ford, Carter, Reagan, Bush and Clinton. The United States is now the world's largest debtor and hence no longer has the economic power to create unilaterally a civilized international economic order as we did at Bretton Woods, and with the Marshall Plan later in the 1940s. The virtue of our earlier actions, however, cannot be erased from the history books. So while the actions of the American Administrations since 1973 have wasted much of the good will created by Nixon's four predecessors, some credibility can still reside in our words and actions. The United States did commit its economic resources to a civilized international economic order when we had the opportunity. Now others share that pleasant vantage, and its accompanying responsibilities. But the United States can help by word and deed to design such a civilized system.

Taxed-based Incomes Policy (TIP). TIP provides an external disincentive to those who, motivated solely by self-interest to increase their share of the GDP pie, contribute to inflation. Unlike the conservative policy of a natural rate of unemployment to fight inflation, however, TIP's effects are directed solely at those whose behaviour generates inflation – not at the economy as a whole including innocent bystanders. Although built upon external incentives, TIP also requires the establishment of civic norms which place TIP in the context of an economic system which promotes excellence in entrepreneurship and full employment.

Commodity Buffer Stocks. Buffer stocks allow governments to pre-empt volatile (and unproductive) swings in commodity prices, such as those experienced with oil, grains, etc., in the 1970s and 1980s. Government buffer stocks can be released to fill the shortfall when natural calamities occur. Moreover, the existence of these buffer stocks will deter the economic aggression of foreign and domestic suppliers which induce artificial shortages (as did OPEC). Moreover, if producers innovate and increase production from existing resources, a buffer stock policy assures the entrepreneurs who increase productivity that their income will not be adversely affected by any resulting temporary glut. Thus, there is never a self-interest in suppressing any technological improvement that might otherwise cause temporary overprotection. In other words, a properly designed buffer stock policy will not only prevent the disruptive effects of any temporary (natural or deliberate) shortages but it will also help stabilize the income of commodity producers at a level which encourages the rapid growth in productivity of essential basic commodities.

Fiscal stabilization of the business cycle. In an entrepreneurial economy, the independent decisions of millions of independent enterprises will sometimes move the economy towards recession. By increasing its purchases from the private sector, government can insure full utilization of America's productive capacity. This not only makes it possible to provide better government services, but also generates income into the hands of self-interested businessmen and households who will spend it elsewhere in the economy as they see fit. Fiscal policy should be designed not to fill in the valleys of recession and shave off the peaks of prosperity in the business cycle. Fiscal policy should be designed to insure that the economy moves continuously along the peaks of prosperity.

Tax Reform. Civilized tax reform can enlist the voluntary compliance which is necessary to reap the billions per year in taxes which are never collected due to noncompliance. More importantly, tax reform is needed to re-establish the civilized relationship between taxpayers and their nation. When we choose as a nation to require citizens to pay taxes, we take on the responsibility to create (and maintain) the civic context which supports such activity. *In a civilized society where civic values and self-interest flourish, the citizens must be willing not only to die for their country but also to pay for it.*

Unfortunately, the current conservative culture regarding taxpaying does not promote the civic virtue in paying one's taxes. Even worse, it provides a veneer of self-righteous encouragement to tax cheaters.

We have identified here a number of civilized alternatives to the way we govern. If we try to enlist both self-interest and civic virtues, we may be able to muster all of our resources to address whatever new challenges emerge. However, a civilized perspective is not enough. While sincere efforts are a necessary beginning, there may not be enough virtue in sincerity to govern our nation. We must be as wise and shrewd as possible, so that we can see justice through the haze of circumstance that surrounds our complex public issues, and so that we can out-think those whose self-interest would otherwise take advantage – and pervert – our government of laws.

THE EVOLVING ECONOMY

In his *Tales of a New America* Secretary of Labor Robert Reich suggested that the evolution of our economic system is reducing the applicability of the conservative economic vision. Economic conditions which once may have provided some support for the conservative myth have continued to evolve. This conservative view envisioned business as a small, single-factory firm led by a single, profit-driven entrepreneur. In the last half century, however, the evolution of our enterprise economy has accelerated. Today, a typical business must coordinate hundreds of factories and other facilities to efficiently provide the thousands of diverse products and services that make up the current American standard of living. As production has become more complex and interdependent, coordination and finance of these complex production processes has emerged as a major entrepreneurial problem. This evolutionary trend increases the value of cooperative patterns of behavior as compared to the individualistic competition of the conservative philosophy.

The failures of some of the liberal practices instituted in the 1960s made the conservative picture *seem* attractive once again. But the nature of the development of our economic environment has not reverted back to this earlier era of the individualistic entrepreneur – only our economic philosophy has. And it is this regression toward nineteenth-century Social Darwinism which threatens the viability of our 21th century global economic community.

REVITALIZING THE NATIONAL COMMUNITY

> We will ever strive for the ideals and the sacred things of the polis, both alone and with the many.
> We will unceasingly seek to quicken the sense of public duty.
> We will revere and obey the laws of the polis.
> We will transmit this polis not only not less, but greater, better and more beautiful than it was transmitted to us.
>
> Oath of the Athenian City State

By this oath the ancient Athenians committed themselves to the pursuit of excellence in the practice of citizenship – an excellence demonstrated by how well the people governed themselves and their nation. We practise our citizenship by actively participating in our national institutions – by which we mean customs and traditions as well as more formal structures. We are all participating in the real government of our nation in the way we lead our lives, whether it be by apathy or activism, by cheating 'the system' or living up to our commitments. The ultimate responsibility for maintaining our civilization is in the same hands that have created it – We the People. If we strive for our national ideals, seek to 'quicken the sense of public duty', and voluntarily comply with the rules necessary to govern society, we will be able to transmit to the next generation an American Civilization of which we can be rightly proud.

The pivotal word in the Oath of Athens is 'transmit' – the Athenians understood that time brought change to all institutions, and that the duty of each generation was to overcome the challenges that history brought in order to bestow to their children a better world. The United States Constitution echoes this spirit in proclaiming that we are 'to secure the blessing of liberty to ourselves and our posterity.' A society thrives when its members can sustain the integrity and strength of the values of its civilization across history. This practice of civic excellence requires that we adapt our social institutions to changing economic and political conditions. It is not enough to create a set of civilized institutions at one moment in time. As a changing world leads to the erosion of the old understandings, we must be prepared to recreate our institutions; to reaffirm the meaning of 'We the People'. It is our hope that this volume will help our society rediscover the way towards a civilized economy as we attempt to resolve the economic problems of the last years of the twentieth century.

Sources and References

Preface to the First Edition

William Stanley Jevons, *The Theory of Political Economy* (New York: Augustus M. Kelley Bookseller, Reprints of Economics Classics, 1965).

1   The Pursuit of Civilization

Thomas J. Peters and Robert H. Waterman, *In Search of Excellence* (New York: Harper & Row, Warner Books, 1984).

Gary Wills, *Reagan's America: Innocents at Home* (Garden City, New York: Doubleday, 1987).

Milton Friedman, *Capitalism and Freedom* (Chicago: University of Chicago Press, 1962).

George F. Will, *Statecraft as Soulcraft* (New York: Simon & Schuster, Touchstone Books, 1984).

Adam Smith, *An Inquiry into the Nature and Causes of the Wealth of Nations* (New York: Random House, The Modern Library, 1937).

John Maynard Keynes, *The General Theory of Employment, Interest and Money* (New York: Harcourt Brace Jovanovich, 1936).

John Cornwall, 'Notes on the Trade Cycle and Social Philosophy of Post-Keynesian Economics', in *The Second Edition of the General Theory*, edited by G. C. Harcourt and P. Riach (London: Macmillan, 1996).

Amitai Etzioni, *The Moral Dimension* (New York: Free Press, 1988).

Thomas Hobbes, *Leviathan* (Indianapolis: Bobbs-Merrill, Library of Liberal Arts, 1958).

Jeremy Bentham, 'Principles of Morals and Legislation', in *The World's Greatest Books*, vol. XIV (New York: McKinlay, Stone & Mackenzie, 1910).

The example of goal displacement comes to us from Gary R. Orren, Professor of Public Policy at Harvard's Kennedy School of Government.

Robert B. Reich, *The Next American Frontier* (New York: Times Books, 1983).

William Safire, 'The Crisis of Institutional Loyalty' in the *New York Times*, 18 August 1986.

Robert N. Bellah, Richard Madsen, William M. Sullivan, Ann Swidler, and Steven M. Tipton, *Habits of the Heart: Individualism and Commitment in American Life* (New York: Harper & Row, Perennial Library, 1985). The Madison quotation is from Theodore Draper, 'Hume and Madison: The Secrets of Federalist Paper No. 10', *Encounter 58*, February 1982.

Lester C. Thurow, *The Zero-Sum Society* (New York: Basic Books, 1980).

Niccolo Machiavelli, *Discourses*, in Bondanella and Musa, *The Portable Machiavelli* (New York: Penguin Books, 1979).

Stuart M. Speiser, *Lawsuit* (New York: Horizon Books, 1980).

2   The Demise of Liberal Economics and the Emergence of Conservatism

Blinder, Alen S. *Hard Heads, Soft Heath: Tough Minded Economics for a Just Surely* (New York: Wesley-Addison, 1987).

George Gilder, *Wealth and Poverty* (New York: Bantam Books, 1982).
David A. Stockman, *The Triumph of Politics: How the Reagan Revolution Failed* (New York: Harper & Row, 1985).
Niccolo Machiavelli, *The Prince*, in Bondanella and Musa, *The Portable Machiavelli* (New York: Penguin Books, 1979).
W. H. Auden, *Selected Poems*, 'The Shield of Achilles' (New York: Vintage Books, 1979).
Edith Stokey and Richard Zeckhauser, *A Primer for Policy Analysis* (New York: W. W. Norton, 1978).
Aristotle, *Politics*, Book III, as translated by Ernest Barker, *The Politics of Aristotle* (New York: Oxford University Press, 1981).

3 The Political Economy of Civilization

Christopher Lasch, *The Culture of Narcissism: American Life in an Age of Diminishing Expectations* (New York: W. W. Norton, 1978).
Mancur Olson, *The Logic of Collective Action: Public Goods and the Theory of Groups* (Cambridge, Mass: Harvard University Press, 1965).
Thomas J. Peters and Robert H. Waterman, *In Search of Excellence*.
Lee Iacocca with William Novak, *Iacocca: An Autobiography* (New York: Bantam Books, 1980).
John T. Dunlop, *Dispute Resolution* (Dover, Mass: Auburn House Publishing, 1984).
Steven Kelman, *What Price Incentives? Economists and the Environment* (Dover, Mass: Auburn House Publishing, 1981).
Robert N. Bellah, *et al.*, *Habits of the Heart*.
Nation's Business, April 1968.
Pertschuk, Michael, 'Language Matters', *The Nation* 26 June 1995.
Berque, Philip J. and Scott, Robert E., *Washington Post Op-Ed Page*, 17 July 1987.
Barry Schwartz, 'Reinforcement-Induce Behavioral Stereotypy: How not to teach people to discover rules', *Journal of Experimental Psychology*, vol. 111, no. 1, 1982.
Thomas C. Schelling, *Macromotives and Microbehavior* (New York: W. W. Norton, 1978).
Benjamin Barber, 'A New Language for the Left: Translating the Conservative Discourse', *Harper's Magazine*, vol. 20, November 1986.

4 What's Wrong with Economists?

Robert B. Reich, *The Next American Frontier* (New York: Times Books, 1983).
Walter Bagehot quotation as given by J. M. Keynes in his *Treatise on Money*, vol. II (London: Macmillan, 1930).
Robert M. Solow, 'Economic History and Economics', in *The American Economic Review*, vol. 75, no. 2, May 1985.
Paul A. Samuelson, 'Classical and Neoclassical Theory', in *Monetary Theory*, edited by R. W. Clower (London: Penguin, 1969).
J. M. Keynes, *The General Theory of Employment, Interest and Money*.
John Maynard Keynes, *A Tract on Monetary Reform* (London: Macmillan, 1923).

5 The Entrepreneurial Market System vs. State Socialism

J. M. Keynes, *The General Theory of Employment, Interest and Money.*

6 Why Taxpayers Pay their Taxes

Jude Wanniski, *The Way the World Works* (New York: Basic Books, 1978).
David A. Stockman, *The Triumph of Politics.*
George Gilder, *Wealth and Poverty.*
Forbes, 'Good amnesty or poor enforcement', 4 June 1984.
Trend Analysis and Related Statistics: 1986 Update, Department of the Treasury, Internal Revenue Service, Document 6011.
Business Week, 16 April 1984.
Income Tax Compliance Research, US Treasury Department, Internal Revenue Service, 1983.
Reducing the Deficit: Spending and Revenue Options, Congressional Budget Office, February 1984.
Taxpayer Attitude Study, Final Report, prepared for the IRS by Yankelovich, Skelly, and White, Inc., December 1984.
1987 Taxpayers Opinion Survey, conducted for the IRS by Louis Harris and Associates.
1990 Taxpayers Opinion Survey, Final Report, conducted for IRS by Schulman, Ronca, Bucuvalas, Inc.
Charles W. Christien, 'Voluntary Compliance with the Individual Income Tax: Results from the TCMP Study', *The IRS Research Bulletin*, 1993/1994.
Burkhard Strumpel, 'Contribution in Survey Research', in A. Peacock (ed.), *Quantitative Analysis in Public Finance* (New York: Praeger, 1969).
M. W. Spicer and S. B. Lundstedt, 'Understanding Tax Evasion', *Public Finance*, vol. 31 (1976).
Joachim Vogel, 'Taxation in Public Opinion in Sweden: An Interpretation of Recent Survey Data', *National Tax Journal*, vol. 27, no. 4, 1974.
Robert Mason and Helen M. Lowry, *An Estimate of Income Tax Evasion in Oregon*, Survey Research Center, Oregon State University, Corvalis, January 1981.
Y. Song and T. E. Yarbrough, 'Tax Ethics and Taxpayer Attitudes', *Public Administration Review*, vol. 38 (1978).
Mancur Olson, *The Logic of Collective Action.*
Jerome Kurtz testifying as head of the IRS, US Ways and Means Committee, Second Session on HR 6300, 'Bill to Improve Compliance with IRS Laws', 9 May 1982.
Mark H. Moore, 'On the Office of Taxpayer and the Social Process of Taxpaying', prepared for the International Conference on Tax Compliance, Reston, Virginia, 16–19 March 1983.
Clara Penniman, *State Taxation Policy* (Baltimore: Johns Hopkins Press, 1980).
Fair Share: A Program to Increase Taxpayer Compliance in California, State of California Franchise Tax Board.
N. Machiavelli, *Discourses*, in Bondanella and Musa, *The Portable Machiavelli*.
'Workshop on Increasing Tax Collections through New Enforcement Methods', National Association of Tax Administrators, National Workshop No. 4, 25–8 July 1982, Chicago, Illinois.
An interview with Harry Durning, Director of Public Affairs, Massachusetts Department of Revenue, 28 February 1985.

Remarks by Ira A. Jackson, Commissioner of the Massachusetts Department of
    Revenue at the National Conference of State Legislature, 26 July 1984.
William M. Parle and Mike W. Hirlinger, 'Evaluating the Use of Tax Amnesty by
    State Government', *Public Administration Review*, May/June 1986.
Hobart Rowan, *Washington Post*, 'Tax Amnesty: Mischievous Nonsense', 21 March
    1986.
Thomas K. McCraw, 'With the Consent of the Governed: SEC's Formative Years',
    Journal of Policy Analysis and Management, vol. 1, no. 3, 1982.
N. Machiavelli, *The Prince*, in Bondanelle and Musa, *The Portable Machiavelli*.

7 The Basic Problem of an Entrepreneurial System: Unemployment

Alfred Malabre, *Beyond Our Means* (New York: Random House, 1986).
J. M. Keynes, *The General Theory of Employment, Interest and Money.*
Barry Bluestone and John Havens, 'The Microeconomic Impact of Macroeconomic
    Policy', *Journal of Post-Keynesian Economics*, vol. 8, 1986.
John D. Donahue, 'Efficiency, Rent-seeking and Privatization: Ten Propositions',
    in *Economic Problems of the 1990s*, edited by Paul Davidson and Jan Kregel
    (Edward Elgar Publisher, Cheltenham, 1991).
Ronald C. Moe, 'Public and Private Sector Relationships in the Age of Privatiza-
    tion', in *Economic Problems of the 1990s*, edited by Paul Davidson and Jan
    Kregel (Edward Elgar Publisher, Cheltenham, 1991).

8 Unemployment Develops because Money doesn't Grow on Trees

Milton Friedman, 'The Role of Monetary Policy', *American Economic Review*,
    vol. 58, March 1968.
J. M. Keynes, *The General Theory of Employment, Interest and Money.*

9 Fighting Inflation: Controlling the Money Supply vs. Buffers and Tips

Sidney Weintraub, 'An Incomes Policy to Stop Inflation', *Lloyds Bank Review*,
    1970.
Henry Wallich and Sidney Weintraub, 'A Tax Based Incomes Policy', *Journal of
    Economic Issues*, June 1971.
J. M. Keynes, *The General Theory of Employment, Interest and Money.*
Paul Volker's remarks in *Economic Policy the 1980s*, edited by Martin Feldstein
    (Chicago University Press, 1994).
Muliglime Frum, *New York Time, Op-Ed Page*, 1 March 1987.
Lester C. Thurow, *The Zero-Sum Society.*

10 Policy for a Civilized Global Economy: Whose International Debt Crisis Is It Anyway?

Irma Adelman, 'Long Term Economic Development', *Working Paper No. 589*,
    Giannini Foundation of Agricultural Economics, Berkeley, California, 1991.
The Economist, 6 June 1990.
Lewis, Flora, *New York Time Op-Ed Page*, 4 April 1986.
Financial Times, 7 February 1987.
John Maynard Keynes, *The Economic Consequences of the Peace* (London:
    Macmillan, 1919).

Sarah Kerr, 'The Confidence Men', *New York Review of Books*, vol. 42, no. 13, 10 August 1995.
Rodney Clark, *The Japanese Company* (New Haven: Yale University Press, 1979).

11 A Final Summing Up

Robert B. Reich, *Tales of a New America* (New York: Times Books, 1987).

Index